CW00496968

THE YOUNG GUVNORS

RODNEY RHODEN

EMPIRE
PUBLICATIONS

First published in 2012

This book is copyright under the Berne Convention. All rights are reserved. Apart from any fair dealing for the purpose of private study, research, criticism or review, as permitted under the Copyright Act, 1956, no part of this publication may be reproduced, stored in a retrieval system, or transmitted, in any form or by any means, electronic, electrical, chemical, mechanical, optical, photocopying, recording or otherwise, without the prior permission of the copyright owner. Enquiries should be sent to the publishers at the undermentioned address:

EMPIRE PUBLICATIONS
1 Newton Street, Manchester M1 1HW
© Rodney Rhoden 2012

ISBN: 1901746 887 – 9781901746884

Printed in Great Britain.

CONTENTS

INTRODUCTION

This is my story. The story of the Young Guvnors. The Young Guvnors fought not only on the streets of Manchester against their fellow hooligans but with other firms up and down the country. We sought out rival fans to fight (and on many occasions were sought out ourselves.) To say it is not a pleasant story is an understatement. From our formation in the mid 1980s when organized football hooliganism was at an all time high it's a vicious account of how we operated – our bloody battles with opposing mobs and ultimately about our demise at the hands of the police.

As the Young Guvnors, we were a younger offshoot of the Guvnors. We were involved in violent attacks on hooligan rivals almost every weekend and where there were newspapers stories of rival fans battling it out in town centres, train stations and outside football grounds, you could almost guarantee that the Young Guvnors were involved. We were gaining a reputation as one of the most feared up and coming football mobs in the country.

Increasingly, as lurid accounts of large scale violence and damage to property was taking place, the football authorities were putting pressure on the government to act. And act they did. They were about to start putting a plan into action to combat the spread of what was being called at the time 'the English disease'. For many years during the 80's the police were powerless to stop it. But the plan the government came up with was going to change the way the police patrolled and co-ordinated policing of football.

This book tells the story of how a team of police officers set up an Undercover operation, code named 'Operation Omega' to infiltrate and break up this gang of Manchester City hooligans. They had obviously been catching the eye of the Greater Manchester

Police force and other Police forces throughout the country. Within earshot of our most hated rivals, a covert operation was run from Chester House Police Headquarters in Old Trafford whose sole intention was to rip the heart out of the football hooligan scene at Manchester City.

From what I knew and saw at City it was kicking off almost week in and week out at games we went to during the 1987-88 season. And towards the end of the season before, 1986-87, with the weather getting hotter and with summer approaching, everyone was out and the mob was getting bigger for each game despite relegation looming.

It wasn't always about going to games to fight because sometimes the opposition never showed up, or the teams we were playing never had a mob, so we would just go to show what numbers we had. We even went to shitty little towns as the police didn't know the score and we would take the piss by walking around the grounds like we owned the place. We would often go in the home end and if we scored everyone would get on the pitch, which would hold up the game for a few minutes (which would no doubt be in the papers the next day). We would then get escorted to the away end like a victorious army returning from war.

It was all about the buzz of it all, as the lads I was with, like me, didn't drink or smoke or to my knowledge take drugs. Football hooligans are stereo-typed as drunken, drug-fuelled morons but the only drug we were addicted to was fighting for City. We only fought with people who wanted to fight us and very rarely did members of the public get done in, except perhaps the occasional 'have-a-go-heroes' and that would only ever happen when shops at away matches got rushed by mobs (other teams as well as ourselves). Ordinary scarf wearing fans were not deliberately targeted even though some people still seem to think that organised football hooligans just went round doing in opposing fans at random.

EARLY DAYS

At a very young age I was doing certain things by myself without the help of a big brother or sister, small things like walking to school on my own. As I am the youngest in my family I was learning to stand up on my own two feet and stick up for myself. I was left behind in primary school as everyone started secondary school. Here I met new friends and started to hang around with them in school. We played out, usually kicking a ball on the local park but quite often we would be getting into fights.

I was beginning to follow football and began supporting Man City from the early 80's, and occasionally watching them on TV. I was at that time attending Holy Name Primary in Moss Side and our headmaster occasionally took our class to games when they had tickets available.

The first ever game I went to was against West Ham. We were all in the north stand family section. I can't remember much of the match but I do know that we won 2-0, I also remember it kicking off in the Kippax stand with City's Kool Kats. I heard a lot about them, they were mostly black guys from the Hulme and Moss Side area, and because of the primary school I attended, these lads all lived round that area and the older lads at our school had brothers who were in it and they would speak about them – what they heard them talking about, about the kick offs they had and the trouble with City's NF in the Kippax.

They would only have been about 16 -20 years old because we were only 11 at the time and didn't really understand what was going on or what it was about. I attended another game; this time with some of the lads who were in school with me and their older brothers – these were the lads I heard about – the Kool Kats.

Simmo was one of them. He came from Hulme. It was an area made up of council housing but no one could be described as deprived or struggling to live – everyone dressed the same and they all had the similar things – no one was worse off or better off than anyone else.

The next game I went to was Huddersfield. This time I was with my mate Jason Broughton and Paul and Danny Gaye who brought us in the first place – that's how it all started and from then on it went from bad to worse. I was going to most games and there was a buzz about it. When I started in the second year of senior school in Whalley Range, I was always getting into trouble and suspended by the headmaster. I don't think he liked me that much because I found out he never got on with my brother who had attended the same school. He tried to take it out on me and I wasn't going to stand for any shit off him. Everyone said he was an ex-policeman and he had a serious problem with me and some of the other kids in the school, so you can imagine that he and the other teachers were on my case.

In the end I got expelled in the middle of the third year for head butting him. The best thing he did was to kick me out. Some of the City hooligans went to my new school in Chorltonl; Carl Stewart, my brother, Michael Ossia, Brendan Murray, Anthony Barnsley, Peter Wright, Dennis and his older brother called Paki (who is white). Later I went to a school in Oldham where I made some more friends and who also started to go to matches with me; Rob Hulme, Damo, Daz Millers, Winners, and Craig Gill who was later in the pop group the Inspiral Carpets.

A load of City fans used to come down to the matches with me, there was about fifty of us including the older lads who used to go down – they were in another gang from Chadderton called the Mills Hill Villains who used to fight with the Moor Close boys from Middleton/Rochdale. These boys ran with Oldham's firm the FYC (Fine Young Casuals).

From Oldham we used to travel down on either the 82 or on the 182 bus and we had to go down with that many because the bus used to always stop on Oldham Street outside the Merchants pub which was always full to the brim with Cockney Reds, Yorkshire Reds and Brummie Reds. In fact the whole of the red army who were really doing it back then. Every time I said to Rob and a guy called Lloydy, "I bet it stops there" and nine times out of ten it did and nearly always we got clocked and ended up getting ran by the whole pub, which used to spill out on the streets.

In those days, well before the game, there were always 100 plus United boys in town. All the City boys, the Guvnors and young Guvnors used to meet in town as well, to go to away matches. For instance if we were playing Leeds or Liverpool or Everton, teams that were not too far away, there would always be a big mob in town by midday. There were often about 2–300 City. Then you would get me and the others that were on the bus in the first place run to meet up with the rest of the boys and my brother and tell them that the famous Red Army had chased us from the bus stop and we would then get it together, march down to the Merchants and have it with them. No windows would get put in because that would have brought it on top with the Old Bill, who would eventually arrive to witness the running battles through Piccadilly with shoppers and by-standers running for cover.

The city centre made for an ideal battleground. For instance, when West Ham came to town to play Man United in an FA Cup Match, City played Middlesbrough at Maine Road the same day. That was the only time I can remember that some City joined up with United and the numbers were adding up to about 400 that morning. Benny and about 30 City were waiting in Piccadilly when West Ham came off the station and they did so with some force – the police didn't know what to expect but it kicked off at the monument at Piccadilly Gardens.

United and City were together in battle but it was mainly United doing it all. West Ham got ran and the police were on their toes because they couldn't believe only weeks before these two sets of Manchester hooligans had been at each other's throats and had now joined forces.

This was a short lived alliance… After our match at Maine Road we headed to town. There were about 80 of us in my group and we were all talking about United and City joining up and half of the boys couldn't believe it. I could see a load of them were happy because nearly all of us were scared of United at the time, who wasn't! They had the biggest hooligan firm in the country boasting over 1000 boys.

Anyway, back in town after the game some of the City lads didn't feel comfortable being around the Munichs as they called them. They were all saying that with the numbers they had it would just take one of them to start tripping about earlier fights that had taken place between City and United to start them all off... No sooner had Benny said that, than the main group of United's main men came along – the likes of Coventry Rob, a guy called Messer who was from St Albans who was said to be the top man and a black guy called Cockney Sam from Tottenham.

I was 13 at the time and I can honestly say I was shitting it; these guys looked mean, well they were from my point of view anyway. When everything in town eventually settled West Ham got off back on the train and the police were at the station approach scratching their heads. I bet they were flapping for the simple fact was that there were now well over 1200 thugs in town, there would have been 300 City there mixed in with United. Then someone in the crowd shouted Munich a sick reference to the Munich air disaster To this day I don't think any of the City lot shouted it ,I think it was one of the United boys because he was upset that we had joined up with them. Either that or he had been done in by City in the past and there was some sort of truce being planned. Whatever he was thinking, his plan worked.

Some of the known Guvnors and Mayne Line crew got a dig or a beating and the rest, like me, the Williams brothers, Keith, Clement and Floyd, got away unnoticed. There were too many thugs there to start picking out faces. How most of the City lads got noticed was when they stared to back out of the group – they were the ones who got chased off. You had to be there to see that none of us would have dared shout anything for fear of or own safety. Remember these were among the most feared and dangerous hooligans around and from that day when they turned on us, they were never trusted again.

Later on that season, City were due for promotion but we had to beat Notts County away. All the talk was about if we went up we would meet up with United for revenge for turning on us. We needed a point or a win to be sure of promotion but it wasn't to be because the game was going so well at 2-2 before they scored a late winner. It ended 3-2 to County. Then all hell broke loose. City fans started ripping the fence apart to get on the pitch and after that I couldn't say what happened, only that the trouble was captured on TV.

It was the second time that season City had been captured on TV fighting. The first was on Bank Holiday Monday back in April when we lost 2-1 to Leeds at Maine Road. All the City boys; the Kool Kats, the Mayne Line and the Young Guvnors, backed up by the beer monsters, were in the Platt Lane stand behind the goal when suddenly all City's mob ran for a gate that separated the two sets of fans. City got in and it kicked off – there was toe-to-toe fighting and it took the police a very long time to get there. Eventually they came and separated the fans. That was all I saw that day. It was a shocking experience for me at my age but I liked what I saw.

The next day the news came on and it showed the fighting. Then the broadcaster said that there had been cameras installed at the ground for the first ever time and no one knew about it. This explained why the police took so long to react - although I don't think anyone ever got nicked for it. However it did give the police a good reason to take a good look at City's mob.

Following City's promotion the Old Bill began watching us closely.

COVENTRY (A)

City were in the news again, this time at a match at Coventry. I heard City fans were kicking off after the game only because they were provoked and they only wanted revenge for the FA Cup game the previous season when City had been knocked out of the cup – they started to rip seats out and throw them onto the pitch. Coventry fans invaded the pitch and City's boys tried to get on and were stopped by the stewards who in turn got done in.

The government had attempted to clamp down on hooliganism following the Heysel disaster back in May which had been the worst of a series of well-publicised and often fatal incidents at football matches. Then there was the Luton-Millwall cup-tie when the South Londoners ripped up the seats and started hurling them toward the home fans. What made the incident worse was that it was televised on Match of the Day with a disapproving commentary by John Motson.

In the past few years there had been a number of TV documentaries glorifying hooliganism. One in particular followed West Ham's ICF (Inter City Firm) following their team around the country. I think that is how the Old Bill put two and two together and came up with their undercover operations, mingling in with the thugs and really getting to know how they operated. Dawn raids would follow but they were still two years away as the various police forces collected information on this new threat to national security.

The first to be targeted was West Ham's ICF in "Operation Full Time" before Chelsea's Head-hunters were the subject of "Operation Own Goal". Later Millwall's Bushwhackers were the focus of "Operation Dirty Den", then Arsenal's Gooners got hit in "Operation Spoonbill" and they even rounded up Luton Town MIGs "Men In Gear".

These raids started moving up the country – Birmingham's Zulu Warriors were nicked in "Operation Red Card" before the GMP put a close watch on City during the 1985-86 season as the police turned up the heat. A few weeks after the Coventry game we had Tottenham at home. They brought a good mob down and there were loads of black guys in their mob at the time, one of whom I had met a year previously. He was a lad called ET. He was one of their top boys and I knew him to talk to but at that game I found out he was locked up for a fight at one of the Spurs games the season before.

Their mob known are known as The Yids and they were in the Platt Lane end in full force, while we were in the Kippax stand.

Nothing much happened off the pitch and after the 2-1 home win I got off straight after the game. I heard it kicked off with The Yids but that wasn't unusual back then.

UNITED (A) 85-86

The next game I went to was the derby. This was the big one – the one everyone was waiting for because of what happened the previous season. Everyone was hanging about outside the ground waiting for the so called Red Army. They came alright… with a police escort and nothing happened before the match. However afterwards it was a different story. There was mayhem outside the ground – it was kicking off all around the forecourt and no one knew who was who until the fighting got down to Claremont Road outside the Sherwood pub.

There was a stand off with us and the reds with the Old Bill in the middle. They got pelted with all sorts when suddenly everyone ran at each other, there were scuffles on the way to town and then in Piccadilly. City got ran from the Gardens – there were just too many reds there. Those who stood trying to fight got done in badly. I was stood in the amusement arcade Sun Spot when City turned up. They were fighting outside Hurley's sport when suddenly I saw a mob of City rush the shop while it was going off outside – that was the in-thing in those days! I later left town and didn't see anything else after that, I didn't really go to any games after that only a few home games that I managed to go to.

*

The next Manchester derby which was in March 1986. I went to the ground with a few boys Stefan and Danny Gaye (RIP) , David Maynard, a lad called Lloydy from Oldham who is white and just to make it clear so there is no mix ups with the names with the lad in the Oldham mob, Jonh Sheehan from Moss Side and a few other lads. We got to the ground late so we missed all the fun beforehand but we got in near the end and it had just kicked off in the K stand. We all stayed back and watched because we didn't want to be clocked by the Old Bill. The dust had settled and the match was nearly over so we had to get it together because this was their patch and we knew that the reds had brought everyone out from all over the country. They were even more likely to be pissed off as we had recovered from 2 goals down to draw 2-2. A great result for the Blues!

Bizzarely, City were due to play Chelsea the very next day at Wembley in the final of the Full Members Cup - so we had to put our name on the map somehow off the pitch. We left the ground with all the lads I was with and waited under the Munich Clock -that was where everyone wanted to meet as it was right outside City's End and most of the lads didn't want to get split up.

Anyway, by this time the fans from both teams were pouring out, everyone was walking away from the meeting spot when we heard a big roar and then all you could hear was 'war, war, war'. We ran towards Chester Road and by the time we got there the Old Bill were there. It was going off and we didn't know who was who until Benny spotted some City he knew. It was kicking off all over the road. A lad from Oldham called Splodge was there and his brother Simon lost a shoe in all the commotion - not that he was involved or anything just in the wrong place at the wrong time and he came out of it one shoe down!

After all that, on our way down towards Hulme there were a lot of cockney reds trying to attack some City fans near the wall of some flats but the group I was with on the road ran over to see what was going on and gave one of these cockneys a sly dig in the head and got off over the wall with the rest of the City group. We had to go past the cockneys making out we had nothing to do with it but they got on to us and were shouting 'come on Niggers' and all the usual shit but we couldn't stop as there were too many of them. City's main mob were nowhere to be seen so we got off to town and down onto Deansgate where the United's pub was.

We were near the Evening News building when Danny said 'look it's going off at the Sawyers Arms' and we ran and crossed the road to watch because then again we didn't know who was who. This mob came charging out of the Sawyers with stools, bottles and anything they could lay their hands on. They were shouting 'United' so the mob outside were obviously blues.

They backed off before a few fights started and the City fans charged back at the United mob who had started entering the pub. The City boys started to put the windows through with the stools outside. I saw some City boys trying to enter the pub but the doors soon got shut – we were still stood across the road, we couldn't have got over if we'd tried because there were about 300-plus doing the business and we then heard the sirens. I thought the police would have got there earlier because Bootle Street police station is just around the corner.

When the police arrived all the City boys fled before anyone got nicked. Me and some of my mates left town and got off home, because it was Wembley the next day and we weren't going to miss that!

CHELSEA v MAN CITY
FULL MEMBERS CUP FINAL, WEMBLEY

We we're off to Wembley for the Full Member's Cup final against Chelsea. It was going to be a big test for the Guvnors against the Head hunters who were well known for getting on the pitch and holding up games, so we were expecting something to go on in the ground. I got the supporters' coach with pure jokers. After a long drive we finally got to Wembley. I couldn't wait to get off that coach, my ears were fucked with all the singing the jokers were doing – all I could hear was 'Wembley, Wembley were the famous Man City and were going to Wembley'... for five hours!

As soon as we came past the pub at the bottom of Wembley Way we saw it was packed with Chelsea boys. Our coach went fucking quiet. I thought to myself 'why don't they carry on singing now?'

This was definitely the Chelsea mob and when I got off at the coach park I ran up Wembley Way to find where City were. I met up with Benny, Danny and his brothers. Keith, the Spinner brothers, Carl Stewart, Lloydy from Oldham and Maynard from the Moss who was also there. In the end there were about 40 of us

- I told them that Chelsea's mob was at the bottom at the pub and we marched down Wembley Way and in turn they were on their way up so we clashed with the police watching. Again we heard all that nigger shit, that's what got us mad so I thought fuck the police they are stood there listening to them Chelsea shouting that shit and we ended up running them back down Wembley Way. I clocked a black guy with their mob 'what a dick', I thought. Moments later the Old Bill ran us all off .

That little disturbance would soon get round the ground. Once inside we were all sat to the left of the managers and players. I was with Pat Godfrey from Oldham who has been everywhere and been watching City for years, Danny Gaye, Keith Williams, who was my age at the time (13), his brother Clement and some other lads who had sneaked in. We were sat in that section to get on TV as we thought that this game was going to be live on telly but it wasn't to be, the Full Members Cup wasn't that important after all then!

The game had started and City played well for the first 15 minutes, then we saw a few tired legs out there, this was because most of the team played the day before in the derby. I think we were losing 1-nil at this time and the Chelsea fans were on a high. A few minutes later on the opposite side of the pitch to us, in the terracing section, we saw a mob in Chelsea's end run to the fence where the City fans were. The Chelsea fans looked like they were getting very angry it's like the City boys in their end were telling them to come on and fight as their was some City trying to climb the fence. They didn't get very far...

By this time the police would normally be on the scene but they were nowhere to be seen. They were probably filming what was going on or what was about to go on. I think the argument with the Chelsea fans was about when they came to Maine Road in May 1984 when we lost 2-nil. Chelsea needed to win to get promoted. They brought about six thousand fans up and they took the piss – City got done and apparently they were waving to different sections of the ground because different firms from London had come with them as back-up. I didn't get to the ground that night because my brother spotted me and Maynard on the way to the ground and I got sent back home so I watched it on TV (one of the first live City games on the telly).

I didn't go to any of the two games we'd played against them that season but it's fair to say that City got done so from then on there had been a lot of ill-feeling between the sides. It wasn't only going to be just the Chelsea fans it was other teams who the City fans in the past had pissed off or vice versa – I don't think it was just a City problem at the time it was going on up and down the country with different teams who had scores to settle with one another.

Anyway the City fans tried to climb the fence to get at the Chelsea fans and that angered them probably because they were known for that, after all the fences at their ground had electric wire to stop them climbing onto the pitch. This time they didn't bother. Instead they got about 150 boys together on the terrace, opened their gate and walked at the side of the pitch, opened City's gate and went into the City end. It went off with the Guvnors and Young Guvnors, I thought it was going to be another disaster on the terraces but it was just toe to toe fighting until the police got in to break it up.

This shit should have been live on TV but it was from that day on I really rated Chelsea's mob for what they had done, especially what they did in the ground, there were no more incidents in the ground as the match went on. On the pitch, Mark Lillis nearly got the equalizer but it wasn't to be and we lost 5-4. After the match we all left the ground and there was chaos as soon as we stepped outside. It was dark and everyone was running towards the coach park underneath Wembley Way. There was the sound of bottles smashing and a lot of shouting and by the time we all got to the bottom of the way we saw it going off with Chelsea's so called Head-hunters.

People who wanted it, got off their coaches and had it with them, a coach which belonged to Mikey Williams (RIP) got wrecked by the Chelsea mob. Carl Stewart, Pat Berry, Brian Slater and a load of other known thugs were on that coach, it was a target for CS. gas and a load of other things. I later heard that the police were filming from the helicopter and Terrance Last and his Chelsea boys later got charged with the attack when they got raided in Operation Own Goal.

After that Chelsea game I didn't really go to any more games that season. It was near the end of the season and there wasn't much happening as far as I was concerned. I was still only young and still had a long way to go before I could get to start going with the main mob and needed to grow a bit more as well.

MY FIRST FULL SEASON

LIVERPOOL AWAY

It was a new season in the old first division. I didn't attend the first game but went to the next one which was Liverpool away on the Bank Holiday Monday. It was raining as usual as we all met at Victoria station with a good mob. There was always a mob out for the Scousers because in turn they always turned out for us and the Mancs never got on with the Scousers be it City or United. When United played Liverpool or Everton they would turn out in full numbers and give it them. I don't really think it had anything to do with football from the Scouse point of view I just think it was a case of just Liverpool v Manchester, that's why they all joined up together against them.

Also, at that time, a lot of black guys from City would be on the way to the game because we knew they didn't like niggers and that was from the time a few years earlier when the Scousers were playing each other at Maine Road in the replayed League Cup Final. They came to Manchester in force and headed straight to Moss Side – a perfect time for all the fascists from all over Manchester and elsewhere to get their name on the map. At the time the population in the area was mainly black and mixed race families and tensions still ran high from the Riots a couple of years before.

The NF were out in force that day. This was the last thing the area wanted but they went straight to Moss-side precinct, which was well known as a place where everyone hung about. There were not very many jobs for black people back then so the precinct was just like a chill out zone where the betting shops were and where the Rastafarians would also be. They hit it at about 5.30pm when the shops were about to lock up - 300 Scousers charging in making monkey noises.

Everyone scattered and straight away the Rastas were targeted. There were reports of Rastas getting caught and done in, their dreadlocks ripped out and bags of weed all over the place on the floor and on the road. No doubt the Scousers had it all away, and their favoured red, yellow, and, green tea-cosy hats were knocked off – they looked like traffic lights scattered all over the floor the way their hats lay there.

The Scousers well and truly took the piss, shouting wogs and anything else they could think of. To cap it all off they came on to the Alexander Park Estate where I was living at the time and went straight to a local pub called the Big Western and at that time my dad lived and worked there. There were more Rastas drinking, playing pool or dominoes and smoking weed of course in there but the place got absolutely wrecked. The so called bad boy Rastas shit it, they never even got tooled up in the pub. Instead they just ran through the back doors and more got caught and fucked up badly.

The police were called and turned up three hours later with a very large turn out of the Rastafarian community voicing their objections which, naturally, fell on deaf ears. Instead the police searched a few people who they knew from the criminal underworld and found nothing because all the drugs or whatever they were hoping to find had fallen out of their pockets when they got ran by the Scousers.

So this was the background to our trip to Merseyside. Whenever we played the Scousers, I felt we did it on behalf of Moss Side M16 and Toxeth L8 to give it the racist Scousers. As for the game I can't remember much of it but after it finished we all marched out of the ground with about 300 plus. It was pure confusion because all the normal City fans were coming out at the same time (the non football hooligans), so it was a case of all the thugs to one side and all the straight heads to the other. We soon got it together to find the Mickeys and found ourselves on a long road where it went off with them.

The Police were with us; they had been with us all the way

from the ground so when it did go off the police were after City especially us lot. My brother was there, daft Donald, Maynard and a lot of blacks – we were all watching because we were targets for the Old Bill. It was going off in a Petrol station forecourt across the road and the Old Bill got in the middle of it, the dogs came and that was that. The OB who were with us were cheeky cunts because when it went off the pricks were on their radios saying 'Assistance, Assistance, Black disturbance, Black disturbance!'. I never knew what that meant until later – it was police slang for blacks rioting. There were just too many of them and they held us there until the coaches came to take us to the train station.

TOTTENHAM (H)

Five days later we had Tottenham. Their mob was ok, they were all in the Platt Lane end behind the goal which was all wooden bench seats back then. You could see all the Yids because they were stood up on the benches a few rows from the front. I think they wanted everyone to see their mob and how many they had brought. There were a few black guys there and the Jewish community too, some of whom I got to know a few years later – Sammons, Browny and Ricky who I had a run in with a few years later, me and him are the best of mates now . They were some of the main heads of the so called Yids. I didn't see Trevor Tanner with them in all the times we were kicking it off.

I knew one of the Yids very well but I think he was locked up at the time for other football related matters. His name is ET Niki Carrington. He is a City fan as well and one of us but he never got involved whenever it went off with us and them, which was understandable and he never slagged them off, why would he when he chills with them? Anyway as the game was coming to an end everyone was piling out of the ground to give it the cockneys. They thought they were better than us because there from the big city but that proved to be a load of shit.

When we came out them days the Old Bill didn't really know the score. You could take a mob of about 400 round the ground and those clowns wouldn't even get onto it. These days it's red hot of course and a group of a dozen or so would be spotted straight away. Eventually we bump into their mob and all we got out of them was 'Yiddo's Yiddos'. They were calling the attention of the Old Bill to rescue them and sure enough the OB intervened.

*

It was fairly quiet a few games later and I did not attend because I was still at school having just started the fourth year aged 14. I was the youngest in my year, I soon started to recruit a few lads in my year and although I didn't have a lot of money to travel to certain away matches, our parents always used to sort us out with spends. If not we would go on my brothers rail card or jib the train, we had to hide in between the seats. Loads of us used to do it because we were all small, so when the ticket inspector came for the tickets, the older lot would surround us, show their tickets and pass them on to us or just block us or terrorize the guard. Either way we weren't paying. It got to the point where we'd just say 'Do you know who we are? The Guvnors or in our case the Young Guvnors and yeah we're from Manchester'.

CHELSEA (A) 86-87

Chelsea away saw the same routine with the train jib and this time we had a very good mob out especially after the Full Members Cup at Wembley when it went off proper. We took about 250 there. We came off at Euston and met up with Larry Philips and ET who had just got out of the pen and Bobby and Paul Langley, Colin White, Scott McAllum, Bootsy, Anthony Costello (COZI) who was one of Man United's boys at the time, then we got on the bus outside the station, there were about 80 lads packed on our bus I think the rest got the tube.

There was a lot of Old Bill on the station because a few teams were passing through including Wrexham. There were a few of the Yids hanging around, it was just their scouts though. Nothing happened then we got on our way on the bus. We wanted to surprise the Head-hunters and loads of us were excited about this game because City hadn't won in nine games and hadn't won an away game in sixteen. City had just signed Imre Varadi who had a very good goal scoring record. We got to the ground just as the game kicked off and we could see a big police escort. It must have been the other lot on the football special, the mob that we left early would have been there ages ago and probably got ran. No offence to the lads but them Chelsea boys are no push over on there own patch. We did see their mob; it was a surprise to us because we were behind them after getting off the bus thanks to Benny's directions. We just ran at them and had them on their toes for a minute or two until they turned and had it out with us. It wasn't long before the OB got to the scene and rounded us all up and marched us straight into the ground.

Me and the lads at Euston 1986

It was good news for us because we were one nil up after five minutes, although we all missed the goal of course and guess who scored, yes Varadi on his debut. Sadly, the game finished 2-1 to Chelsea and without any further incident because we were boxed in and the only place we were going was straight to Fulham Broadway and back to Euston where I ran right up the escalators. I was always excited and wanted to be up front, it was a bonus for me being young, I never really got spotted being so young, the mob behind me was top of the range there must have been 250 plus, that was what I liked, to see us getting it together and sticking together.

As I got on the forecourt I could hear a slight noise coming from the other side of our escalators which were the stairs to and from the tube. As I approached I could see a mob coming up and a flag with a dragon on it. I heard one of them say something like 'look at that nigger' I could only take it they were talking to me. There was a big fat cunt giving it all the mouth, not forgetting I was only 14 and he didn't know who the fuck I was as I didn't have any colours on.

I took it that he thought I was just some little black cockney kid from Brixton, I called him a fat bastard and backed off until they thought they could just pick on anyone, they came up looking straight ahead and did not see the City boys, there were about 80 of them and no police that was when I shouted to everyone and it went off with Wrexham. They didn't know what had hit them, let alone who we were or how many we had. They soon scattered back down the steps, the fat guy was their main man who was called Foulkes, and I found that out when I was in Kirkham Prison seven years ago locked up with some guy from Flint. The Transport Police came out in numbers after seeing it on the CCTV but there were no arrests as we only ran them but we were to meet them again before the end of that season.

A lot of lads went home on the next train but there were about 50 of us who stayed behind as always: me, Benny, both Spinners, Splodge, Danny G, Maynard, Martin Travis and the rest of the Young Guvnors. We went for a drink with ET and Larry in Somers town in the pub called the Lord Somers then onto the Lion and Lamb. We stayed until about 8.30 then went back to Euston which was only ten minutes away. Everyone was expecting to see the Yids after the match but no one did and every time ET used the pay phone (there were no mobile phones in them day) so I know he was blagging it so he wouldn't get spotted with us off the police who knew who he was People would say he was shady but no one would say it to his face, I should have told him what they were saying but just wanted to keep the peace, he never ever got involved whenever Tottenham came, he just stood to one side and kept out of it.

Funnily enough by the time we reached the station the forecourt was filled with black guys backed up by 30 odd white guys. They charged at us, took their belts off and ran us back out of the station and onto Euston Road. We got back together at St Pancras station, charged back at them and fighting broke out in Euston Square. We ran them back into the station, who knows why they went back that way unless they were going to re-group. The BTP arrived with the dogs and there were verbal exchanges, after that you would never guess who was there again, the same faces who were at Maine Road the season before Brownie, Ricky Pryce with the glasses on and Sammons with his ear ring.

Funnily enough City went to Tottenham early in the season and give it them, although I did not attend but I heard it went off and one of the City lads dragged a police man off his horse. The wrong man got nicked, Callam Frizzell the son of City assistant manager Jimmy – the police just grabbed anyone, luckily enough he didn't get prosecuted for it. Everything settled after the run-ins with the Yids at the station and we all got slung on the next train out of there. We arrived back at Piccadilly too late to meet up with United so home we went.

CITY v UNITED 86-87

The next game we had was United at home. it was a Sunday game but it was a bad start to the day as about 50 of us who lived in Oldham had to walk half way from Oldham to Manchester because the buses were on strike. On the way we bumped into some United boys who were meeting outside a pub in Failsworth. I could see there were about 20 lads there. We knew they had a mob in that area so it was almost certainly them. The next stop we got off the bus, ran at the pub and they scattered – what a waste of time! It then took us half an hour to get to town!

As we approached Oldham Street we could see a load of police at the bottom end near to the Merchants pub – a regular meeting spot for United. There were a load of lads outside so there would have been a load more inside because when you see the odd police van and a car and some on foot but that wasn't the case there were more than usual. We knew the Cockney reds, Yorkshire reds, and Brummie reds were here – what a day it was going to be! To round it all off who did the police come for? Yes City as always! Don't forget the game was at Maine Road so they should have been escorting the United mob to the ground but no it was us, unless they were scared of the red army who were well known just like the likes of Coco, Tony O'Neil and Messer from St Albans not forgetting Coventry Rob, Cockney Sam, P. Dobson and P. Chris from London.

So once again the police got hold of us all and marched us to the ground. Half way there we saw a mob about 30 lads and we soon noticed it was City lads: the Samms brothers David and peter, Linford Taylor from Birmingham, Maynard, Traves and the Williams brothers. The police started to get excited, getting on their radios for back up not noticing that half of the lads who were making their way towards us were black and it was not as if Man U had that many blacks in their firm. There were only a few including fireman Sam, Henry Ferguson, Joby Henry, who the mickeys had slashed up years before. We then ran at each other and one of the OB who I would say was on the ball we knew then we were all mates, they even asked me if I was ok with this lot and asked me if I was lost because I was small and very young looking.

He thought that I had got dragged into this crowd I said 'officer I am just trying to get to the projects'. What I really meant was Moss Side, I think he knew what I meant. We approached Whitworth Park and suddenly they got a radio call from what I could hear was that there was a very large group of United fans on Princess Road. That was about 15 minutes away from where we were. They left us and all the vans and dog vans just took off we continued past the park down Wimslow Road to the Clarence pub where City's mob were. So there was about 80 in our mob and about 400 in and outside the pub so it was a good turn out Pat Berry, Scotty, Brian Slater, Bernard Chaisty, ET, Larry, Danny Paul and Stefan Gaye, Benny, Spinner, Micheal Ossai, a load of beer monsters, the Mayne Line crew and the Guvnors and the Young Guvnors so it was a good turn out. Another 30 lads shown up Chris (Bez) Beswick and his mob from Bury. There were a lot of blacks with City at the time about 40 in total but their had been a bit of unrest with some of the lads at meeting at the Clarence because it was a known NF pub and a lot of the City lads at the time followed them. We could clearly see Scotty was their with his full crew. Some of them never blinked an eye at any of the black lads or said hello for that matter, the fifty lads who I was with from Oldham were all white and never bothered with that shit.

The older black lads I went to school and grew up with were mostly white lads and I fought together with them over the years. We were all going to get it together and give it to City NF at some point but this wasn't the day to be fighting each other so everyone left it. Those lads would carry on over the next few games not that everyone mixed with them they had their own mob the so called beer monsters, we soon told every one that the reds were on their way and every one who was inside the pub got tooled up and joined us outside.

A lot started charging across the waste land (where I got a good photo of United's boys) over the road while everyone else told them to wait for the United boys to come to us but they wouldn't listen – they ran across and no less than a minute later we could hear the sirens and we knew then that they were not far off at all. That mob soon came running back with bricks and bottles flying over their heads, that was it, the reds were here! Everyone was running everywhere it was like a proper battle! We could see there were at least double numbers to what we had it was almost certain they had 850, they had at that time the biggest hooligan mob in the country so it has to be believed. Bez got hit in the head by a brick so I had to get a photo of him outside the Clarence pub ha ha!

The police were on the scene but could not control it. There was so much running back and forth and missiles going every where, they were not getting in the way until the dogs and horses came. Then everyone scattered; no one knew who was who but all ran to the ground, there was a lot more police presence at the ground – they were taking no more chances, we all got in the North Stand with or with out tickets. That was our stand and no one else was coming in... or that's what we thought! The game kicked off incident free. Police were everywhere – all over the ground there were horses and dogs on standby even some Old Bill with cameras taking pictures.

It was a good game until City gave away a goal then all hell broke loose. The City fans started taunting the United fans shouting 'Munich' and then fights started in the North Stand after the United fans jumped up to cheer the goal. They were there in large numbers and from what I saw the police waded in. At least five people were arrested and the other United fans were taken out and put in their own end. Late in the game Mick McCarthy scored for us. We all went wild and tried to get onto the pitch but were stopped. There were ten minutes left so a load of us left the ground; me, Benny, Peter (Frithy) Frith, Maynard, Danny and we all got it together and waited outside the ticket office at the back of the North Stand.

In the end there were 200 lads outside and then it went off as the United boys came round the corner. They must have spotted the mob leaving early and came for us. They were everywhere. Chrissy James knocked one of them out on the forecourt then fighting broke out all around in the end we all got ran off. United were all over, there was too many of them as usual. City's full mob didn't get it together quickly enough but United did every time. City turned and had a go but it was pointless – there were 200 onto 800 and they took over all the streets. We eventually got away from them onto Wilmslow Road where City were back at the Clarence in large numbers having a pint while we were getting ran half way across Moss Side.

Well anyway, everyone came out straight away. Now we had numbers and all the main men were there who we all had a lot of respect for that including Pat Berry, Benny, Bernard Chaisty, H from Oldham who is Colin Whites big brother, Duffy, Charlie Sow and we had to keep it together and we did. By the time we got to Oxford Road by the BBC the United boys showed up as if they were waiting for us. This time no one was getting ran, they got a good kicking but were still turning and fighting. Toe-to-toe it was going on all the way up to Oxford Road train station. Police were scattered everywhere, I could see a mob of City double back and storm Cotswold's ski shop while it was going off - yeah well niggers were broke at the time. Some police saw it but just had to stop the fighting. The City lads piled out and got off with all the Peter Storm and Berghaus jackets and distress flares. Two of the shop staff came out shouting and grabbed one of the City boys which was a bad mistake because some City were outside the BBC at the bus stop as if they were waiting for a bus. They ran over and give it the shop staff which went a bit over the top but the City lad had to get free or get nicked the heroes always had to get it.

The fighting went on all through the night until there were only fifty lads left in town and the pubs were all shut. What a great derby day it turned out to be!

UNITED V CITY (FA CUP) 1987

From then on it was a fairly quiet season. Not much was happening on the hooligan front and a load of shit games, games such as Charlton, Watford, Oxford, Sheffield Wednesday, Wimbledon – a load of teams who loved to turn up when we went to their ground but never took fuck all to ours.

Funny enough the next good game was a few months later with United at their ground in the third round of the FA Cup. This time no one met in town, everyone was meeting in Moss Side on Great Western Street. It was a good turn out – 400 or so again and we set off at 12 o clock through Moss Side, Doddington Close, where I had a few photos taken of us then through Gooch Close and the tension was good in Moss Side. No war going on but we had to give the two estates respect and march through saying hello to the lads I knew on both sides telling them that we were on our way to Old Trafford.

Those who under stood what was going on said we had a good firm, so we carried on to the Whalley Hotel which was only a few hundred yards up the road and another photo taken there. It was good getting there unnoticed, that is why we kept it quiet – there were no police so everyone got in the pub and sorted out how we were going to storm Old Trafford. It was said that everyone stays put until we knew where the United mob were so a few of us young ones like Benny, David Maynard, Paul Urban (aka Johnny the Mugger an ex-United hooligan), Stefan and Paul Gaye. There were only about six of us who went scouting about for them and we were five minutes away from the pub when we saw United's mob on Ayres road in Old Trafford.

We walked straight into them, the only thing we could do was walk and mingle with their mob which we did apart from Maynard who ran off straight away to tell City that United were on their way and that Me and Benny were walking with their mob. No one believed him because he was young and they didn't think that we would be walking with United because we were hot and would certainly get spotted but we didn't and Maynard came half way down the road and had to stand in a doorway as if he lived there.

He told us when we got up to him without United hearing him

The Guvnors on the way to the derby 1986

so we stood with him and waited until the red army got to the end of the road to see if any City had come out but they never and that is when we could hear the windows in the pub going through (they were warned!).

The City lads came out with pool cues, pool balls, stools, table legs and a few fights started. The United mob got chased off back down the road and a load got caught. We were in the middle of it, the City boys tried to attack us thinking we were reds. Pool balls were bouncing off cars, stools flying everywhere, that's when the police sirens were heard. The road and the pub looked like a real war zone, the road was littered.

The Guvnors approach the Whalley on the way to Old Trafford

Everyone was told to 'fucking walk' when the police did get there so no one got nicked on our side. Either way they were heavy handed with us again probably because there were pure niggers with us, and it didn't take the police long because they stopped the escort and gathered the niggers up against the wall. Carl Stewart, Chris and Mickey Francis, George, Ricky Campbell, Mickey Williams and his brother Pebbles, my brother, Linford Taylor, David and his brother Peter (Samson) Samms , big Warren W, Neil Crawford, Scooby, Raymond Pilling, Paul Urban, Jamie Roberts, Danny and Stefan Gaye. It was a blatant piss take. We all thought their had been a hand bag snatch or a mugging that had gone on the way we were all rounded up because that was there usual excuse.

They stopped and searched the niggers in the hood, then they asked us all what we were doing around here so I said at first 'Are you going to ask all them 400 in the escort as well?' He wasn't impressed then I said 'we live round here'. I was just playing their game,. Just because we were all black and there was a lot of blacks living in the area that was all and don't forget the Moss Side riots were six years before so why didn't daft Donald get pulled out too because he starred in the riots and done his bird for it? Yeah they wouldn't fuck with him in his prime and he was a lunatic and well known throughout the football hooligan world. I stopped being lippy to the officer. I knew he couldn't nick me as I was only 13. That was one advantage of being that age.

By now the dust had settled and we were on the move again. It took ages to get to the ground and we were expecting the United boys to try and attack our escort but they were nowhere to be seen until we marched onto the forecourt. The police left us and the cockney reds were there straight away calling us black bastards thinking that because the police were over the road and watching nothing would happen. Well police or no police we would kick it off . One of the so called black bastards knocked him out and the rest got ran through the crowd and that was it.

It was on top from then on. The plod came to the City end and were asking who had tickets. That fucked us all up because we were all going to jump the turnstiles but instead the hundred unlucky ones including me never got in and just got marched well away from the ground. That was it – the United boys thought we were flapping and they got their result when they smashed our pub. We left it an hour and came back to Old Trafford and found some of their mob outside. It went off again and yet again the police were not far behind, chasing the City fans off as always. We then decided to fuck off from the ground altogether and wait for all City's mob back in town where everyone was going to meet at Brannigans.

This was a United pub in the Royal Exchange but City had taken it over, it was a shady pub which you had to walk down a load of steps to get to. Anyway we settled in there. It was pointless trying to walk about with 100 lads round town and get nicked or chased all over by the police. An hour later the mob started piling in – it was soon full to the brim, no one else could get in there. There were about 300 in and about 200 in the Royal Exchange and outside the building on Cross Street. Everyone had to move quickly if we were going to get a result by smashing one of their pubs up with their lads in it. Don't forget they put the windows in at the Whalley.

We came out and ran them but to them that was a victory which it was. They smashed the pub and that was it, we all marched up Market Street the mob was chanting 'Guvnors, Guvnors' all the shoppers were all running out of the way as we marched up. I was right at the front and felt good. I wanted every one to see me with a mob. There were then chants of 'City, City, City' everyone was up front including all the main heads Pat Berry, Bernard Chaisty, Paul(Deno) Derry, Duffy, Mickey F, Chris F, Benny, the Foulkes brothers, Colin Jones from Oldham, Martin Townsend, Ged Ganson (RIP) who was totally off his head, we never knew who was the worst lunatic out of him, Daft Donald or Chrissy James.

We had a lad with us called scouse he was from Miles Platting he was one of the main heads as well. We had a few NF lads with us lads like Scotty from Openshaw. Brian Slater, a lad called Mark (Chappy) Chapman who was from Burnage and who brought the undercover police with him in the first place, and a lot more which some people were uneasy about but only time would tell. It was going to kick-off with them lot at the derby at Maine Road back in October but it was the wrong day at the time, but that fight was not far away.

As we were approaching Piccadilly near the corner of Oldham Street everyone was told to keep it quiet but what did they do, United were just round the corner in the Merchants public house which was their pub. About 2–300 City lads who were walking at the back of us rushed past us and attacked the pub with the United mob inside .They never came out, they never had chance to – all the windows were put through it was pure chaos by the time we all got round the corner the pub was smashed to bits, worse than the Whalley pub because City stayed and made sure every window went through and that those inside could not get out.

There were chants of 'City, City' the buses on Oldham Street were at a stand still as they could not get past as the road was littered with pint pots, broken tables and chair legs which the United mob used to try and back City off by throwing them out of the broken windows but there were too many of us – we just kept on coming and coming round the corner. In the end everyone turned and made their way to the Brunswick pub (which is now called Finnegan's Wake) on Piccadilly near the train station. That was when the sirens started – the landlord of the Merchants must have called the police out and you could see behind you all the City lot running towards us being chased off by United and the police doing nothing. They knew the United boys would soon give up the chase when a lot of City lads started getting nicked.

We started running towards the Brunswick while the police were busy nicking the others, the cockneys reds were in the pub waiting for their next train and so the windows went through once more. It was more like a hit and run this time – either stand smashing it to fuck or brick it and run before the police got to us. From that point on we left town, got onto Oldham Road to the Thunderdome club and waited there for the City lot from Oldham. This was our meeting place whenever we got ran off by the reds or the police. It was out of town and the 82 bus stop to Oldham was right there. We eventually got off home. I heard 20 City got nicked later that night for fighting near Victoria station with Ely and the Bury reds.

QPR (A)

QPR away saw another good turn out if only because we were going to London and we knew that the Yids would be waiting for us there. 200 lads may not have been as many as on derby day but it was good enough and would do anyone on our travels. We jibbed the train again and stopped at various stations including Birmingham New Street. There was a heavy police presence there because of a bit of bother. There had been a bit of bother at Stoke with a load of Port Vale fans so the police were waiting for us and made sure none of the City boys got off the train again until it reached London.

When we did get there I was walking on to the main station with my brother when one of the Yids pulled out a CS gas canister and sprayed us. We ran out of the station – our eyes were fucked for ages but ok ten minutes later after we'd splashed water in our eyes. The City lads were mad but the guy just ran off, we later met up with ET and Larry Philips and made our way to the QPR ground by tube. Everyone jumped the barrier at Euston station. When we arrived at White City station twenty minutes later we came out on a main road. (Benny) Andrew Bennion was up front, he was one of the main men from Wythenshawe and he had been to every City game you could think of from Portsmouth to Carlisle.

He was there kicking it off and every thug from nearly every club that City had visited knew who he was. Even though he was small he was game as fuck and always there to back you up. Another lad who was their was a guy called Chris from Prestwich, he was off it too. I think we should have been called the lunatic fringe, we marched through chanting 'City' and 'GUVNORS' 'GUVNORS'. We wanted every one to know that we had arrived and who we were.

They saw us from way across the park, they were all gathered outside a picture house but never approached us because they we well out-numbered. We carried on our way, shouting 'MUNICH' 'MUNICH'. It was getting louder and louder, we turned on another road which had market stalls on both sides. There were a lot of people there who looked like they were shitting it seeing a mob marching through them. There was a chant of 'City we're from Manchester' that was for the shoppers and the QPR scouts as we got through to a housing estate near some flats we were met by a black guy who was from Longsight called Egghead who had moved to the Shepherds Bush area a few years before.

He was now one of the QPR boys and was talking to Benny and a lad called Anthony Rowan and told them that QPR's mob were on their way from the BBC. We knew they had a mob as I had seen it less than twenty minutes before. We were only a few minutes away from the ground and could see the floodlights of the ground. We turned a few corners and ended up on the road to the ground and saw their mob heading our way. We bumped into them outside a betting shop at the ground and kicked it off. We ran them to the other end of the road near the BBC Studios. The shit bags got one punch and fucked off. The police came with a dozen officers like they were going to do something, like they could they would have got done if anyone would have got touched.

We made our way to the City end and people were saying to get into the bottom tier so we can all get on the pitch if we score, so it was over the turnstiles as usual and in, no trouble. The mob was behind the goal. The game itself was shit – we were getting beat as usual and City were on the way down. The next thing there was a pitch invasion by the QPR supporters that made about fifty of us go on thinking it was their mob and that they wanted it but it was just a demonstration, we soon came off.

After the game was over we were kept behind for ages. We were let out at five thirty, got back to White City and there was fuck all so we went back to Euston. We went to go to a pub in Somers Town only to see them Yids heading down Eversholt Street. We didn't waste time in chasing them off and made sure they wouldn't come back. We had enough of them coming over to fight us all the time and when they got ran, they didn't come back so we fucked off back to Manchester. The next day the news showed the demonstration and people getting interviewed outside the ground only to see ourselves running the QPR lads past the camera!

MAN UNITED (A)

It was derby day again only two months after the last one at Old Trafford. This time there was none of that going in and out of pubs waiting for the United mob to put a few windows through and say to everyone they done us. The trick those days was if you smashed a pub up and caused the maximum damage possible it was almost certain to get in the papers and the local radio the next day. It was 11 am and Chadderton was our meeting spot.

At the time I lived directly across the road from the 182 bus stop so everyone met at my house. My mum wasn't too pleased that there were at least 80 lads across the road and about five guys knocking on the door. She could clearly hear the lads across the road saying tell Rodney to hurry up or we will miss the bus. From that moment on she knew that these weren't just ordinary football fans I hung around with, she hadn't had any idea for two years up until then. Some of the lads she knew which were my age or just a bit older and she knew we all hung around in Chadderton Hall Park with a load of lads but she had never seen that many before.

She called me back in the house and said 'I hope you ain't going out getting yourself in trouble'. I just said 'no' and left to get on the bus which was on its way round the roundabout. I eventually got on the bus and we headed straight to town. We were all meeting at 1 o'clock at United's pub in Piccadilly, the Brunswick, the idea this time was to get the train to Old Trafford cricket ground and storm the place. As we were on our way down to town we were approaching an area called Moston and the bus driver stopped for ages and everyone thought he was taking a rest because his bus route was from Rochdale to Manchester but was he was really doing was radioing a ticket inspector who turned up with the police – what a prick!

The excuse was that the lads were singing stamping and chanting on the bus and that only about 35 people had paid on so most of the tickets were checked until they got half way down the bus to a lad called Andy B who started kicking off saying he lost his ticket then everyone who didn't have tickets started kicking off with the hector who then radioed for back up. I said to a lad called Cozi 'for fuck's sake, we ain't ever going to get to town at this rate', the Old Bill said 'either some of you pay the fare or get off', he was a cocky cunt but when he said that Clanger (David Clayton) said he would pay for some but not all. Everyone had money but just wanted to bully it and no one wanted to get kicked off we just wanted to get to town and meet up with the mob.

We eventually got there and there was a buzz of excitement around us all as we marched through Piccadilly towards the Brunswick. Shoppers always looked scared when they saw big mobs marching through the city centre every weekend. There are two main train stations in Manchester which teams would have to cut through in order to change for other stations and that would always bring trouble to the city centre. No wonder the shoppers were so worried especially when there was no police presence.

We were now on the main stretch of Piccadilly and we could see that the traffic from there on was at a standstill, as City's mob we spilling out onto the streets and into the road. I tell you it brought a smile to a lot of faces that day including mine because the mob was now one of the biggest turn outs in history. You could see face after face, people who you had not seen at games or anywhere else in ages and people who you didn't think would show up. The only lads who were missing were ET and Larry which I thought was strange, it was estimated that there were 500 lads from City out that day.

This was a game where everyone was out. The whole of Manchester and the shopping public were well aware what day it was, you couldn't miss all the normal City and United supporters gathered in the City in their thousands with their team colours on. The local paper the Evening News were reporting in the papers in the Friday and Saturday edition that the police were expecting trouble in and around the City because their was trouble when these teams met the last time. Word soon spread for everyone to make a move and move we did. It was like being in a football crowd already, the amount of people who were there singing.

The police weren't called because their was no disturbance because the only thing missing were the United boys who were always in town and especially on derby day. Some of their scouts must have seen the size of the mob and reported back. They didn't even try an ambush which was unusual. We start piling onto the station and by this time it was silent – no one wanted to bring it on top but there was no point, the BTP were there and they knew exactly who we were, what we were up to and where we were going . Out came the dogs to bark at the niggers – it was as if the B T P had a picture of a black guy in the kennels for training!

We get on the train without any arrests being made which was a surprise because the police had it in for City, all the carriages were full and to no surprise the police kept the train at a standstill for almost half an hour. We thought the police were on the way to get on the train with us because their were so many of us, then we heard on one of the B T P radios as they walked through the carriage that all units were at the Grey Parrot public house in Hulme and were escorting the United mob to the ground. That pub was another stronghold for the red army, the transport police then radioed through saying that their was 4 to 500 City hooligans on the train making their way to Old Trafford they must have thought that the B T P were exaggerating the numbers.

The temperature in the train was getting to minus whatever degrees it was as if some one had opened every window in the train, it felt like snow was on it way, it really was fucking freezing. The train was taking time to get to Old Trafford cricket ground and everyone was getting pissed off. People started shouting and swearing then cans started flying everywhere then there were chants of 'City, City'. The train was going slowly probably on police advice, so they could get the United scum to the ground first and no doubt about it, that they would be at the station waiting for us. There were about 50 B T P officers there. I marched out at the front with the main lads. We had everyone there: the beer monsters, the Guvnors and the Young Guvnors – the police soon radioed for back-up.

I loved all the attention we caused as we marched down Warwick Road to the ground. It was approaching 2.30 pm and by now the road was not only full of us but other fans. They seemed in a hurry to get out of the way of the thugs who were now under very heavy police escort with dogs all barking beside us, the horses shitting and spitting everywhere, the foot police and the hoolivan which was filming us all the way from the cricket ground. Then as we approached the cross roads to Chester Road there were chants of 'Munich' – by this time the road was full length ways and width ways with boys and as we approached the forecourt the police reckoned that their job was done (far from it) and backed off.

I could see ET a few yards in front of us. I thought he wasn't coming. He was with Larry and a few of the Gooners from Arsenal who I knew and I could see they were having an argument with some big lads. The lads had their backs to us. We were approaching them unnoticed and as I looked to my left I could see under the tunnel the United boys were there but were just watching as were got within a few feet of ET.

The United mob who surrounded him said to him 'where's your boys' meaning the City mob – these guys were cockney reds who had known who he was. He wasn't running he just pointed over their shoulders and said they are behind you and as they turned round they got the shock of their lives as they just got attacked and the City mob were now all over the forecourt which attracted the attention of the police but everyone just ran at the tunnel where United's mob stood. They couldn't be bothered to come to us, they ran off.

That was it! What a waste of time! Now the kick-off wasn't far away and I don't think any of us had tickets to get in as the snow started to come down. Everyone wanted to get into the ground but it wasn't to be because as we all tried to storm the turnstiles it was on top with the police and at least forty of us never made it in so the police just moved us on. We weren't too bothered about not going in the game because most of us had never been in a derby at Old Trafford, we just stayed outside all through the matches, looking for their fans who were also looking for us.

As the snow came down the day was soon going to be over for us. We made our way to town on the bus so we could get in a pub. Don't think ET was too happy with the weather and said that they were going to get the next train back to London. He was with fellow Yid Larry and the Arsenal boys basher, big Corbet, Russel, Sneakers and Half-caste. Pal, who was six foot odd young and still growing the gooners said that they didn't know we could pull a mob like that. Only a few hundred used to travel but they had never seen or heard of the beer monsters which built up the numbers even more, as far as we were concerned the day was over we heard City were getting beat two nil so we all fucked off home because of the score and the snow.

NEWCASTLE (H)

I showed my face for the Newcastle game at Maine Road and it was as if nearly every game or every team we played there was going to be trouble. I was in Moss Side about half an hour before kick off on the Alexandra Park estate waiting for some of the lads to go over to the ground. We eventually set off across Princess Road to knock on for Neil Crawford when a lad called Alvin, who was into kung fu and who died a few years later of a heart attack, spotted a coach full of Geordies who were directing their attention to us making arm signals. Then were shocked to see a few white lads with us who then ran off down a nearby alleyway while the rest of us were telling the Newcastle boys to get off which some were trying to do.

The coach was moving slowly in the traffic which was also not going to get to the ground on time for kick-off. The white lads, Simmo and John Sheean, came back from the alleyway and to the Geordie's surprise they had a few bricks. I took two off them and as I turned back to the coach two police officers on motorbikes spotted us and told us to drop the bricks, which we did and ran off to Crawford's house. He was taking ages to come out and when he did we were going mad because it was now five past three and we thought we had missed them. As we ran through the estate and met up with other lads who were heading in our direction and asked them if they had seen the coach, they said that no coach had passed them.

There were now thirty five of us heading to the ground at some speed. By the time we were on the corner of Claremont Road and Maine Road it was dead – it was ten minutes into the game as we turned to go back towards the estate one of the lads who were scouting about on Lloyd Street saw the coach and by the time he got his words out, he was out of breath and was told to stay on the alleyway with some bricks which he did.

The coach pulled onto the corner of Maine Road and they saw us and got off their coach. Some fat cunt and a skinny cunt who I thought looked like Laurel and Hardy were giving it 'come on nigger' (the usual shit which didn't bother us). Alvin dropped him straight away then the rest pilled off making monkey noises which at this time as there were ten blacks and twenty five white guys with us we all got ran down Maine Road. We were near the main entrance on a facing street they were still coming. By the time we stopped because we were fucked there were now at least twenty of them as the rest had stopped as most of them were big fat beer monsters and the only running they would have been doing now was running for a pint!

Alvin said to the lads 'fucking stand, we're City and this is our ground' we stood fighting toe to toe with Manchester Evening News signs which backed them off as Alvin drop kicked another Geordie before more Geordies were heading our way and we thought we gave them a good go and it was time to get off. And get off we did because no doubt the CCTV had picked half of it up.

As we got round the corner we made our way to the Parkside pub where we took shelter, looking out of the window constantly just in case the Newcastle gremlins came back for us. We were all tooled up in the pub either way and some of the locals were ready, they had to be because if they didn't help they would get caught up in it. Anyway they never came, instead the dog van and hoolivan arrived. The hoolivan was an ugly looking thing – a transit van which looked to have a big spring on it with a big TV camera on top of it. They came in the pub with their dogs and half of us had to hide in the toilets or under tables as we were too young to be in there and that they might now who they were looking for. Obviously the other Geordie who got dropped off Alvin must have been still dizzy when the police got to the scene and that the Geordie's must have grassed us up.

No one got grabbed in the pub and by the time the police left, the pub had emptied. Some of the lads went back to the ground; the rest of us got off back to the estate and told them we would give them a ring to sort out where we would meet and what time for the Leicester game. We then saw one of the lads who we told to stand on the alleyway with bricks coming out of a shop stuffing his face. We asked were did you get to? And he replied the police came. We just looked at each other and walked off.

LEICESTER (A)

It was a rainy Saturday morning and very dull outside. I had stayed at my dad's house in Longsight, I had to do that to get money off him for the match. I didn't want to go to the game because of the weather but as I'd told some of the lads that week that I was going I had little option. So I got up and got a shower after which I felt much better.

As usual I went to the shop for my dad to get a paper. He used to take the piss sending me to the shop all the time but if I didn't go I wouldn't get any spends, sometimes I wish them Scousers would have done him in when they rushed The Western a few years earlier! When I got back from the shop, Smiler was there waiting as he didn't live far from my dad's. His real name was Jason Miles and he was in another gang from Lonsight mixed with United and City fans called the Inter Longsight Firm who used to go in the City Gates pub on Hyde road. I got my money off him and got off straight to town to meet up with everyone. Smiler told me on the bus that he thought that my dad, Mike, was onto us going to the games with pure lads and asking if we ever got into any trouble. He had seen us chatting to some big guys one day and knew they were football hooligans called the Guvnors. Smiler told him that they were just lads we see at the match, he must have looked in my school bag like dads do and saw MCFC Guvnors written on my books but he never ever said or asked me about them.

I knew he was onto me, though. As I got to the station I saw my brother who told me we were going to the match by coach. I was buzzing because I couldn't really be arsed getting the train. The turn out was good – the guy who organized the coach got £5 off the older ones and £2 off the youngsters. As the coach got full twenty more lads turned up but were told the coach was full but some lads said he had to let them on or if they got the train the Baby Squad would have them at the train station, so they jumped on but had to sit on the floor half way there.

It was a good spot where we met at the coach station – the BTP and the GMP didn't see us and that way they could phone through to Leicester to tell them that there were no troublemakers on the way which was a good thing for us. It was the first time I had been to Leicester and I wanted to see their mob. I even heard that they had a few Asian lads in their firm who wore turbans. I had only ever seen two Asian hooligans at United who were Dobson and Chris (Cockney Reds) and three lads who came with City who were local lads.

As we were on the M1 we stopped at a service station which got its shop ransacked by certain members of the coach party and then a few fights started with some have a go heroes who got slightly injured so the coach party had to make a very sharp exit. Most away games were not just about the fighting it was also about the buzz that came with it and going by coaches with mobs hoping to bump into different firms at other services but on this occasion their were no other firms around.

We were soon on our way again – some of the lads were not happy at what went on at the services and were saying at this rate we would get nicked if this shit carried on. As we were approaching the outskirts of Leicester some one told the coach driver to pull up at a shop but that was really the signal for everyone to get off and the driver was told to meet back in the same place and not the ground at six because if he went there it would more than likely get smashed up.

So we all pilled off the coach and some lads were at it already bringing it on top by shouting Guvnors and chanting songs about United until told to shut up – that was a good way of attracting the attentions of the police or their mob. As we marched down a road cars were sounding their horns because people were now walking onto the road singing 'Where's your famous Baby Squad'. It was unbelievable the amount of noise coming from them – they might as well of just started smashing car windows because it wouldn't be long before the OB would get there. We didn't want that, we just wanted to get to the ground and kick it off straight away before the police came but it was like everyone was on a hype it wasn't as if anyone took drugs or there was anyone drinking.

As we got to the end of the road there was a corner shop which you could not miss, so again everyone piled in, me included and the shop got rushed. Everything in the shop was going missing and that was including the money in the till. To round it all off the shop got smashed up so that cause the shop keeper and the assistant to set off some kind of alarm but as we left we carried on walking like we owned the place. Needless to say, by the time we reached the end of the road the police arrived. Out of the 80 odd lads the police stopped and came for, a group of fifteen black lads and five whites were pulled out to make it look good.

Benny was going mad with the OB - the usual black suspects getting rounded up again, it was becoming a common thing this with the blacks getting picked out and we were beginning to wonder if the GMP were telling every force every time City were visiting to arrest the blacks and find out their addresses. Every time we got nicked we never got released until police in Manchester went to every house of those arrested then rang the other force back to confirm it was all correct.

What the police failed to do was to go to the houses of the white lads also arrested. They must have thought that we were not going to ask them if the police had visited theirs! One of the lads gave an address of a house which was boarded up so how did they work that out. We couldn't figure out why we were getting nicked and no charges were ever brought.

We were taken to the police station and kept until after the game and let out only to see their mob outside the fucking police station. They must have thought we were some kind of dick heads like they were going to do us. Like fuck they were - we ran them back up the road and kept on running at them until they fucked off. We never knew what happened at the ground only that City had got beat again (0-4). We were on our way down for sure - we made our way to the train station as it was now 7.30pm and the coach had fucked off. We boarded the train with what we had and got off back to Manchester.

ASTON VILLA (A)

This was only a week after we had all got nicked at Leicester. I was wondering whether to bother because the OB had visited my dad's house the week before and he was going on with himself. If he was in any doubt before, he was well and truly onto me now. At least the police never went to my mum's, but that little lie-down the week before didn't bother me and I didn't really want to miss this one (because we had it with the Villa youth earlier in the season on Euston station when they were cutting through to go back to

Birmingham). One of them started to mouth it to me, Travis, ET, Larry, Maynard, Danny G, Carl s, and a lad called Arron Burns and Benny until he got a sly dig in the face off someone.

The other City lads come out of the buffet bar area of the station you have to give it the Villa lads they never ran even though they were heavily outnumbered. There was a slight stand off with them and a bit of banter – shouting and swearing – then I think it was one of their main men who appeared out of the crowd to make himself heard and was upset that one of his lads got a dig in the face, even though they had started it, when they thought there was only a few of us.

Well Benny, who was one of our main men, calmed all the City lot down and from then on Benny and Travis were talking to them which from that moment on everything was sorted out and there was no trouble. There hadn't been any real problems in the past with City and Villa, their main man or their spokesman was a big fat guy who looked like that guy Roland Browning off Grange Hill. He was ok to talk to not like the others snarling away at us behind his back.

Anyway he shook hands with some City lads and all was forgotten everyone went their own way before anything got out of hand. That day we travelled to the game on one of the football special trains which were laid on for scarf boys and singers. They were the ones who would wear the team colours sing their heads off and the train would never stop at any stations, just the nearest station to the football grounds. The fans would then get a police escort to the ground. No football thugs anywhere in the country wanted a police escort to any ground because the other firm would think that they were shitting it.

If you came by normal British Rail without getting spotted by the local police, that was ok. You would get more respect if you got to fight different firms first before getting picked up by the OB and escorted. At least you had the kickoff you wanted. This time as our mob was in Piccadilly railway station with the normal fans waiting to get the next train to Birmingham the singing fans on the station started to get a bit louder and at the time it was very busy with women and kids passing through. The BTP were called out and that was time for us to jump on the football special or get the police on our case so we had to sneak there somehow and the thought of been followed by them shady guys who wanted to join up – we didn't want to wait around for them as we got on the special.

I went straight to sleep and as my eyes closed I could hear singing non-stop – I couldn't wait to get off! We eventually arrived at Witton station and the police were waiting to escort us. We all made a sharp exit across the road but as I ran across with the rest of the firm I felt dizzy as fuck. All the singing on the train had given me a headache. We were approaching the ground and someone said them lads who we had trouble with on Euston would be out for us, so one of the lads said 'everyone in their end'. In them days you could pay in without tickets so some of us paid in and the rest brought it on top with the stewards by jumping over the turnstile and the unlucky two were me and Raymond Pilling who were right at the back of the mob and never got in.

The police were called they were known to take no shit off anyone and were notoriously heavy handed, so we were not sticking about to get nicked! So we fucked off around the ground and by the time we get to the City end it was closed so we were well and truly fucked! We were gutted so we walked round the ground until we went back to their end where the City mob had gone in. Then our luck changed. We saw a load of police going in that same end and we knew it had kicked off. Even if the City boys got done or not it was a result because we got in their end!

As we got to the entrance I noticed Tony Daly who played for them but was not playing that day. I had met him before so he recognised me and I asked him if he could get us in, which he did. The only thing was we had to follow right behind him because we looked like tramps in the Players Lounge with jeans and trainers on while everyone was dressed in suits. We got through then Tony disappeared. We were now in the main stand where the manager sat but we were right up at the top of the tier looking for City's mob which we soon spotted because they were now surrounded by police. We went over and sat with the lads who told us that they give it their boys in the seats just before half time – that was a victory in their end and they had taken the piss.

From where we were sat we could see Villas mob not far away from us. They were also surrounded by their local police as well. I noticed that fat guy who we had seen at Euston sat with all they boys and this time putting up two fingers to us. Someone stood up to do it back and some police quickly grabbed the lad and put him back on his seat. Nothing happened after that in the ground as we were now under tight guard, only that it was a shit game even though I only watched half of the second half and it finished 0-0.

We left under the watchful eye of the WMP. They walked us down the road before being diverted to another incident on the other side of the ground so we were now well in the clear to go and find their mob. As we mingled in with the fans leaving the ground, we found their mob waiting in a nearby park near the City end of the ground. It looked as if they had been fighting with City fans coming out of our end and that the police had backed them off into the park with the dogs and horses.

As we came from behind them there were chants of 'war, war' followed by the shouts of 'City, City'. There were about 100 lads who were in their end charging at the villa youth in the park some of them ran as the main bulk of their mob stood fighting toe to toe (which everyone loved) until more City joined in to back them off. Other fans who were nothing to do with the pitched battles were scattering everywhere and that made some police, who were at this stage escorting the City fans to the station, divert their attention towards us who had nowhere to escape.

Everyone got on the train and the BTP were already on the special to make sure no one pulled the emergency cord. They stayed with us all the way back to Piccadilly and as we pulled in there were a lot of police on the platform with dogs. They were on the concourse of the main station where we met some City lads who had not travelled to the game but who were in town for most of the afternoon watching over the United fans who were now waiting in a backstreet pub called Mother Macs.

They had a few lads on the station earlier to see what time the train was due back so that was how the police got onto it and they were there to stop any potential trouble with United. But they were wrong and so were the United fans, as trouble was waiting right around the corner. The police now thought town was clear of all United fans they let us out of the station unescorted and as the United fans thought that we would not be back for a few hours, their pub got attacked. I could see all the windows getting put through, the sound of the whole scene was now reverberating around the narrow streets which was full of thugs on both sides.

We were backed off by the United mob who had now got out of the pub through the back doors. They were tooled up with bottles, pool cues and any weapons they could find. Most of the City lads soon returned with bricks and sticks which they had found nearby and the mobs now attacked each other. You could see lads from both City and United on the floor I heard sirens which were only one street away. The fighting continued when the police got there, they couldn't break it up until the dog vans and more backup came.

People were now getting hit with police truncheons – everyone scattered, some got nicked and the rest of us fucked off back to the usual meeting spot out of town – the Thunderdome then straight home on one of the buses to Oldham.

TOTTENHAM (H)

It was two games after the Leicester one and we were playing Tottenham. I had a funny feeling that the whole of City's mob would turn out for this one as all the times we had travelled to London to different games the Yids would be waiting for us. We used to stay until late fighting with them so we were going to see how brave they were outside London.

It was only early afternoon as I left my house to meet Splodge and the rest of the lads in Chadderton Park. As it was three o'clock, I had to keep out of the way because school was nearly over and I never went in that day, so I didn't want to be spotted. I got the bus there and could see some of the City lads making their way across the road to the park. I jumped off at the next stop and met up with them. Marco Rossi brought me a sheet and a spray can I had asked him for the day before. I was spraying on it 'Swales Out – Young Guvnors' in to put up on the fence that night.

The game was on the local soccer night on ITV so we were hoping the cameras would pick up the banner which was about the chairman who the fans wanted out because the results were not going City's way. The team had now gone twelve games without a win and the league table was looking bad for us with only six games left. After I finished the banner we jumped on the 59 bus which went the opposite way from my school – it went the long way through Middleton to town. We reached town an hour later and went around to a few pubs to look for some City thugs. We found them in Brannigans in the Royal Exchange. Most of us were too young to go in but because the lads on the door were too shit scared to say anything just in case the older lot would kick off.

We left soon after to go to Sunspot Arcade – from there we could see right up Station Approach, so if any mob were on the way down towards Piccadilly that is when we would strike. It was now six thirty and town was busy with people making their way home from work or shopping and as the late comers started to arrive in town, all the older lot went and sat in the Brunswick pub while we went up onto the station to see where their train was.

The London trains had arrived and the next one wasn't due until eight pm, they were known for always turning up late at grounds. We would call it making a late entrance but in their case a very late one, one of the lads said that when they came the season before they went to Old Trafford they always would come on coaches or mini buses and stop off at Warrington so we checked the time of the Warrington train and it was due in fifteen minutes time.

So we went back to the pub to tell the rest who thought they were not going to show. As we got down the approach we saw about 200 lads making their way up towards us so we stopped to look in a shop window thinking it was the Yids but it wasn't, it was City. The numbers were swelling because everyone wanted them for all the times they would always turn up for us. Some lads whistled down to the others who were outside the pub which then emptied, there were more and more coming out, everyone stopped to stare at what was going on there were over 300 boys in total marching up towards the station but everyone was waiting outside to see if they got off the Warrington train.

The CCTV outside the station was zooming in on us but no one cared as far as we were concerned these Yids had to get it tonight. A few lads who were still in the station keeping watch came running out at ten past seven saying that they were here! We let them get out of the station, there were only fifty or so lads them which was a piss take to bring to Maine Road, after what we had brought to their ground and to London all the time but knew that these yids were up for it and game for it so respect to them.

They came bouncing off like they were running the show; Browny, Ricky and Sammons at the forefront as always these were some of there black firm who were always there and wanted it they ran us enough and vice versa. Either way we always had good battles with them they never backed down . Then they had no time to turn and run which I knew they wouldn't, or they wouldn't of bowled out the way they did, City lads got them and gave the ones who stood a good kicking. There were City boys everywhere; they had been waiting for this day for ages. Browny and some lads got done in and Ricky, who I think was from Birmingham originally, got punched in the face and his hat and glasses flew off. Someone picked them up as this disturbance was going on before the police arrived which then brought the BTP out. You have to take your hat off to them they stood and had it.

Someone shouted 'everyone walk' so the police called for more back up and as they did most of the lads got on their toes back to Sunspot with some police in a van giving chase. Everyone stopped running and turned on the police then started banging on the van. I could see someone had thrown a brick as the police got out which made them get back in as it was going to go off with them as the full mob were now getting chased down the approach towards the police van.

They were under the impression that the mob was coming for them and sped through the crowd – everyone scattered before the rest of the GMP got there. They were surprised that the mob had turned on them for the first time and they were pissed off. As we got to the ground we saw Ricky again. He had some front walking about on the forecourt but with a police officer looking for the mob who had his hat and glasses away one of the City lads, Ady Gunnings, went up to him and told him to fuck the police off and he would get his glasses back for him.

When he had done this he soon put them on and could see properly again just in time to see another mob walking towards him – he was soon on his toes but wouldn't anyone if they were at Spurs. We all went into the north stand buzzing like fuck but there were a few people who were upset at the fact the Yids brought fuck all really. The game was underway as we were all busy talking and not paying any real attention to it as we were getting beat one nil and as half time approached the police were on their travels walking past the sixty or so lads sat in the seats in the north stand.

Some thought it might have something to do with what went on with the police in town but I wasn't arsed because I had done fuck all wrong. But then again if they were going to start dragging anyone out for nothing then that would have been a different story. As the second half was underway the police fucked off, so we all moved down to the front of the stand right behind the goal. That was when I took the banner off the lads and climbed up on the fence to put it up so the TV cameras could see it. Ten minutes later Neil McNab got an equaliser and everyone was on the fence trying to get onto the pitch and on TV at the same time. It didn't work out; there were too many police presence and stewards.

After the game there was a demonstration outside the ground. We never bothered with that shit; we just got it together and went looking for the Yids. We couldn't find them; they must have made a sharp exit, so we all marched through the dark streets of Moss Side. As we entered Moss Lane East near the traffic lights, we saw three mini buses which were full. There were no markings on them, so some of us doubled back to get some bricks from an alleyway. As we got back onto the road it was too late, someone had already thrown a brick through one of the windows which caused the rest to speed off through the lights. That was the end of the Yids for that night, they really took the piss the amount of times we went to London stayed and kicked it off nearly all night, Yet they come up here turn up late, get done and then after the game fuck off straight back to London without putting up a fight – the fucking shit heads.

SHEFFIELD W (A)

As the mob met at Victoria train we were met by a large crew of photographers but it wasn't the press it was police officers. They were now on City's case as they took pictures of us. Everyone started to put hoods up and hide their faces with newspapers. We all walked through the ticket barriers and sprinted for the train as the police continued to take photos. When we boarded the train the BTP jumped on then as did a load of GMP to travel with us. They were obviously up to something and although it was only a short journey across the Pennines to South Yorkshire, we knew why the police were coming with us.

The mob was 200 strong so that was probably why they came but on the other hand it might have been a bit of intimidation from what went on the other week in town before the Tottenham game. As we left Sheffield train station on the way to the ground, the camera crew were there again taking pictures, so everyone put their hoods up – me and the young ones never bothered because we were only juveniles and didn't give a fuck about having our pictures taken, in fact we liked the limelight and so did Daft Donald, who was one of the older lads and a complete lunatic, didn't bother about hiding his either.

We were under heavy escort to the ground it was probably for the Wednesday boys safety and the skinheads that were in their mob. As we approached the ground under escort the police led us straight to the City end and left us. Me, Daft Donald and Maynard fucked off for a walk about to see if we could see any of their mob. We came up with nothing. We were then spotted by the local police who tried to give chase so we mingled in with the crowd but could be easily be spotted as we were the only three black guys there. So we had to jump the turnstiles and go in their end.

We had lost the officers outside the ground. If we would have stopped for them they would have probably nicked us for something just to take the piss because we went walking about the ground, we sat in their end in the bottom right hand corner and we could see all the City mob to our right in the top tier and below them were the other City fans in the bottom their. There were six and a half thousand City fans which had travelled to the game to give the team support, even though we were almost certain to go down. We started shouting across to the City mob and telling them that none of their mob was in that stand but as we went into the tunnel at half time to get some drinks there were about thirty lads heading our way shouting racist remarks, which didn't bother us as we had heard all that shit before.

Daft Donald wanted us to kick it off with them even though we would get done in, but to their surprise we stood bouncing about saying come on then you sheepshaggers. They then started to hot us up with all the fans Wednesday fans saying that we were Mancs so with all the attention now turned on us, we made a run for it back up the steps and into the seats. This time we went straight to the very corner of the ground which was at the corner flag but still in the stands at this stage and shouted up to the lads to tell them that their mob was in that stand after all, not that they could have got down to help us...

Half way through the second half a City player, Paul Simpson, was coming over to take a corner when Daft Donald who was constantly looking over his shoulder for most of that half all of a sudden said 'they're here'. As we looked around there were about fifty Wednesday hooligans who call themselves Owls Crime Squad making their way over the seats towards us. At that point the three of us jumped up and over the wall at the corner flag where Paul Simpson was about to take the corner with their mob now within feet of us shouting racist abuse again. A skinhead was their spokesman, shouting most of the shit saying 'tell your lads we will have it in the housing estate near the ground'.

The police and stewards arrived pushing them back and then grabbed the three of us. The City mob in the top tier was now shouting down to us to do the Old Bill. I think they were trying to get us nicked! We were put in the stand behind the goal as the kick was being taken and the City fans cheered us for going in the Wednesday end. The game soon ended and we all met up outside and told them where the Sheffield mob wanted us to meet. They must have thought that we had about fifty lads as well. The police put us all on buses – everyone was gutted because now the Sheffield boys would think that we shit it and got off. As we got a mile down the road all the buses in front came to a halt as one of the windows were put through on the very first bus we could then hear it going off.

We jumped off with the police at the front and back of the buses on motorbikes; they were radioing for back-up but could not leave their bikes. As we got near to the fighting the Sheffield mob realised that there were five buses full of City thugs and were soon on their toes. They had thought that the first bus full of lads that they bricked was the only one, and as more police arrived we were charging down the road. This soon came to an end as the heavy handed police started pushing everyone against a wall and held us there until the buses caught up. They were telling us if we ever came to the Wednesday ground again they would nick us all. Obviously they didn't look at the league tables because the next time we were in Sheffield would be at Sheffield United.

As we got to the train station the Manchester police were waiting and taking pictures. On our arrival back at Victoria train station there were no United fans waiting for us, instead it was more police backed up by their cameramen. Some of the City lads were pissed off at having their photo taken and were on their way over to ask them why when some over excited police officers ran over and started lashing out with their truncheons. Then they started chasing the City fans towards the Arndale centre until one of the main lads shouted 'everyone fucking walk', so we did and the police backed off.

We were heading towards the Cypress Tavern where United might be. As we marched through Piccadilly we met up with some City lads who had not travelled to the game who told us that they were definitely there. So we marched through the Gay Village and ran a few ginger beers (Queers) off before reaching Princess Street as we could see some United boys going in. Some City lads shouted Munich and they spotted the whole mob and ran into the pub to tell the rest that we were on our way.

As we approached the pub the police appeared from the side of it. It was all over we got ran off by the police and the United fans never came out.

EVERTON (A)

As the mob met at Victoria for this fixture it was unclear whether a big mob would turn up or not because the last game City played the week before was at home to Arsenal, (the game finished incident free as most of the Gooners were with most of us as we knew them) but as we all walked down Wilmslow Road, we passed The Clarence and there was a large crowd of City lads and drinkers outside, most of whom knew us. Most of the older black lads had an argument with some of the City lads who were said to be members of NF, which didn't go down well. It had been coming for months because that pub and most of them lads who went in there were known to support the NF, even though they stood side by side with one another on the terraces.

On this occasion a couple of the more sympathetic white lads who were with us decided that enough was enough, it had to get sorted out there and then. The NF lads in question were attacked by some of the lads (both black and white) and this then caused people to break it up with a little stand off and a few verbals being exchanged. As the full mob came to the pub to try and sort it out, all most of them could say was 'we are all City together'. After an hour or so at the pub and with people trying to sort things out everyone left. The Arsenal lads went half an hour earlier to get their train back to London.

Anyway for the Everton game as a large mob of City thugs turned up at the station. There were over 200 plus there were forty black lads who came, this was the biggest turn out of blacks for a Merseyside game ever and as we knew them Scousers didn't like us, we had to turn out in force. We were hanging about waiting for the train to arrive, talking about the troubles the week before with the NF when most of them arrived on the station. Everyone was eyeing each other but nothing was said until everyone was on the train. People were asking questions as why it kicked off and what had brought it on but as the train arrived at Lime Street the mob marched off and the NF went their own way.

So it was back to the same 200 that we started off with and the tension was building up as they split up. There were only forty blacks in the group of 200 so why did the other 100 or so get off? As we marched to the ground with what we had, we got to Goodison where we saw all of their mob outside the front of the ground one of them who I always spotted because he was always at the front of there mob and is one of there main heads he is half Chinese and had a pony tail his name is Kenny Chan. Then Big Warren said all the tan heads to the front (meaning all the blacks) so the 40 of us walked upfront with the white lads at the back. The idea was to let the Scousers see us all at the front and to see what they would do. As the mob marched down the road towards the scousers chanting Guvnors, Guvnors, the police came from nowhere and grabbed Big Warren W who was right at the front and told him to tell his boys to turn back and go the other way. Warren then said 'you tell them, I ain't the main man'. The officers then tried to arrest him which caused everyone to surround them including all the black lads saying to the officers 'he's coming with us' and 'if he gets nicked we all get nicked'.

Then one tries to say we only want you lot to turn and go the other way, that caused the other officers to get on their radios and put a call out saying 'assistance, assistance – black disturbance, black disturbance' (now where had I heard that call before?) the response was delayed for a few minutes because we never knew at the time one of our lads, Chrissy James, had wandered off into an estate to kick it off with some Scousers and got his neck slashed. Chrissy must have been off his head to follow the Scousers into the estate in the first place. As back up came we were marched back to the turnstiles at the City end as there had been no trouble with the

Scousers to this point. So we entered the ground and went into the standing area.

As we all went towards the corner section of the ground, Everton were now in the corner section singing a song about Chrissy James whose neck one of them had slashed no less than forty-five minutes earlier. So the City boys replied with 'Barry Green how's your back, you scouse twat' referring to one of their boys who had had their back slashed in London. Then there were more chants from the City mob of 'Euston station' where the incident happened. After all the banter I spotted my mate from school Paul Lowie who was in their end and with their mob Kenny Chan was also there, we shouted to each other then he shouted again to show me the black guy who was in their mob. He told me he was called Emmy, I never believed him until then that they would have a black lad in their mob.

As it got to half time there was a fight it the tunnel with a few of the NF lads. The police were called but it was the thugs who sorted it out without anyone getting nicked, then the shouting got worse on the terraces with everyone swearing before the older lads had to stand in the middle and stop all the shit. The scousers were having a field day at this point watching all that going on with City's mob arguing among themselves. The game finished goalless and there was no trouble after as the police had us under tight escort back to Lime Street. As we were taken on the long walk back, the Scousers tried to attack the escort twice but the police were onto them. We reached the station without further incident and then back to Manchester. Everyone was in good spirits as if nothing had happened in the ground as they all chatted to one another.

We made our way off the train at Victoria and marched up Cross Street towards Market Street with the police driving next to the City mob. We knew then that United were not far away so we marched up Market Street in between the Arndale Centre and the police tried to stop us. By the time we got to Fountain Street, United were heading in the same direction towards us but in the end the police split both groups up by chasing everyone off with the dogs. Nothing was going to happen now as the police were going to follow us or chase us everywhere until we left town, so we all called it a day.

WEST HAM (A)

This was to be City's last game in the top flight for sometime as it looked certain that the team was on the way down. We all met at Piccadilly and forty of us left on the early train. We made our way to London, most of us were wearing t-shirts as it was a very hot morning. The tee shirts read '061 - we prefer to call it Manchester' which some one had robbed the day before out of Affleck's Palace, it was reference to the Manchester telephone code. So they were all handed out to us that morning to put on in London so everyone knew who we were as we never wore the team colours.

We got to London at 10.30am and Euston was dead, so we went to a pub which was called the Lion and Lamb, which was five minutes away in Somers Town. Benny knocked on the door as the pub was shut as he knew the landlord. He would always let us in no matter what time because he had some trouble there a few months before with some Walsall fans and Benny and a few City lads were in there and gave him a hand to remove them from the pub.

We stayed in there until midday when the next Manchester train was due but the British rail train was running late as always so we waited on Euston. As we were in their we saw about twenty lads walking out of the station. There were three mixed race lads with them, one was wearing a Liverpool top which I thought was strange as I thought all the Liverpool thugs were all white. We followed them out as they were heading for the pub which we had been in as most teams used to visit it as it was the nearest to the station. As they got half way down the alley we shouted 'come on then Mickeys' which was a bad idea as bottles and other bits of rubbish were used to back us off onto Eversholt Street. As we dodged the missiles which had been thrown at us we stumbled upon a skip which soon got emptied and the Mickeys were on their way back down the alleyway with us not far behind. As they turned again, bricks and bottles came flying over our heads which the City mob had been throwing, they then turned and ran into the pub. We followed as they ran straight through it and out the back doors.

We then turned back and returned to the station to see if the train had arrived but still no sign, so we waited as there was no where else to go and we couldn't go walking about London without the full mob. When the train finally came and the mob came off in their hundreds on Euston. This was a mob to be proud of – they had travelled 200 and odd miles to be at this fixture to show all the cockneys that we were now top boys in Manchester. We made our way out and on our way back to the Lion and Lamb we left a few scouts on the station to wait for Tottenham as there were rumours going round that they were coming out in force because of what happened on Piccadilly a month before. They soon arrived and the City scouts got spotted and ran out of the station by the Yids. The usual suspects were with them; Browny and Ricky who were not giving up for some unknown reason. The Yids were just out for a fight with City all the time (well at least we always stayed to fight and not fuck off in some mini bus ha ha) but we had been ran off them a few times but not today. The City lads made it back to the pub to call everyone out. The Yids soon turned back on the alleyway towards Eversholt Street when half way up they turned bumped into some City lads who had ran back to the skip to remove more weapons.

There were now fist fights and broken chair legs were involved. The fighting continued for a while until a policeman came out of a building with a pair of overalls on clearly marked Police. The two sets of thugs were fighting on Eversholt Street outside a Police garage of all places where their vehicles were being repaired. Anyway he ran back in and came out again on his radio asking for back up which wasn't far away. As they arrived the fighting had stopped the Yids made off in the other direction as we headed back. But we all got stopped – Cozi and Splodge got nicked and the police reckoned that they had seen them remove items from a nearby skip and use them as weapons, that was one of the best toe to toe battles ever with them.

(When they attended court a few months later the police were warned about future arrests of so called football hooligans as it was proved that they had made up a false story between them and arrested the wrong lads over the incident).

After that we were escorted towards Kings Cross Station and more and more City thugs joined the escort. The police didn't stop and call for more assistance – it was red hot which made sweat start dripping off most of us. The mob was getting frustrated and started to chant 'Tottenham cop he is dead, big machete in his head'. There were about 400 in total on the way to fight the ICF of West Ham. We set off from St Pancras tube and after ten minutes it came to a halt. No one knew what was going on as we were sat in the middle of nowhere for ages. One woman passed out because of the heat before we set off fifteen minutes later and it stopped again at a station and everyone jumped off.

As we tried to get through the station we were blocked off by a heavy police presence. The OB said they would not let anyone through and then there was a surge forward and it just kicked off with the police. As we backed them off they came back at us with truncheons drawn. We were blocked in and had to give up and as we walked out of the station there were rows of police vans waiting for us. Obviously that was why there was a long delay on the tube – they had no intention of letting half of that mob go to the game and after the chanting that was going on. We were taken to different police stations, I ended up at Snow Hill – there were about fifty of us in there with twenty to a cell which was like a big double room me.

Lappo, Maynard, Benny, Taves, Arron Burns, Marco Rossi, and a load more lads were in there. We never knew why we were held but we weren't let out until after the game. We were released without charge although all our addresses were noted and a Polaroid was taken. We were then told that there had been a pitch invasion by City fans and that we had been relegated. As we were all let out together one officer laughed and said 'you didn't think we were going to let all you lot go to West Ham did you? There were just too many of you!'

We made our way back to Euston to see if the mob had arrived back. They were waiting and we marched to another pub in

Somers Town just down the road from Euston where all City's beer monsters were drinking. As we joined forces again we were all going back to get the train home ET got to the game and was pissed off. We had gone down. When three Chelsea and two Liverpool lads said that they wanted to join up with us as we had the biggest mob in London that day, they got fucked off – we trusted no one! As we got onto the station the Tottenham lads were on their way off the train as they came back from Watford, the BTP moved quickly to stop anything and as they took the Yids out of the station and down Euston Road we ran down for the tube with everyone jumping the barriers.

We got the tube to the next stop which was Euston Square and got back onto Euston Road. We were now in front of the Yids. It kicked off and we got ran twice before running them past Euston Station down Euston Road. There was some fighting in the McDonalds where some Yids ran. Police were now on the scene and wading into both groups then there were fights starting down side streets and down a long road where we could see the big Telecom tower in the distance. Eventually the Yids backed off as we were chased back towards Euston. We split up and met back at the Lion and Lamb where Simon Skelly, Dave Goodall, Steve Kinsey and a few Wythenshawe lads were.

We told them we were leaving before we all got locked up. Ten lads had just been nicked and it was like the police attention was turned all day on City so we left for the train. This time there were more police on Euston as the mob made their way through the ticket barriers without even showing a ticket. The police just wanted us on that train and out of London.

On the train back we were trying to work out why we were nicked in the first place and had our pictures taken but this time names and addresses were put onto the back of the photos which we had to sign our names onto. It was strange but we didn't get onto it then although we'd soon find out why the OB had taken the trouble to do that.

WREXHAM (A) FRIENDLY

During pre season we played a testimonial match which at Wrexham for one of their players. That day I was in town with a few lads as we were getting a bus to Wythenshawe to meet the rest as we were going by car and mini buses. The game wasn't until 7.45 so we had to wait around until the older ones finished work. There was a good turn out from Wythenshawe who had black Dennis Edwards, Crossy, Adrian Miller, Gilly (RIP) who was Man U and Raymond Pilling from Prestwich brought a good mob of thirty over from that end. In the end there were forty of us who travelled from Oldham. We were off down the M56 with a convoy of six mini buses and a couple of cars. As we got into Wrexham we parked up at a B&Q and made our way towards the ground where there was a town centre. We spotted a few lads stood watching us so we just ran at them, they fucked off straight through the town, I don't know why they bothered coming out for us. As it was still only seven o clock, fans started to arrive in the town centre we made our way back towards the ground when we heard sirens it was two police cars minis, 'what the fucking hell is that?' the lads started to sing.

The minis pulled to a temporary halt to have a good look at us before driving off, so we made our way to the B&Q car park where we stayed until the others got there. As we headed to the ground we had a tidy mob of about one hundred but we were held up near the ground by the police and the good thing about it was there was no GMP there to push us around. The Welsh police didn't know the score so we just carried on walking as they tried to talk to a few lads at the front who were just blanking them.

As we got to the ground we saw a line of police in the middle of the road with the Wrexham Frontline mob behind them. There main man was at the front – that big, fat fucker Foulkes who had been on Euston with his mob the previous season. As the two firms charged at one another there were a few fists flying and City charged through the police line properly. The police were just trying to grab anyone as they were obviously clueless as to how to control the disturbance. Eventually the Welsh ponies and sheepdogs came to restore order and march everyone to the right end of the ground. The turnstiles got jumped – there was no trouble, everyone got over, so much for raising money for the player.

Everyone was talking about the forthcoming season as someone had a copy of the fixture list as we read through it their was some very good games to come and a lot of trouble that would follow. Halfway through the second half all the mob went to the left of our end where their was a cabin selling food and, as some lads were getting served, Me, Raymond P and Dennis E, were at the back of the queue some City lads started to help themselves as there was only one girl serving. She then started to shout at the lads robbing, and a copper heard her and came over. She told him what had happened and then pointed out 'the niggers' (the cheeky bitch) when we had fuck all to do with it.

The officer then made his way towards us telling us he wanted a word, so I said to the other two I ain't getting nicked for fuck all so I climbed over the fence and onto the pitch to get away while the game was still going on. The City mob then got on thinking that it was a one man pitch invasion and came to join me. The ref stopped the game for five minutes while the police got us off and out of the ground, it was then time for us to get off before we all got charged.

THE DAWN RAID SEASON

This season more or less started off where the last one had finished, the first game of the new season was at home to Plymouth Argyle. It was a quiet game which City won 2-1, it was a pity they could not do it at the end of last season – they were all the same players in the team that had got relegated. The game finished trouble free, Plymouth's mob did show up with about 70 lads from the Central Element who looked like they were up for it. There was at least one mixed race lad in their mob which was good for race relations but for some reason City were not up for it. What a waste of a journey for them!

OLDHAM (A) – THE NIGHT BEFORE: FRIDAY NIGHT FEVER

It was a Friday afternoon in Oldham the day before City were due in town. All the City lads who lived in different parts of the town met in Chadderton Park to discuss the game the next day when one of the lads came and brought to our attention a racist slogan being sprayed around the town which read 'O A F C kill all City niggers'. This was almost certainly aimed at me and my brother who were the only two black lads who supported City and lived up there.

I was that pissed off I went to Manchester after I had made a few phone calls to round up some lads and tell them what the sheepshaggers had written. Then we headed back to town to meet up with some more City lads. As we reached town I went to the phone box to call some City lads in Oldham to find out where we were meeting as the so called 'Fine Young Casuals' from Oldham and their NF followers would be in a pub in the town centre right behind Oldham police headquarters. We jumped onto the 82 bus after rounding up a bus load of City lads which included 30 black lads and that was just for starters – they would see the rest the day after.

As we were coming up Manchester Road we were approaching an estate called West Street which was only ten minutes walk from the town centre. We could see about forty lads walking up towards the town centre. We were ready to get off and have it with them when we saw police cars coming in the opposite direction onto the estate. We jumped off the bus only to learn it was the City lot from Oldham and they had just smashed up a house party with twenty-five of the Oldham lads in it. We then made our way through the subway unnoticed by police cars or vans and went the long way round as there was a pub called the Bulls Head up the road from the Oldham pub.

Most of us went into the Bulls Head to see if there were more City fans – which there were and they said they saw the sheepshaggers going into their pub. We all charged about 200 yards down the road and some lads went in and started to kick it off. Soon after the lads who went in were ran back out as the rest of us waited outside. To their surprise we all went back as most of the FYC who were lucky got out of the back as the rest of them and their pub got wrecked.

We chased the rest back up the hill to the town centre when one of their main men Chris Coleman said to me 'you black bastard, you're going to get it'. As he said that coming towards me he got knocked out by one of the lads. The rest of them scattered and some got caught outside McDonalds and got done in. Just then the police arrived and they were running all over the place trying to stop the City thugs. One lad who got nicked had broken his leg and it turned out to be one of the City lads Slashneck Robert Slicker. The lads from Manchester thought he was Oldham!

We all managed to get it together and marched back down to the Bulls Head but the police were now everywhere so we all had to get off – there was no point in sticking around – we had done them and that was that, and there was always tomorrow!

THE MATCH DAY

That morning I was in Manchester early as I was on the way to knock on for a few of the lads who never went Oldham the night before to fill them in with what was going on but we had to be in Piccadilly for 12.30 so we could meet up with the whole mob. This was going to be one of those games which would turnout to be a joke as I knew what the Oldham mob was like and their full numbers in total were well short of the 100 mark. Even if we only had forty against them I couldn't honestly see them doing us at all.

As we met in town with a good few lads already there and some of the beer monsters. We then made our way through the Arndale towards Victoria Train Station. We were going by train as the mob would be as big as ever. City always brought a big firm to Oldham as we all liked going there and taking the piss. The last time City had been there was Good Friday 1984 when City took the ground over, robbed the ticket office, held the game up and done the Oldham lot in. That day there were about six hundred lads up for the local derby – the whole of the Manchester City thugs attended, even the town centre got robbed and the jewellers got done. The police were powerless, they never expected that much trouble let alone that many lads.

By now there were 400 lads backed up by the black community. As we boarded the train for Rochdale we get off at Mills Hill station which on the Middleton/Chadderton border and walked through Chadderton as there were just too many for the bus. It was a long walk to the town centre and once there we met up with even more lads who got the 82 bus up to the town centre which was swarming with local police. Then came the GMP and the photos started again as everyone got it together. We marched down towards the ground and passed a pub called the Brook Tavern. Some of the FYC were at the windows shouting abuse and giving it the v-signs as the police were with us, it then had its windows put through as we passed and still under police escort which the police did nothing about as they just wanted to keep the mob moving towards the ground.

As we got to the top of Sheep Foot Lane we saw the rest of their mob making their way down to the ground. We made our presence felt and chased them and the police could only look on as they tried to stop the charge down the now very busy road. City were everywhere and fighting with some of the more gamer FYC lot which had Burkey, Robin Walker, Pody, Lee Spence, Dave Freer, Scott Morley and Lloyd Scantelbury. But they couldn't do it all and had to back off as more and more City came from all directions. As we headed for the turnstiles Daft Donald and a mob of City who where with him chased more Oldham lads but they soon got lost in the crowd. We never saw where they went as we then made for the City end. The ground was packed – there were still thousands outside as over 100 lads jumped the turnstiles without a problem as the stewards could only watch. Once inside the ground more

A disturbance in Oldham 1987

people stormed a gate to our right hand side as police on horseback tried and failed to get it under control.

By now the ground was open house. From where I was stood on top of a wall, everyone was just walking in. As the match got under way the stand behind City's goal was jammed and no one could move. It was still all standing so the police and stewards opened another end along the side of the pitch which by now was almost

Fans go on rampage at local derby

POLICE SICKENED BY SOCCER THUGS

full of City thugs young and old. There was even some local Oldham lads who I knew and were not into the violence but just came along such as Cliffton Muir, Jerome Hurbert, Christian Parker from Chadderton and Pratt (Matthew Fitton) from Oldham who was a United hooligan who we still all hung about with.

The game was now well under way and it was still 1-0 to Oldham until Imre Varadi popped up to score the equaliser. Everyone went wild and jumped onto the fence trying to get onto the pitch but failed – there was now a heavy police presence with most of them taking photos. Another twist to the tale was that they now had a big shoulder sized video camera filming us. This was the start of the dawn raid season and the police must have said to one another 'enough is enough'

So we got off the fence and started putting hoods up. The video crew were now directed to the famous Chaddy end where all Oldhams FYC hooligans were housed and Daft Donald and about twenty City lunatics who had got in their end unnoticed until they jumped up when City scored. Then Daft Donald started fighting with the Oldham mob who obliged and started to get stuck into Donald and the City lot, I can honestly say the City lads got done as they got surrounded and outnumbered.

As police and stewards arrived to arrest Daft Donald, his mates all ran to the other end of the stand to get to the Oldham fans on the other side of the fence but were held at bay by the now hyped up police force. That was the kind of thing they were good at coping with – keeping the fans at bay. As the game came to a close we could see the Oldham thugs clearly leaving, so the whole of our end down the side of the pitch emptied as the police could only watch from the opposite side of the fence, we left in our hundreds and were met by a heavy police presence outside the ground. They now had their truncheons drawn with the dog section and the pony section to back them up as they then escorted us up Sheepfoot Lane and then onto Rochdale Road.

As that was going on there was a breakaway group of some of City's main and older lads that went in the opposite direction and there were reports fifteen minutes later that a large group of City thugs were fighting with Oldham and were attacking each other as units rushed to the scene. This was taking place on Chadderton Way which was where I lived. I then thought that my house would get attacked but I heard it had now moved to outside the Trap Inn, a pub at the other end of the road from where we were but I couldn't see it.

By now the police wouldn't let us move and when we eventually reached the Trap Inn the police had rounded up the City group on the corner of Chadderton Way and Rochdale Road. The police marched us up a hill and left us there as they were called to another disturbance back at the Brook Tavern. More City latecomers had spotted the Odham mob going in there and attacked some of them. The pub windows were now boarded up from the earlier incident. As we reached the top of the hill we were now outside the Tommy Field pub just by the market and now parallel to Henshaw Street (which was only five minutes from where Richard Edgehill lived at the time but was unknown to us all at the time) when we saw a mob of about 80 of the Oldham FYC coming our way.

They had spotted us, you couldn't miss us! The FYC ran at us throwing missiles on the way as some of the City lads shouted 'everyone fucking stand, no one run'. As that happened the FYC stopped and turned with only Pody, Lloyd Scantlebury, Scott Morley, Lee Spence, Burkey, Dave Freer, and a few or the main men just stood their and ready to fight us. But as more City came piling around the corner and most of the FYC had ran off, his left them with no choice but to turn and run.

Now we could hear the police (give away) sirens once again, so we made off through the market and into the town centre with a few shop windows going through on the way. The police finally got us at the bus station – it was like they brought the whole of the police force out just for us and they were filming and taking photos again. They would not let us in any pubs as they just got us back to Mumps train station and back to Victoria.

We eventually marched up Deansgate as I was taking a few of my own photos on the way when we bumped into a few stray United fans who got weighed in before running off towards Piccadilly and we followed –we arrived to find all United's mob backed up by the main boys and the Cockney Reds which I then took a photo of. Then there was a running battle in Piccadilly which the police got under control as hundreds of City and United thugs were on either side of the road with the police in the middle with vans and dogs. Eventually we were dispersed and me and the City mob from Oldham got off to Oldham town centre to see what the FYC were up to. The only thing they said was that they couldn't stand and fight as we brought too many meaning that our mob was too big for them to fight with, it would have just been like City trying to take on man u back in the day.

ASTON VILLA (A)

This game was to be more or less the same as the one the season before but with a few differences. This time it was more organised and sorted out the week before at the Oldham game. We travelled to Birmingham New Street by train and as we arrived to our surprise the West Midlands Police were there waiting for us and escorted us straight to the ground but for some reason no one wanted to go into the City end and those who hadn't travelled their the season before wanted to go in the Villa End. As we got to the ground the police took us to the City end and left us all at the turnstiles and we kept it quiet so we could go in their end without being spotted.

Their mob would never think we would go back in their end for a second time in a matter of five months but we did and they never knew – not even the police got onto it. This time a 200 strong mob were sat in the bottom tier which ran along side the pitch not far from the manager's dug out. But we managed to keep it quiet for most of the game apart from the odd cheer and a jump up when a City shot just went wide of the post.

It was one-nil to Villa who had scored early on in the game and it looked very odd when the villa fans jumped up to celebrate and there were 200 lads just sat there watching. It was a poor game overall. With ten minutes left City had Paul Simpson warming up on the touch line to make a change when Ian Scott popped up to score. That caused all the City thugs to leap over the wall near the manager's dugout and onto the pitch. A load of us ran to celebrate with City defender Steve Redmond who was in the middle near the centre circle.

As the mob stayed on the pitch, the stewards came on to usher us off and we continued to walk when the police arrived and we speedily made a sharp exit back to the seats. The game was only held up for a few minutes as the stewards sat near a wall to keep an eye on us. Of course Paul Simpson wasn't happy as he never got on but City earned a draw so it wasn't that bad after all, Simmo!

The game soon ended and the police were following our every move. As we left the ground the police let us all go and the Villa mob soon arrived and a small skirmish broke out with a few fights starting as some City lads backed away from the Villa youth. The police were soon on the scene and we were all put against a wall and searched. As this was happening I noticed two guys who were sat in the game with us but funny enough they never got on the pitch. One had fair ginger hair and the other had glasses on and black hair. The police never searched them and as I was being given the once over I said to one of the officers 'what about them two?'

As the officer approached them I clearly saw the ginger haired one pull something out of his pocket and show it to the officer at which point he let him go as the police told us all to leave the area or we would be arrested. As we walked down the road the two guys came up to me in front of everyone and said 'hey mate you nearly got me nicked back there'. I told him I wasn't his fucking mate and that I had never saw either of them before and asked them what they were doing with us? He said that they were City fans at which point I told everyone that he flashed something to the police and never got searched. I told him I thought he was police and he laughed and said I was being ridiculous. He thought because I was 15 no one was going to listen to me! Clearly he hadn't done his home work or he would have known that I had been there from day one. At that point one of the older lads intervened and said 'Just who the fuck are youse? Show us what you showed the officers then! If you're not the police' Then they ran off. They were chased but got away in the direction of the ground and the police

As we headed down the road people were checking the mob to see if there was anymore Old Bill around. There wasn't and everyone was told that if anyone was trying to get into the mob we should all give it to them. As we approached the Asda car park not far from Villa park, their mob appeared from nowhere and then there was another disturbance as shoppers abandoned their trolleys and ran out of the way of the bottle and stone throwing Villa fans.

They managed to back us all off but the City lads turned which caused a stand off as missiles were still being exchanged. Then we heard the sound of sirens to let us all know that they were coming and to disappear. We were soon blocked off back on the main road as the police and dog unit came running towards us. We then had an escort back to the train station and out of Birmingham.

SHREWSBURY TOWN (A)

On the morning of this game we all met at Piccadilly train station as usual. Nothing much went on at the station apart from a larger than usual police presence who were now making a habit of travelling with us by train. They had been there at Oldham and Villa and the video team were with them as they filmed me, Lee Boots, Scott McCallum, Peter Price, Pete Munday, both of whom were from Oldham near me, Benny, Carl Stewart and the rest of the lads. I think that they were intimidated by the number of lads that turned out – they must of thought that there would be no mob after all the grief we got off at Villa Park. What they didn't realise was that Division 2 was the place to be because if they had studied the fixtures carefully they would have seen that every game we were going to play was going to go off without out a doubt except maybe Bournemouth and Ipswich. Those were the games the police turned out in force for, the undercover police were giving them the wrong information.

As we all travelled to Shrewsbury we had to change at Crewe and as the train pulled in there was a mob of Cardiff City on the opposite platform. We don't know where they were off to but they spotted us and tried to get over to us as we tried the same thing, forgetting that we had GMP on board with us. Nothing happened and the Cardiff mob finally got on their train while we had to wait an hour for ours.

So we all piled out of the station and into Crewe town centre where we saw some of their boys. One of them shouted racist remarks at us and we chased them through the traffic lights. They ran into a pub to take shelter and the doors were locked behind them which was a mistake as the only way into the pub now was through the windows so they got put through.

On our way back towards the City mob the door then got kicked in and as that was going on some City lads started to climb through the windows. At that point police sirens could be heard, which caused the City lads to retreat back to the station which was no more than 500 yards away. The police came back into the station but no arrests were made as there were no witnesses as their mob had scarpered out of the rear of the pub.

Our train arrived soon after and we were off with the police now keeping a close watch on us. As we arrived in Shrewsbury there were no officers at the station so we went on our way and the GMP left us alone, we marched through the town centre and soon bumped into their huge mob of twenty as we chased them into a McDonalds where they asked the staff to ring the police!

So we left them to it and went to the ground. As we arrived there we knew it was sold out so it was just a matter of getting in.

The fans went in leaving up to 800 of City's large group of loyal fans left outside. The police were now debating whether to turn us all away and fear the town centre getting wrecked or give in and let us in for £3 each – which they soon did and opened up half of their end. The attendance was a poor 6,280 with City's travelling army bringing half of that.

All our mob were situated behind the goal and as the game was nearing an end City were awarded a penalty – was this going to be our first away win in thirty away games? The last time City had won away was in January 1986 and it was now September 1987. As Neil McNab stepped up to take the spot kick we all jumped up onto the fence ready to go onto the pitch – then he went and missed.

On the police video which was shot of us in the ground it just shows a mob of us on the fence and then it says that we can clearly be seen waving our fists in the air (which I never knew was a crime). As we left the ground at the end we were taken straight back to the train station. On our arrival we heard that Smiler and a few of the lads who never got into the ground had been nicked during the game for kicking it off in the town centre with some of their boys who then grassed them up to the police. They were later released without charge.

As we got back later than expected we bumped into some United boys in the Burger King in Piccadilly and it went off in the premises. Tony O'Neill was there and called us all black bastards with Mickey and Chris Francis wanting his blood. This 15 year old (me) knocked him to the floor as chairs and tables were used. It spilled outside onto the street as police units from the train station arrived and for once chased the United mob off. Tony Cannon, who got slashed up on the ferry by West Ham fans, was with the United mob and got nicked at the scene but no less then twenty minutes later was on the 82 bus with me and some City lads on the way back to Oldham. He lived up the road from me so we all knew him so there was no trouble with him that night.

MILLWALL (H)

This was a game not to be missed! As the Young Guvnors met in town most of us that day couldn't wait to finish school. From three o'clock onwards there were more and more thugs gathering outside Sunspot which was more a less a stone's throw from the station. As the day dragged on everyone was now in the arcade and in the Brunswick pub – the time was now reaching six thirty and there was still no sign then few of the lads who were on the station came running down the approach.

We couldn't see anyone but all the older lads were still taking it easy in the pub until we all went running past. Suddenly they all came out as we saw the Millwall mob come down the Approach with only about thirty lads. They just came down walking and they all had bubble coats on with fur around the collar and they were shouting 'bush bush bushwacker', they must have thought that we were going to run!

We let them get onto London Road before we had them on their toes with one of them telling the rest to 'stand they're only fackin' Mancs'. He was said to be called Scotty – he was tall and skinny with short black hair. They got ran down London Road before they turned onto Store Street and ran up the stairs back into the station. We fled the scene before the police arrived and got off to the ground.

We all met at the Parkside pub and as we rushed down the alleyway we were now on Maine Road. We saw the Millwall mob were queuing outside the Platt Lane end and we ran into then and give it them – they had nowhere to run and had to fight back. They were up against a brick wall until the police eventually came and we scattered. Most of us stayed outside the ground and never went in as we waited to see if anymore came. There was no trouble in the ground and after the game (which we won 4-0) we were all outside the ground but were chased off into the estate by police dogs. They carried on chasing us until we got it together, got tooled up and started to brick them and their dogs.

We managed to back them off onto Lloyd Street where Millwall coaches were passing and we bricked at least three of them when the police came charging back with their dogs. We chased them out of the estate and cornered one who got bricked before we all fled into Moss Side's notorious estates.

W0LVES (H) CUP MATCH

The season was now well under way and the fighting was getting a bit out of hand as every week it was going off. The police never seemed to be acting but it was now more obvious that we were going to get raided. As we gathered outside the ground there was the odd camera flash from time to time and when I told most of the lads they told me I was being paranoid. All I could say is 'we will see'. The plain clothes police were seen by everyone outside the ground with a big tv camera on a tripod filming the mob stood about. Then there was the Hoolivan parked nearby taking pictures of the mob.

Later that evening I was with two lads when we were approached outside the ground by the two guys who were at the Villa match who had run off. They said to me that they were not undercover police but when I asked them why they wanted to join up with City's mob so badly, they couldn't answer it and after a brief chat I punched the ginger haired one in the face and left in a hurry as there was dibble all over and they were after the blacks.

They never made an arrest for the Millwall game when the officers in the estate were attacked, from that game on every home game I was a target for the cameramen and after this we were all in town waiting on the arrival of the Wolves fans when a white van with the words British Gas kept driving past us. It was the same officers from the match who had the big TV camera on top of the police box. They saw that I had spotted them. We knew then that there would be a car driving about but didn't know which one.

As we went down onto Deansgate near Kendals I noticed a car full of men but I couldn't see who was in it. As I approached it with a brick in my hand two of the City lads jumped out and one of them was Bernard Chaisty and said 'if you put that through the window you will be paying for it'. Kevin O'Rouke then said 'what were you trying to do'. I apologised and told them just to keep an eye out for that gas van, which obviously sounded weird.

LEEDS (A)

This game started off with a running battle in town with United before we even set off to Leeds. There was trouble all the way down Tib Street and back to Oldham Street to the Merchants pub where the rest of their mob were.

It all started when me and about twenty lads got off the 82 bus outside the Merchants pub and ended up getting ran towards the direction of Victoria where there were over 300 City boys about to board the train. Then a load of lads came to join in the chase – there were lads with all different accents. I noticed one of the United boys who I knew from Moss Side called Craig Moss. He was a white lad originally from Blackburn and was once on their books, he got locked up in 1991 during Operation China which was aimed at the Gooch Close gang. The police claimed that he was drug dealing.

Mossy wasn't really involved as he knew most of us. It was mainly the Cockney Reds mouthing it as City chased them back to Oldham Street. The pub windows started going through as shoppers ran for cover. The United mob would not come out as they were all cowering at the back of the pub. If the Manchester lads had been with them they would have put up a fight.

Anyway as we ran back to Victoria through the Arndale centre the police were searching the area for those responsible. We then saw ET and Larry. They were making their way to Piccadilly to meet up with the Yids as they were playing United at Old Trafford. We all made it back to the station as we met up with even more City fans, this time the beer monsters.

When got to Leeds an hour later and the police were starting to hold most of the mob in the station and let most of the young ones go. As me, Benny, Carl Stewart, Desmond Phelps and a load more left Leeds station, the mob was waiting as we all got to the bottom of the approach the Leeds mob attacked us, so we fought back in self-defence and give it most of them before the police arrived. It was a set up from the police as they walked us back up the station

Undercover police can be seen infiltrating our group
- dibble are easy to spot, just look out for car coats and moustaches

approach as they filmed us. I was the first to spot them and covered my face before telling everyone else but they never got the fighting on video. However on the transcript of their video this is what they said:

"A large group of Young Guvnors can be seen leaving the station and walking towards the town centre (at the forefront of this group are Ossai, Big Spinner, me, Benny and Splodge) who make their way to the front with others, the group is then taken under police escort and several of the males on realising that they are being filmed, attempt to disguise their identities by putting hoods up, reading newspapers etc"

That was when the police started to target certain individuals who they knew were up for it as well as mad for it. They had been filming every game but now had evidence of who was mainly involved. As we escorted to the ground there was a disturbance with the Leeds mob as we got near the ground. There were about 200 of the service crew and 450-500 City thugs which were in the escort. We had almost the full mob out with the Beer Monsters, Guvnors and all the Young Guvnors as most of them who sometimes got cold feet had to be threatened to come or not come at all as most of them only turned out for shitty games. However that day there was no hiding place!

There was no more trouble en route and as we entered the ground, City had filled their end as usual. There were a few shady guys who were stood near to us but it wasn't the ones who were at the Villa game as we had caught up with them the week before when I assaulted one of them at the Wolves game at Maine Road in the cup match. So it was obvious that those two had been taken off the operation and more sent in. I would say their were eight undercover police in total. When we all got nicked we could see three undercover officers stood behind my brother and the others listening to their conversations on a photo and they took a photo of me with all City's mob in front and all around me (see photos).

The game ended, which was of no interest yet again as we lost two nil, and as we left we firmed up marching up a hill away from the ground without a police escort. They were waiting close by and waiting for it to go off ready to film it again. We saw the Leeds mob then show up at the bottom of the hill. We charged at one another and there were bricks bottles and other missiles thrown as the fighting started. They backed us off as most of the lads shouted "Stand! Don't run from these Yorkshire rippers". So as the order was given we all charged back down the hill to the Service Crew racist scum with everyone getting stuck in with a few City casualties including one who had been hit over the head with a bar.

As both sides backed off there was another charge and one poor Leeds lad got caught and dragged in the middle of City's mob. As he was getting a kicking the police came to the scene as the two groups fled. The City mob was going nowhere as we got escorted back to the station. Desmond Phelps got dragged out of the group by the police and arrested for the fight which had taken place before the match at the bottom of the train station – he got fifty-six days in prison. As he got nicked we were all put on the train and as it set off I saw a mob running towards the train. Someone pulled the emergency cord and the train came to a halt and the City lads jumped off only to be met by police dogs as the police ushered the Leeds fans off the station. Ady Gunnings and myself were to get the blame because the cord was right next to where we were stood.

The train set off without anymore trouble. We arrived back in Manchester with a train load of thugs and went to the Three Legs of Man pub which was near Victoria Bridge. As we marched through the tunnel with 500 boys shouting Guvnors we approached Deansgate and more or less bumped into United who were making their way to Victoria station.

As they saw us all their tools came out: bats, sticks and whatever and we saw a lad with a knife, they must have got ran off Ricky Pryce and the Yids after their game with them. They were outnumbered as they were not expecting that many to turn out after the Leeds game. This was it! We ran them all over all: the main lads were with us including Pat Berry, Benny – they were the gamest. We chased them down Market Street and into Piccadilly smashing windows along the way. This then attracted the attention of the police and from then on that was it for City – we would be targeted yet again and nicked for fuck all in the process. They really hated us now, especially the blacks because of what happened at the Millwall game with the police in the estate.

HULL CITY (A)

This was a night match. We all decided to travel by coach as the City mob were meeting in Manchester that day. Most of us stayed in Oldham and waited for the coach to come and pick us up as it had to drive through Chadderton to get onto the M62 towards Leeds. The coach party arrived later on and we got the rest of the firm out of the Chadderton Tavern pub – it was only five o'clock and at least half of them were pissed but they still managed to travel. It was a shit day to travel as it had been raining but we still had to show up for the rest and not lot them down. More thugs were going by train.

We all met up outside Hull's ground, it was a nice tidy mob. All the older lads turned out and a few beer monsters we had never seen before the game. We knew they had a good mob who would be up for it, I don't think that we had ever played them in the league because City had nearly always been in top flight football but that didn't mean that they had no mob. Nearly all the lower league teams had mobs but the lower down you went, quite often the worse it got. Some of the bigger teams assumed that places like Hull would be a pushover so when a few of them got done, they had to wake up and take notice.

During the game nothing much happening, just a lot of walking up and down on the terraces from one group to another just chatting. I was called over later on in the game to a lad called (Shady Ady) or just Adrian Gunnings, he was sat down on the steps of the terraces with a coat over his face as everyone was stood near by. We looked at each other and laughed and thought that he had lost it. He then said that we were being filmed. I soon moved out of the way. A lad called (Wacker) David Foulkes, put his coat around his face then looked at the camera. Then Chris Francis put one hand on his face and turned away, then he put his other hand over his face and looked away before looking back at the camera. He then took his hands down and said "fuck it, we haven't done anything!"

As I spread the word down the terrace nearly the whole mob was now watching the game with their faces covered. It looked funny because all the Hull police would now have known who all the thugs were I wasn't arsed in the end. From that moment on I was going to make sure I was on every police video and picture possible because something just clicked into my head that I was still only fifteen and not much could happen to me. I soon told the others who were my age as well and from then on we just stepped up the violence!

After the game we all left the ground together. We walked through the car park and did a right onto the main road walked down for a few hundred yards until we came to a pub. We were all hanging around to see if their mob was in the pub but they had come from behind us from the ground and it kicked off on the pavement and in the road with the football traffic screeching to a halt. As the fighting continued I never knew there were so many black people in that part of the world. There was this mixed race lad with them, he must have been in his early twenties. He charged at us throwing a punch and the odd kick. These were all big lads, so I more or less had to take a back seat.

The police arrived and to our surprise the Hull mob stayed and fought us. Then the police ran at us and so did the Hull mob! It was fucking unbelievable! We were now trying to stand and fight both the police and Hull. We were getting slaughtered and we then all got ran off both the police and Hull's mob. Me and Mark Timperley, from Oldham, got ran off the police down a long street. He got caught while I carried on looking for an alleyway half way down. There was none. It was different from Moss Side or anywhere else I knew. As one still gave chase I carried on – them big boots of his were not catching my size four Nike trainers! In the end I kicked off a big gate which looked like it had an alleyway behind it but it was only a tunnel which had been blocked off… that was it, I was nicked.

I came back out of the tunnel to get taken away because I was now tired and had given up. As I walked out the police officer was running back down the road and helping with the arrest of Timps. I couldn't believe my luck! I was fucked and had given up only to find the Old Bill had given up on me. I made my way back down the road slowly. By the time I got to the end everyone had disappeared. I made my way back to the ground where I saw our coach and it was surrounded with police. I walked over and thought 'if I'm nicked, then im nicked'. It wasn't to be. My brother and everyone had been waiting for me so they could go. As the police was giving everyone an escort well out of Hull,

Timps later went to court and was banned from the Hull area for life – I couldn't believe the shit I was hearing – he got stitched up.

SHEFFIELD U (H)

As we travelled down to Manchester together by bus, the rest of the mob from Oldham were looking for trouble. Well we didn't always go looking for trouble it just found us at every away game we attended!

We were not going to make everyone at City think that no one would take us seriously, so the mob got recruited even more as I rounded up lads who were older and aged 17-21. Then Mickey Francis and his group would have to be broken up as well as Pat Berry and his Guvnors Crew but when we did kick it off we were still all together one for all and all for one, but our mob was the one who were out and about while everyone else was in the pubs that we were not allowed in because of our school kid looks. We all used to chill in Sunspot arcade. The landlords always had visits from the police on match days but it was good that Mickey and his mob and Pat and his mob never roamed the streets because they would have got clocked off the police and other firms that were looking for City.

To everyone else we were a bunch of kids and they didn't take us seriously. We were the Young Guvnors and from the end of the previous season when the mob was just getting too big, it was now the right time for the two groups to split as we couldn't go walking about in big mobs we would get spotted. We knew that certain people following us in British Gas vans were taking pictures.

As a separate gang we were doing everything to get our name on the map. The best thing about the two gangs splitting up was to see who should not have been with the mob. For example, the undercover police knew that they were in the mob but there must have been about eight of them but only five were in with us now, saying that we had two guys with us who clamied to be from Middleton called Paddy and Arthur who claimed to be painters and decorators. Hmmm now where have I heard that one before?

Once the Guvnors and Young Guvnors split the undercover police were one step ahead as they now got hold of Mark Chapman who was in the Guvnors but for some reason distanced himself from everyone and went with the Beer Monsters thinking he was in the National Front as he didn't mix with any blacks at all. That was how the undercover cops befriended him, so they never were with us and half of what they knew was what Chapman had told them...

To get close to us they had to step up their surveillance and after one of their officers got twatted at a game, they knew we were on to them. They filmed us almost everywhere they could to get that much evidence. They were going to get it off us as we were pissed off at getting filmed and guys jumping out of cars taking photos was becoming a joke. We were young and we decided to start giving them what they wanted because as and when they were finally going to raid us, we were only going to get a slap on the wrist because of our age.

When we started kicking it off in front of them and as they were filming, we knew we would not get nicked because if we did it would blow their cover wide open. They wanted me out of the way as they knew I was sometimes in the right place at the right time. For instance, once City's mob were all in the Brunswick pub in Piccadilly. No one knew they were there and as me and a few others never went in the pub we were always on the step of the Sunspot arcade keeping an eye on the pub and we saw two guys come out who we didn't recognise. (They were, of course, undercover) at the time but they walked past Sun Spot without seeing us and went straight to a phone box. They then made their way to the bus station and within minutes a police car and a van had parked up across the road watching. Then the white British gas van arrived and parked up taking photos.

As I attended the Sheffield United game at Maine Road we were all in the North stand. There must have been thirty of us in our spot and it wasn't until later in the game that I noticed two guys sat near us. They looked like the two who had phoned the police from the phone box but they looked slightly different. One had grown a beard but the other one with glasses on was clean shaven. As Paddy from Blackley pointed out he was now wearing glasses but the thing I noticed was that the jacket he had on was the same one from town. It was blue and green and it was one of those one cut jackets that you just didn't see back then.

I climbed over the seats and fronted him. Jamie Roberts and the others followed me and the guy denied everything I said to him. I told him that this corner was a no go area and it was for thugs only and out of all the hundred or so seats that were empty, he had to sit right near us like he was listening to what we were all talking about. He carried on in denial as the whole North Stand turned their attention towards us. Having a short fuse I leant forward and pushed him making him stumble backwards. He was now surrounded by the mob. Some fat City prick with a bobble hat and badges all over it jumped up and thought he was some hero as he started mouthing it off. I spat in his face as my brother came to pull me away.

We were all going to fuck him up but the police arrived in force which was strange as they never turned out like that normally… We all turned and leapt back over the seats. No one got grabbed and outside the ground we were outside the Kippax End where the Sheffield United fans would come out. I was walking from mob to mob fuming telling them that if them two guys show up again we all give it them there and then. There'd be no talking this time.

I watched the Operation Omega video that the police took in the ground and it shows just what I described. In their statements they state that I threatened a Covert Officer which explains why so many police came in the stand in force. They must have thought that when I pushed him he was going to get a crack. I didn't care, I knew the cameras were on us. If I would have got nicked and charged they would have had to say that he was an officer.

Two hours after the game we headed away from Maine Road. The police were still watching our mob and we were followed so I told everyone to follow me onto the Alex Park estate. I knew that the police were not far off and there were about forty of us. The gang war was still ongoing between the Doddington and Gooch gangs and a few of the lads were shitting it at going through the estates as we had to walk through Doddington Close then through Gooch Close to get to the Whalley Hotel where we were going to chill until the police fucked off.

I told them that me, Maynard, Crawford, Stefan G and Simmo, who was a white lad and from the area, knew both sides and that we were nothing to do with the gang scene, only the football scene. Then some lads started chatting shit saying that they will get shot we said "don't talk shit and stereo typing the area". I told some of them to fuck off the estate then and get nicked as the police did not come on there. As we would probably have joined up with one of the gangs and attacked the police who were following us I then said "to Scotty and his NFs amongst us, you'd better run!" and then laughed, We eventually got to the pub but the police turned up again. As a mob we were hard to miss. I knew that the police were on my tail after the North Stand incident. We left the pub in twos and three and made our way to town and then home as town was quiet.

SWINDON TOWN (A)

I missed four games in a row after the Sheffield game as I was keeping a low profile. Also I had to play for the school football team which I couldn't get out of as the teacher knew the score thanks to some loud mouth kid. When I did play I could no longer be arsed about it so I would go in with late tackles and if I got fouled that was it, that player would be a target for the rest of the game or until the teacher thought that I was going to get sent off. Then he would sub me. I was doing nothing good on the pitch, I was just the same as everyone else. I didn't want to play again but saying that I didn't get picked again – thank god.

During my time away from the City match I hung around Chadderton Hall Park and met up with friends and school friends. We would hang around the area for an hour or so and go up to Oldham town centre to do some shopping and meet up with a few lads. Most people would go there as there was not much to do as it was boring. Sometimes Danny Gaye and Maynard would come up as it was also boring in Moss Side. I trusted that the diehards: Benny, Arron, and Traves were keeping the flag flying as they went to every City game home and away even when results were not going our way. They were there with the followers who refused to give up on the team and show their loyal support. There were certain games that the undercover police travelled to on pointless journeys following a lost cause. At shit games like Bournemouth in midweek and Ipswich, where there would be no trouble, they would hype it all up to the local police making out that there would be a riot. They would be left with red faces at the end of the day just because they would see a big mob of thugs travelling that were now known for kicking it off and they automatically thought that meant a riot!

It's a pity they didn't do all their homework on certain teams. They thought that they had evidence by filming the mob in grounds but after 26 games of videoing us everywhere in front of them they then said this was a meeting between Guvnors and Young Guvnors when we were all watching the game. However they did have it right at the Swindon game. As we set off on the long journey from Manchester we had company all the way. Most of us had to pay on the train this time as we were under the watchful eye of the British Transport Police. They only came along as they saw how many we were taking.

Everyone was out yet again but most of all it was the simple fact that nearly all of us had never been to Swindon before and it would be a pleasure for us to bring a mob there to show them what we had and see if they were up for it like most teams were there mob was called the aggro boys or the SAS . We were all just having a laugh and just walking about the train taunting and buzzing off people and then bulling our way into the first class carriage until some bitch grassed us up to one of the guards. That was when my big brother told me to calm down before I got thrown off. So me and some of my little followers had to calm down the rest of the way.

Everyone was out: Pat Berry, Chris and Mickey Francis, Benny and Spinner, my brother as always, Martin Travis and Splodge and a load of City fans from Oldham. As we were approaching London Euston, word had got round to watch out for the Yids as they were always waiting for us and we were going to lose the police by going straight to Summers town which was five minutes away from the station.

As we arrived the station was empty with no football fans but it was still only early as the mob walked through the station. I went to phone ET and Larry Philips to let them know we had arrived and was on our way to the Lord Summers pub in Summers town. We later met and everyone got off as we now had to go and change stations to get another one out west to Swindon and it was also stopping at Reading before that. But no one was there and there were no police on our train but as soon as we arrived at Swindon station the police were everywhere. They had obviously been tipped off how many we had and were taking no chances as the dogs were waiting for us. We loved all that attention – getting marched under heavy escort through the streets as people stood and watched (and any other thugs who would say they never had that buzz from all the attention would be lying) as if they had never saw that many hooligans. But I'm sure they were more concerned at all the blacks in the mob more than anything and yes they were right when we used to hear whispers about they're from Manchester and them blacks must be from Moss Side where the riots were. As if that was the only place that rioted. You would get the odd cheeky bitch putting their hand bags under their arms.

When we finally get to the ground their mob was on the forecourt so we ran at them and they scattered and that gave the police the chance to have their long awaited fun and games with us pushing us about then telling the whole group "anymore and we are not going into the ground". Everyone from then on kept it quiet until we just got in but the police were a bunch of punks thinking that they were top notch. We had the bigger firm of 300 that day, not like these guys who were new to the game and were only acting like that because they knew that we were under surveillance and thought that nothing was going to happen or we were all going to behave ourselves.

In the ground we were penned in two sections so most of us had to climb a fence to get into the right bit where the mob was.

So one section was now packed out with City's most loyal fans but the police did fuck all. It was a good close game and as we were winning everyone was in a good mood. It was 4–3 and the hyped-up police didn't do anything about us on the fence for most of the game. Right near the end the City fans were singing "on the pitch, on the pitch, on the pitch" so we obliged.

Chris and Mickey F were the first on, and then everyone got on unchallenged by the police. There were now about a hundred lads on and more following as we ran to greet the players and still no police. They knew then that we were not fucking about, that's probably why they did nothing. We were on for a good few minutes as our end was right across the other end of the pitch and as we all walked back slowly to the corner nothing happened. Swindon's end had no fences it was only the away end that did and they never got on so we didn't know where they were. As soon as we were all going through the gate back into our end, Swindon decided to get on from the far end and we piled back onto the pitch only for the police to now come on trying to push us all back.

They pushed Chris Francis, who pushed them back, as more and as more police came out the Swindon boys started kicking off. They had had five minutes to get on and never showed where they were until we were walking back on the terraces. We were not going to start going in an end kicking it off if we didn't know where their mob was. The GMP made sure they got it all on video and it shows how long we were on the pitch for. As we left they were nowhere to be seen but the police soon got hold of us all and that was it – right back to the station and back to London for our long trip back home. This time the BTP made sure that they were with us all the way back to Euston and once we were there they tried to put ET and Larry on the Manchester train. They were kicking off with some of the Manchester police who were also with us until one of the Euston BTP officers noticed them and cleared it for them. Even that officer made the GMP officer look stupid by telling him that they had cockney accents, meaning that they were Londoners. His face went red as all the boys cheered – no undercover police with us today. On the way back on the train almost everyone had gone to sleep but not me I stayed wide awake − I didn't want to nod off in case the Old Bill handcuffed the lot of us on the sly, ha ha.

We got back to Manchester for 2 am and we were overwhelmed by the amount of police out at that time of the morning. Sure enough they were filming us as we left. We couldn't be arsed with them but the hoods soon went up as we left the station and near enough everyone got in a black cab. We had a convoy of about six cabs and made them drop us in Oldham town centre outside Butterfly's night club which had just finished. So there was a big crowd still outside as our taxi came to a halt. The taxi came to £30 but we all just got out and walked away towards the crowd and to people we knew. The taxis sped away in the direction of the police station and some of us went missing down a side street and home. The older ones stayed to get some bitches to take home as most of them Oldham ladies were up for it and as the Oasis lads said 'Mad for It'.

Talking of the Gallagher brothers, they used to be at a lot of City games but didn't mix with the thugs even though they knew some of us. We'd always see them in Dry Bar on Oldham Street and after games we used to let on to each other as we were never really on speaking terms but they did know (Benny) Andrew Bennion.

MIDDLESBROUGH (H)

It was a hard few days in school as I was now in my last year. All the work was getting harder as we were preparing for our mock exams so I was getting a lot of homework which I often didn't do as I was always out with my mates at night and by the time I went home I couldn't be arsed. There were times when I had a dead line to bring it in - one of the days was the Thursday after the Middlesbrough game. I never had any time to do it as I went to the match.

All these games were new to me as most of the teams we were playing had mobs and I wanted to see them. The lads told me that Boro had a mob who called themselves the Frontline and that we might get a run for our money because they were no pushovers. So on the day of the game I met up with a few lads as normal and travelled to Manchester. There were more of the City firm in town outside the Sunspot arcade waiting for Boro to arrive. I couldn't be arsed staying in town as the police were there keeping an eye on everyone, so I just jumped onto the 100 bus to Moss Side. On the bus also making their way to the ground were Daft Donald and Ged Ganson. These two lunatics were much older than me. They had been in a lot of fights, we were still on the bus now on Princess Road in Moss Side.

Daft Donald was telling more or less the whole bus how he petrol bombed a shop in the 1981 Moss Side Riots. Everyone on the top deck of the bus turned to have a look at him but as he was so proud of it, I asked him did he see any police officers with guns because when the riots was on I used to walk past Moss Side police station and there would be an officer outside with one, as we went to school. As I was at Holy Name school which was on Denmark Road right next to the station we had to walk home past the station and we were all in groups as most of us were scared as our dads told us about the police stopping and searching blacks – stitching them up and beating people up for nothing and not to forget the police station had been attacked. I won't deny that there were bad people about but the ones who kept out of trouble got trouble.

It seemed that the police's job was to make sure that every black man and child had a criminal record! That was why so many people were being set up. It's more or less the same today but they now struggle to get convictions.

When the riots took place there were a lot of Man City's Kool Kats involved but only two got locked up for it as one was unlucky as he was visiting friends at the time and was then pick up and locked up that was Jimmy G who never took part in it, he just happened to be in the wrong place at the wrong time. Daft Donald was involved and all he said to us was that when he got caught by the police he had been walking past a shop and saw a petrol bomb that wasn't lit properly, so he lit it and threw it. On one of the nights of the riots I was living on Doddington Close. The place was like a war zone, far worse than a football riot as petrol bombs, bricks, knives, bats, and other weapons were used.

From my bedroom window I saw the police at the front line

with truncheons and guns but none were fired as they chased a group of lads down the path and onto the Close. Everyone scattered and they chased a guy called Simon Chin into his house then a lad called Jason Gillard who lived across the road was on the front of his drive way with his family as there were other families outside on their doorsteps just having a look and seeing that the rioters didn't damage their property. As the police came they were attacking anyone on the street and Jay, who was one of the lads, was still in his slippers was attacked and as they went back into their house the police hit everyone within reach. Following incidents like that, no one trusted the police again and they wonder why they don't get any co-operation with things in the area.

As we eventually get off the bus in Moss Side for the short walk to the ground I went to knock on for Maynard, Danny and Stefan Gaye. We walked to the Platt Lane End to see if Middlesbrough's mob had arrived which they had. There was no trouble as they were surrounded by the police. We saw a few black guys with their mob, some had Afros. I spoke to one of them. His accent was a bit funny to hear a black who sounded like a Geordie was unbelievable even though he was a smoggy. I didn't even know that there were any blacks up that end. He said they were called the black bishops. We had a short chat and then left to go into the game.

It went surprisingly well on the pitch after we had been under pressure losing 1-0 and nearly conceding a second ten minutes later. In the second half and with not long to go Andy Hinchcliffe, who was having a good game, made it 1-1 as the crowd urged the team to get a second. There was a good turnout that night − 18,500 including the 2000 that had made the journey from the north east. They were all behind the goal and their mob was on show as there was up to a hundred or more lads stood up all the way through the game and we could spot about five black guys mostly with afros stood in the middle of them. One of those was the guy we had talked to before the game

As the game ended we went round the ground looking for their mob but as the police had let everyone out at the same time they were nowhere to be seen, so as about 80 of us marched through the streets of Moss Side there was still no sign. We made our way down Wilmslow Road and as we reached Whitworth Park we saw it was sealed off as there had been a body discovered there the night before. Then we saw some lads in there so the police cordon had soon vanished and now everyone was in the park but the lads we saw were City and then a load of minibuses pulled up and a load of lads jumped out jumping the fence giving it the big one.

By now the police, who were in the incident van in the park, came running over shouting for us all to leave the park but as we reached the Boro boys we were then involved in fighting with them. I will hold my hands up here and say we got done as they took us by surprise as we must have underestimated them, as we didn't think they would be driving and waiting to ambush us. Boro have always had a good mob in my eyes from then on as I remember when they went to Shrewsbury and I had it on tape off the news when it saw their mob wrecking their end and the shop which was behind them in the ground.

Another time, the season after they must got promoted, I was banned from going within half a mile of the grounds and I had just been arrested again a month earlier at the friendly game at Stockport – I was in town on the Saturday of that season I arranged to meet Neil Crawford in town as City were away that day and we were going to spy on the United mob and wait for City to come back if they were still about. As I made my way to town on the 182 bus it pulled up at Stevenson Square. Crawford was there waiting and he said that United were on Oldham Street which was just around the corner. We walked past and as we did some of their bigger lads from out of town were making their way inside when they spotted me. I had just turned 16 and Crawford was 17. There was still a bitter feeling between them and me as the month before I had jumped on one of their lad's heads after a friendly at Old Trafford. Anyway I went into the Merchants as they must have needed more lads to do us two teenagers...

As we continued to walk slowly but still looking back all u could hear was 'come on niggers' to me and Crawford. They all came out and so did a few pint pots and as we ran off glasses were smashing behind us just missing a load of shoppers on the corner of Oldham Street and Piccadilly. We managed to get away from the pissed up clowns who by now were fucking fuming. I ran down a side street and on to a car park looking for a brick as I was going to go back and put the windows through in the pub where they all were. As I returned I couldn't find one and Crawford said sack it because I might get nicked if they saw me as they had grassed me up for the incident on Chester Road which was also on video.

Anyway, we decided to walk down Market Street. We were now going to the Royal Exchange to Brannigans to see if there was any of the Young Guvnors in there. At that time United thought that City's mob was dead and buried as loads were still on remand and banned from going near any grounds. We were still in town kicking it off with them though, so as we were now in the middle of Market Street we saw a mob coming up that put a smile on our faces – it was Middlesbrough's mob. Crawford was buzzing – he was one of those thugs who never really travelled to many away games and would only bother if it was guaranteed to go off. Their mob approached and we told them who we were and they were ok with us, the shoppers at this stage all stepped to one side as they all came through – this mob was long in length and width but I couldn't tell how many there were. It looked a lot as they were now right next to us and before we got run I explained to them that we were by no means looking for trouble and that we were the Young Guvnors from Man City.

They were an alright group of lads as they could easily have told us to fuck off as from the look of us we might have seemed to be a joke to them. Anyway we were still walking on Market Street we spoke about the City game the season before and I think they knew we were not just two little dickheads and accepted us. We were now approaching the top near the monument in Piccadilly and the corner of Oldham Street when we told them what had happened to us and that United's mob was in the pub around the corner. They now gathered around the monument and Piccadilly – this mob was fucking huge, the whole place was packed with thugs. I was buzzing, there seemed to be 400 in total. It was one of the biggest mobs who had ever visited Manchester.

For some reason at that time I don't think that the Middlesbrough firm believed us and thought that it might be a set up so we were told to go to the pub and kick it off while they were now at the top of Oldham Street. Game as ever, me and Crawford ran into the pub, kicked the door in and shouted 'come on Munichs'. As they piled out again the Boro lot knew it was for real and soon came charging forward. The United mob must have had the shock of their lives as they scrambled back to the pub. Some fell over as they fled – they shut the front and side doors which was on the alleyway and sure enough the windows went through as Boro were now chanting 'Munich, Munich'.

There was no sign of them coming out and by now Oldham Street was jam packed with buses and cars coming at a halt outside. The pub was destroyed as the black guy who was the glass collector tried to pop his head through the broken glass window. United were now right at the back of the pub so we left them to it and showed the Boro mob the way to Old Trafford. Meanwhile we walked through the gardens and then onto Mosley Street that was when the police arrived – they were shitting it as they saw the Boro mob and asked them 'are you alright lads' which was a bit different from how they treated us lot! But then they dare not fuck with that mob or they would have been in for a pounding.

As we marched in the escort I spotted an officer called PC Hamilton who had nicked me at the Stockport friendly. I told some of their mob and they pushed me in the middle so I didn't get clocked. As we carried on a car kept on driving past and it wasn't Man U it was the police in plain clothes taking pictures. I told some of the lads and they said it was police from the north east. As we got towards Hulme it was time for me and Crawford to go as I was within half a mile of the ground. It was a fucking joke being banned under that bail condition as I only lived five minutes away from the Oldham ground.

In February 1997 we played Boro in the fifth round of the FA cup at Maine Road and by this time the police were well and truly clamping down on the violence at the ground as the undercover operations had now become a thing of the past. Instead they just had uniformed officers following our every move videoing us. At the same time they still had plain clothes officers following us.

I made it my business to take pictures of them and video them back which they didn't like as the uniformed officers would always arrest me for having a stolen video camera which never was but was there excuse. Whenever I was arrested I would say nothing and get charged and by the time it got to court I would bring proof of purchase and the case would get kicked out. This happened quite regularly.

As for the game itself the Boro lads had nearly all of the North stand and this was going to be a game of revenge for City as the season before they had left the ground early and made their way into the City part of the North stand and kicked it off. It took City by surprise but they made a bad mistake as they got a good hiding from all angles and respect goes out to them for coming in and not running as it was all the fighting was captured on amateur video by me.

As this cup game had finished with Boro winning 1-0, everyone left to go to the Kippax Street End where the Boro mob came out and it just went off with police on horse back in the middle of it all. Everyone then scattered to the Sherwood pub which was nearby before we made our way to a little park in Rusholme (this patch at the time was owned by two brothers know as the Rusholme reds Barron Whitter and Eugene Sobers who were running things in the area), where we met their mob again. As we ran at one another missiles were flying everywhere. The police finally got there and everyone split up – we were now walking through Rusholme when Ian Clarke (clarkey) my mate, who has a nickname (The Town Loafer) he got it for hanging about Manchester Arndale centre or the city centre between the hours of 9am until 5pm seven days a week like he had a job ha ha and Trevor Blackstock (aka JB) came running round the corner getting ran off about 100 Middlesbrough Hooligans.

We were now tooled up so milk bottles went flying into the Boro mob when all of a sudden the police on horse back appeared and the City lot fled. No less than five minutes later just outside Whitworth Park, as Boro were now under escort, it went off again as there were some Oldham and Stockport County fans who had joined up to come and fight us but were caught out on their arrival near the park. As It was kicking off with City and Boro some other City thugs chased the Oldham and Stockport mob away who then retaliated by letting off a distress flare which went bouncing all over the road but no one was injured. As the police spotted who was responsible they gave chase as the fighting City and Boro fans were brought under control. Later we had another running battle in Piccadilly as police again arrived to restore order. On the Monday the Evening News headlines read

'TASTE OF THE BAD OLD DAYS': FANS IN STREET BATTLES

Soccer thugs on the streets of Manchester brought a grim reminder of the game's violent years as fighting broke out in the shadow of City's new Kippax Stand. Police on horseback charged at rival gangs as trouble broke out after the game. The trouble was orchestrated to settle old scores from last season when Boro thugs damaged the North Stand.

By Monday a Boro supporter said that the gang from Middlesbrough called the BBC - Beer Belly Crew and the Boro casuals went by train to cause trouble, he said that there was talk in his town last week that there was going to be a showdown after last season.

"The BBC are a hardcore of lads aged 30-45 and they were not kids, it was a frightening scene afterwards with City fans waiting for us, there were clashes on the route from the ground to the city centre as the away fans walked for coaches and trains".

Police made 19 arrests for violence-related offences and four for pitch invasion, police had feared trouble as extra were put on duty in the ground as the police had more officers on duty than usual. One City fan said that he was approached and told where ambushes were planned after the match, but back at Piccadilly station he saw people with bloodied faces.

HUDDERSFIELD T v OLDHAM ATHLETIC

Only a few months after we had attacked the Oldham fans we were joining forces when fifty of our City mob from Oldham travelled to Huddersfield by train with Latics fans. This wasn't unusual for us as we had in the past had our mob out when Leeds played at Oldham. The rift had healed between us. We went with them but there were lads who were genuine that we got on with 100 per cent but then you had the NF with them most of whom were older but would not say anything to me and my brother face to face. You could tell they felt uneasy.

Then there was the Middleton and Rochdale lot who went with them and who had a problem with the other City lot. That was probably because most were in that other gang we had called the Mills Hill Villiains, named after the train station on the border of Chadderton and Middleton, but we refused to let the Moor Close lads from Middleton come. It was just like defending our territory of Chadderton - if any of us crossed into their patch we would either get run off or get done and vice versa. This was the group that made its way to meet Oldham's hooligans the Fine Young Casuals. Lee Spence and his mob had a bigger turnout than what they had brought out for City. There were 100 lads rising to 150 with our back-up, we were having a good laugh with most of them all the way there and just talking about when City came when some of them didn't want to fight us as they knew us and that we brought too many boys

Lee Spence is someone you can trust to stand with you when it goes off and won't run and leave you. He his known by a few teams as well – he used to travel with Hibernian and the England mob. As we reached Huddersfield we made our way off the platform and in to the town centre only to met by the police and then escorted to the ground. We were all at the back of the mob trying to sneak out of the escort to go and find their mob. With the fifty of our lot some sharp-eyed sheepshaggers spotted us and we were going nowhere from then on.

At the ground we saw their mob but nothing was ever going to go off while the police were there. The game was shit as well as the atmosphere, so as the game went on the City lads went to the other end of the stand just chatting and reading the odd newspaper as you do, this made the Oldham lads paranoid thinking that we were planning something. On the way back to Manchester we were put straight back into an escort and back on the train. We had no trouble with Huddersfield but on the train back it was all whispers and eyes everywhere.

The word from them was that they thought that we would tip off some City fans back in Manchester to wait at the station which was a load of shit. As we reached Victoria they were all walking at a slow pace as we walked at a normal pace and as we got to the exit they were staying on the station to catch the Oldham train. At least forty to sixty of them then backed us off and as we did we got to the waste ground and got bricks and ran them back in before the BTP came out to chase us off.

HUDDERSFIELD T (H)

No less than a month after our visit to Huddersfield we entertained them at Maine Road. We were all outside the ground awaiting their arrival as were the Manchester police who were out filming us. We then entered the ground. We were now certain that there was no undercover police with us as we could account for everyone that was with us. As we met up with Mickey Francis in the ground he was certain they were not in his Guvnors mob but that just left the main mob which was with Pat Berry. This one was as big as the other two put together and contained all the older lot which included all the Beer Monsters. When we had established who was who, we sat down to talk about how we were going to attack the Huddersfield mob without any police or undercover following us. This would have to happen away from the ground as it was dark by then but the ground outside was well lit up.

This proved to be an historic game that would re-write the history books as City hammered Huddersfield 10-1! They had arrived at Maine Road with the worst defensive record in the division and, as City's ninth goal went it, we were all on the pitch. I got as far as the centre circle giving Steve Redmond a pat on the back. As the stewards tried to grab us we just turned to give it them on the pitch but it wasn't worth it as the police were on their way to back them up. We should have thought on because things were kicking off almost in front of the police every week and we were getting away with it now knowing that they would not nick us for every individual game or they would already have done so.

We left before the final whistle and made our way to town. The Huddersfield mob arrived in Piccadilly an hour later and they must have thought that we had all gone or were still around the ground. They then made their way down Market Street without even spotting us on the other side walking in and out of the shoppers and, as they got near the bottom of Market Street we attacked them. Some fought back until they saw that there was a lot more of us than what they first thought and as they ran we gave chase. Some of their black guys ran into Top Man which was on the corner of Market Street and Cross Street. They must have thought 'fuck it we might as well rob the shop as we are getting ran' because the skin tight jeans that they were wearing was making life difficult for them to run. They grabbed a load of denim jeans and shirts as the shop was packed and some City lads had the same idea... The others carried on giving chase down towards Victoria. The mob I was with left the Huddersfield fans alone and grabbed what they could unchallenged as both sets of hooligans went their separate ways. Me, Benny and a few others just walked as the security guards went out running after everyone, not that they could do fuck all. If they would have caught anyone it wasn't like we were a few smackheads who had rushed the shop.

As we walked up Market Street towards Piccadilly two uniformed officers ran past us towards the shop. We fucked off from town; I got off to Oldham town centre to meet up with my mates so I could get an alibi just in case niggers got picked out at a later date for fuck all, even though I never went into the shop.

On the Monday in the Evening News it reported that Huddersfield fans had been chased and then surrounded in Rusholme after the game by a group of mostly black Man City thugs. It also said that a black youth had stabbed someone in the buttock and it reported that some Huddersfield fans had been arrested at Victoria train station for theft from a clothes shop. So in the end they got all the blame. As for the stabbed man, he would learn to stand next time...

Three weeks after that game I was sat at home doing some homework for once when the door bell rang. As I went to the door two police officers from Oldham were there asking for my brother who wasn't home. I was convinced that this was it! They had come to raid us but it turned out that it was for when him Benny, Spinner, Splodge and a load others got rounded up in Reading which I never went to. It had kicked off in their town centre and a policewoman nearly got thrown through a shop window. It became apparent that a black guy was involved. Then they said that he wouldn't have to come to the police station now that it was confirmed that it wasn't City thugs who were involved then they turned around and said to me that they now needed witnesses. I told them to fuck off and slammed the door in their faces. They never came back and there was me thinking that it was something to do with the Huddersfield game.

HUDDERSFIELD v OLDHAM AGAIN

I had travelled to Huddersfield with a mob of Oldham and about twenty City thugs from the Oldham area; this was when I was serving my seven year ban from all games. We got the 365 bus from Oldham town centre. ET from City was with us. As we reached Huddersfield bus station following an hour hour-ling trip through the Pennines, we were met by some Huddersfield hooligans who said they were called the Platform 1 Crew or the HYC (Huddersfield) Youth Casuals. They were mixed group of black and white of about thirty. Some black guy was at the forefront of their mob mouthing it. We just took the piss out of his accent and his woolly jumper. I called him a 'black funky' with his tight jeans on – he looked more like a ginger beer (queer) than a football hooligan.

The rest of his mob started fighting with the City and Oldham lads who give it them and ran most of them out of the bus station there were now only five of us left including ET. Every time City had played them we would just take this game as a joke and were never going to run from them Yorkshire Puddings. We just stood arguing and telling the rest of them that we were not running and that we were Man City, even though it was Oldham's promotion meaning that it was their show today.

We were there as back up but who was backing us up if Oldham's mob and the rest of City had gone? More Huddersfield lads were arriving in the bus station and ET just burst out laughing at the way they spoke. The black guy with the woolly jumper, skin tight jeans and (Claire Rayners) trainers with the tongues pulled so far up his legs that they looked like cricket pads, then said to us "you had better keep quiet the main man's here now". There were now five of us and 20 of them. We burst out laughing again…

This guy was about 30 years old. I was 16 and ET was about 22. Their so called main man was a mixed race guy with Afro hair and a green farmer's jumper on and some tight jeans. This was like a comedy and us Mancs were aliens as far as they were concerned. The lads stepped aside to let this joker to the front. ET then said "What the fuck is he going to do? Look at his jumper and he's the main man, the fucking tramp". The guy then said something about ET's mum. ET replied with "What did you say?" I knew then it was going to go off as ET blasted the black farmer giles in his face. That was it! ET knocked him out cold. As we then give it to two more of them, the rest were all stood in shock at the cheek of us.

We then got ran off them and made our way out of the bus station. As we split up me and ET were running together as ten of them chased us. No way we were getting caught! We ended up on a long road where the police station was. We then saw a police car coming towards us with the sirens going. There was still ten lads behind us so we moved to the middle of the road waving our hands while still being chased. The police drove right past us so we had to keep running until they gave up. Fuck knows where Maynard, Crawford and Danny Gaye got to but we soon doubled back when the coast was clear and got back on that 365 bus to Oldham. Of course this would never have happened if Oldham and City's lads had stayed with us.

The last time we met Huddersfield was back in February 2000. We had arrived there at 3.30 for an 8pm kick-off. There were hundreds of City thugs heading down on every available train and bus. The newspaper picked up on this story.

YOUNG BOY AMONG INJURED FANS

An eight year old boy was hurt as the ugly frightening face of football hit Huddersfield last night. A huge police operation was mounted to keep apart rival Huddersfield Town and Manchester City fans for several hours as the two teams met in a vital game.

But there were 34 arrests, several injuries - including to a young boy - and a massive bill for policing and security. One man was still in Huddersfield Royal Infirmary today after being attacked and knocked unconscious in a clash between rival gangs in the town centre before the kick off.

The young lad was caught up in the terrifying melee involving rival fans after the match out side the sports centre, the game which ended in a 1-1 draw. Trouble had flared in the town centre well before kick-off with clashes between fans in Kirkgate, Northumberland Street and Leeds Road as early as 4pm.

The City fans, who were said to be a gang called The Guvnors, had sent word on the that they were coming in force and were going to surprise the Town fans by boarding every train, every hour with thugs. There were more problems en route to the stadium and at the game itself, with police having to use mounted officers and extra manpower to segregate the fans.

The team had club paid for extra security but there were more than 20 arrests at the ground as fourteen were charged with drink-related offence and 17 for public order. Thirty of those held came from the Manchester area.

There was serious disorder before during and after this fixture. Individuals from Aberdeen, Torquay and York attended to join forces with Huddersfield supporters to fight against the Manchester City's Guvnors. Disorder occurred en route to the stadium as rival supporters clashed. At half time Man City thugs attacked the police. During this attack bottles were thrown and a number of arrests were made before order was restored. There were a number of incidents in the executive boxes where Man City thugs who were drunk became abusive as large numbers of them were ejected from the stands and into their own end.

At the end of the game both sets of fans made their was to the town centre where serious disorder broke out which was soon restored by mounted officers making repeated charges, dog handlers and foot officers backed them up as the Man City thugs numbering around 500 were escorted to the railway station and back to Manchester

30 City thugs had been arrested throughout the day and one City thug was arrested on arrival back at Piccadilly as a disturbance occurred on the train with BTP officers.

MILLWALL (A)

All week from Monday up until Friday all the talk was about the Millwall game which was to be my first visit to The Den. As I was in school all week I was just trying not to think about the game and get my head down with my school work. Everyday I went home it was just another day less but the days were now dragging. As it got to Friday everyone was buzzing including me. I couldn't wait until that bell rang at three thirty so I could go home!

It was a normal Friday – straight in the bath then out for most of the night. First to the Friday youth club to have a laugh then when that was over to Chadderton Hall Park to meet up with some City lads and make our way to the town centre where we met up with the rest of the lads in the club Butterflies. Dele from Bradford came over that night as he was going to the Millwall game too and, as my mum and step-dad were away in Spain for two weeks that meant that I could stay out all night if I wanted, not that I was though as I wanted to be up early.

Back in the club, I was the youngest one in there. Of course I was still only 15 but the door men knew the score. The club was packed out with lads from Manchester. There were football fans as well as lads from Moss Side who were hungry for all the pussy in the club. The football lot from Manchester were Danny Gaye, David

Maynard, Crawford, Benny, Traves, Arron Burns, Carl Stewart and my brother.

The club was ok. It had a few floors so there were different tunes pumping as we all met to sort out our shit for the next day. We knew that everyone would turn up apart from the shitheads who never went but just liked to talk the talk in front of the girls. I don't know why they would try to impress just to get pussy. They know who they are! They made their excuses a week later. They never showed claiming that the police would be filming and that they didn't want to get nicked which was a load of shit as we were getting filmed from twenty games earlier. At the end of the day they were shitting it and we didn't need them.

As the night club was finishing at around 2 everyone was outside. Maynard and the rest got off back to Manchester and the lucky ones fucked off home with a bitch. I had no chance – I was too young even though I had banged a bitch before so I guess I should have stayed in the youth club! Anyway I didn't want them old boilers because that is what they were in my eyes at the time as they were well older than me. I made my way home still happy and just looking forward to the long awaited Saturday 12th December 1987.

It was three in the morning by the time I got to sleep and I woke up at 7am. It was as if I never got to sleep! I got washed and ready as my brother never came home that night – he would meet us at the station. I got in Manchester for eight. As I got to the bottom of the station approach it was rammed. 100 lads were there already plus a load of other City supporters and no doubt the undercover were not too far away but they wouldn't be getting in this mob – as everyone who was there could be accounted for.

As the time was reaching 10am and the last train was at ten thirty to get to London in time their was now 300 lads at the station and Mikey Williams (RIP) turned up with two coaches following behind each other, half of the lads wanted to then go by coach and the rest wanted to go by train so that's what happened as none of us wanted to get clocked. But we could only fill one and a half of the coaches so it was decided to put everyone all on one coach while the other 100 and odd lads were already on the train.

We set off – there was a good team of lads now who were packed onto the coach. We just hoped that mob that just got the train met up with the rest of the mob in London before the Millwall mob did. Our coach was taking ages on the motorway as traffic jams started. It was then that I wished we had gone with the other mob after all.

Finally, we arrived in London late and it didn't look good. We were still on the other side of London and it was now 3.00pm so we were not going to get there for kick off as Daft Donald had to direct the dumb coach driver to south east London. We finally get on the Old Kent Road and Daft Donald tells the coach driver to pull up as we were going to walk the rest of the way. The driver ignored him and carried on driving then from nowhere a mob comes from a side street and they started to brick the coach. The driver carries on driving until shouts of stop were heard as I threw a brick back out of the coach window. We came to a stop and piled off and the Millwall mob scatter. I wouldn't say that was their main mob because they were in the ground at the time but they smashed the coach and got a result.

As we walked through the side streets there was no other attack. They would have been heavily outnumbered as we had 150. We got to the ground at half time and the police were outside the turnstiles like they knew we were coming. They let us in and straight away we got filmed in the ground. We then went to go on the terraces which were in the corner with a big fucking floodlight sticking out of the ground and in our way.

As I couldn't see any of the game we were talking to everyone who had been there all day and they told us they kicked it off outside the ground. ET and just about everyone was in the ground at the end of the game which we won 1-0 thanks to a Tony Adcock goal. All their boys were in the stand to our left along the side of the pitch. The game had well finished and we were left in the ground for ages and their mob was still there.

I rated the way they all stayed behind like that to show us what they had. There must have been 400 still there and the police didn't make an attempt to move them either. They had only seen about 300 City before the game. On the video it shows a barrier which City were at being knocked down and a big fight starts all the way up the road. Millwall hadn't seen the 150 mob that we brought on the coach but no doubt they heard about it but wouldn't be able to tell from all the City fans in our end.

Eventually we get taken out of the ground and the Millwall Bushwhackers' then leave. Nothing happened outside due to the large police presence. We get on the tube at New Cross Gate and still no Millwall. The guy who played Joey Boswell in Bread was on the same tube and got a lot of grief off the City mob. We pull in at London Bridge station and we hear a load of noise then chants of 'war, war'. As we turned around Millwall's mob were now coming down the steps towards us. People were getting thrown out of the way as the Guvnors, Beer Monsters, and the Young Guvnors now charged towards the steps.

There was a stand off at the bottom of the steps as the Millwall mob didn't come down and we never went up. I was right at the bottom of the steps and they were throwing objects. An orange with a razor blade stuck in it missed me as my brother pulled me away. There were other City thugs there who dodged the flying objects and missiles – it was chaos and a bad situation and if anyone had tried to get up the stairs they would have been fucked. Similarly if any of them had come down it would have been the same.

The BTP arrived along with the Met and the Millwall thugs disappeared as more police came and got the City mob under control and taken us back to Euston. As soon as we arrived back on the main station it dawns on us that most never had tickets to get home and the coach was wrecked so Mikey Williams had to pay for everyone to get home which was respect to him. As he was sorting it out, the entire mob was now on the station when two big police officers came over to me and lifted me off my feet and out of the station. I got nicked for what they said throwing missiles on London Bridge station which only the undercover police could have spotted.

I was taken to Kentish Town police station where I was held

for an hour as the police phoned the Manchester police to go to my house in Oldham as I had told them that my mum and step dad were on holiday in Spain at the time. They went and my sister was at home to confirm my story but they were not letting me out as I was only 15 but then my brother turned up with ET and got me out without charge.

We went back to Euston where everyone had missed the train to wait for us – now that's what I call loyalty! We now got on a train to Liverpool as there were no trains to Manchester for an hour. So we all got on that – we had to change at Crewe but before we got there we had running battles between each other on the train. It was all a bit of fun but three carriages got wrecked and fire extinguishers were let off. We were reported to the BTP as we pulled in at Crewe the police boarded the train to inspect it but no arrests were made.

Finally, we arrived back in Manchester at 1 am and the station had police everywhere in one big line. As we marched out I bet they prayed that we had got done in at Millwall but their prayers were not answered. We all jumped in taxis because we just wanted to get home quickly but when we said Oldham the driver stops and said he isn't going nowhere until he gets paid first as a load of lads had jumped a taxi which took them to Oldham in the past. We said it wasn't fucking us but we had to pay up front so we could get home – it was a good day after all.

OLDHAM ATHLETIC (H)

It wasn't so long after the Millwall game that all the lads had met up again. This time we were at home to Oldham. This game couldn't have come any sooner as it was now clear that we had fallen out with some of their hooligans as they tried to kick it off with us after we came back from the Huddersfield game. That day I got the bus to Oldham town centre with a few lads to see if we could find their mob. We turned up a blank but one of them who wasn't going with them told us that they were going by train as they wouldn't dare get a bus to Piccadilly, so I decided to get the train to Victoria from Oldham Mumps station.

As we reached Manchester there were a lot of City lads already there waiting. We left the station as two lads stayed pretending to wait for a train. We went to the ramp which was on the side of the Arndale Centre and waited for the arrival of Oldham. There were only forty of us but that would be enough to do them. A lot of them started asking about what happened at the Millwall game. I didn't even bother to answer it as I knew that they were fraudsters who would turn out in numbers for the Sheepshaggers but never back us up. They were youngsters who claimed to be game but shit it for Millwall and now show up for Oldham.

As we waited the security guards came out to have a look but they didn't know what we were up to. Then Bluey and Vinny George who were on the station came running saying that they were here. We ran down the ramp with the guards just looking on and when we were on the road the Oldham mob were crossing some waste ground on their way over. Unknown to us there was a group of beer monsters in a pub on the corner who had been in there throughout. They came out to give the Oldham lads a chase before we did and ran them back to the station where they were met by the BTP who were already on the station.

They ended up in an escort to the ground. At Maine Road we were mobbed up in the North Stand planning what to do with them as they had been slagging us off all the time saying how they had done us in the past. They must have been talking about the early 1950s as they have never even stood when it had been even numbers. So we decided that everyone would go back to Oldham after the match as them shit bags would only go straight back anyway.

After the game, which we lost 2-1, we went straight to town as they were been escorted. The police went over the top as there was no need for that many police as Oldham's mob was small. They soon caught the train but it broke down at Failsworth station while we were on our way on the 82 bus. It was packed – we then saw the Oldham mob at the bus stop near the police station so we all ducked down. The bus stopped as one of us give the game away by shouting and we all jumped off. Some were caught and given a beating and we chased the rest on Oldham Road before the police came out of the station, some still eating their sandwiches.

We ran to the train station and waited for another train to Oldham Mumps and made our way to their pub the Tommy Fields. The windows soon went through before the police were called as we again fled. Later that evening we had settled in a pub just outside the town centre for a few hours. Some of the lads Stefan Gaye, Maynard, Benny and myself were out and about looking for the FYC while the rest of the City mob were in the pub. The four of us walked up and into town centre – we could have taken more with us but it would have been pointless as we would have got clocked.

We went in a few pubs until we saw their mob on Yorkshire Street in Harry's bar. I knew one of the doormen at the time – he wasn't a thug or a football supporter but he said that he couldn't stand the FYC and never really got on with them. We told him to tell the Oldham lot that one of his mates just came off the train at Mumps station and told him that the City mob were on the station but we told him to tell them in five minutes which gave us time to run back to City's pub and get everyone to hide across the road from the train station in ambush.

As we got to the pub we told everyone that their was about 50 FYC in Harry's Bar and that they would be making their way to the station in five minutes so they all left. Oldham wouldn't have a chance with the mob that we brought; we outnumbered them as we had a good 100 lads up there. We didn't need that many as we could easily do it with 30 but I have to give it to the FYC no matter how many times they were outnumbered they stood and had a go. I should know as I had been with them most of the time but back to that night...

As we waited near the station in the bushes next to the B&Q car park we saw them all coming. They must have bought the blag. Most of them were pissed up but nearly all were tooled up as we were. We had lads scattered in the bushes on the dual carriageway with bricks and bottles. As the FYC came through B&Q and got into the middle we jumped out – they were almost in shock as they were not expecting us to be there. Both mobs now started to exchange blows as the Oldham lads started littering the dual carriageway with bottles which were now smashing off the cars driving by which almost caused a crash.

More City were hiding on the dual carriageway where the bottles landed came over as fights started. We soon ran them, even though a few City lads suffered a few cuts and bruises but that poor cunt from Oldham who fell over while running away wasn't so lucky and came off worse than the injured City lads. I soon had to go into the middle and drag the Oldham lad away as I knew him he had had enough. If I knew who it was before he got a kicking and his head stamped on I would have been over sooner to stop it. He was able to walk off even though their was blood gushing out of his face. I walked onto Yorkshire Street with him as the other City lads were on their way back down from chasing the FYC up. They might have attacked him again so I just made sure that no one else got him.

By now the BTP had tipped off the local dibble as there were bottles all over the dual carriageway outside the station which caused traffic to come to a standstill. The police were now everywhere so City lads started running away. There was a call to walk which they did as the police rounded us all up with their dogs and brought us across the road and onto the station. There was glass and bricks everywhere as the BTP officers swept it off the road and to one side. We could have easily gone up to Harry's Bar in the first place and give it them there but the town centre was too hot and one of the pub licensee's would have called the police when they saw our mob.

The train soon arrived at Mumps to take us back to Victoria. There were at least 50 of us who lived in Oldham but the police were not having it and stayed on the train all the way back to Manchester where we ended up staying and going in the hacienda nightclub until the early hours before everyone went home.

STOKE CITY (A)

We arrived by train for this fixture knowing that this was a grudge match – as we had met up with a load of Stoke fans in Piccadilly when they were all having a drink in the bar. On that occasion we had found out that they were there. As we marched up to the station we entered the bar and it kicked off with pint pots flying. As the pots smashed on the floor there were scuffles as both sets of fans tried to keep their balance. The drink on the floor was making everyone slip and the older lot from City were at the forefront of the fighting. As the BTP had picked it up on the station's CCTV and arrived to bring it under control, one of the lads put a chair in front of one of the officers who slipped on the floor with his helmet flying off which someone grabbed and ran off with. After it was brought under control the both sets of lads were searched and let go.

Now they were out for revenge and as we arrived we were escorted with 80 lads in the mob. We came to a roundabout near a pub when the Stoke mob charged and fighting broke out as there were not enough police. More Stoke lads came as it continued until we were now right round the corner. A slight standoff then took place and the police arrived lashing out at both sets of fans.

We were eventually taken to the ground where we stayed on a big car park with a line of police in front of us. The police now turned their attention to City who had no tickets there were 200 of us without and we were not bothered as we wanted to stay outside. As the game was sold out the police now had to either let us in the ground or let us go to the town centre where they knew it would cause problems, so they decided to do the right thing and let the City fans pay in.

Once we were in the ground the CCTV was soon spinning our way as the undercover must now have been in the police box watching us. That was the only thing they could do without being spotted. We were all putting two fingers up to the TV camera to let them know that we knew that they were watching us. As the game went on the numbers stated to swell in our end as people were now watching the whole game with hoods up and scarves wrapped around their faces but when City scored I pulled the hood down of one of the lads and he wasn't too pleased, so I said "what the fucks up, you aren't doing fuck all! Let them film all they want after all your hot anyway it's too late now, you're well involved".

Without mentioning the individual (he was one of the ones who never went to the Millwall game and funnily enough never got nicked in the raids). He was they type who never travelled with the mob and always drove about telling us where the other mobs were. Whenever we got there he was nowhere to be seen but the police always arrived soon after... His days were numbered – we now knew who he was and he would be getting exposed soon as some rich kid from the Cheshire area.

After the game soon ended, which the best team won 3-1 (we did the double over them that season) we were taken straight back to the station without further trouble.

This was the point at which many of the old faces started to drift away from the game thinking that if they didn't go to certain matches, they would not get targeted. The rest of us were just keeping it together as we didn't care. Everyone came to terms with it but we just could not find who the other undercover police were and where they were.

Mark Chapman, who was fronted a few months before by some of the older lot about the guys he was with, backed up their story by saying that they were his good mates. We should have got onto it from then as Chappy started going to the game by car with these lads and we saw less of him but it was to be his evidence that really brought the case against us.

*

Games started to come thick and fast as it was the New Year. There were games at Everton which was a night match in the League Cup we lost 2-0 as it was on Granada Soccer night and showed most of City's mob which the CCTV cameras also picked up after that game. After a mini disturbance Pete Frith ended up getting slashed which was not his fault.

That was then followed by the Villa game where I arrived at the Sunspot arcade. It was snowing that day and as I was stood on the steps I noticed the same white British Gas van that had been following us for weeks at home games parked across the road on a side street. We went and had a look: me, Clitheroe, Neil Morrison from Oldham but there was no one about. We went back to the arcade when I spotted someone at a window with a big camera, then he hid. I told the others and stood right across the road from where they were filming. I had my hat pulled down and my scarf up to my eyes.

As we left for the ground later everyone was told to keep a look out for the van which we should have wrecked beforehand. It was the same van that the police used to follow and film drug dealers in Moss Side two years later. It's a lucky thing I wasn't in the area at the time or I would have blown their cover. Back at the ground as we were losing 2-0 I decided to get a few lads together and we went onto the pitch while the game was going on. We were too young to get nicked and as we never got nicked when we went on against Huddersfield, I knew they wouldn't touch us now. 10 of us ran across to their end which was behind the goal in the Platt Lane stand.

I was at the front of this group and, as the game came to a halt, the Villa mob started to chant "Bruno, Bruno" as I had a pair of gloves on. The police got us all before we got to the fence as the stewards didn't bother to come on as they now knew who we were. Also they didn't want to get done in by the older lot. After this we ran out of the ground and straight onto the bus to town. Two hours later I met up with Pat Berry and a mob of Guvnors. We were on our way to the Brunswick Pub as we had found out that the Villa youth were in there. As we approached, their mob was already outside kicking it off with some of the Young Guvnors. They were getting run as the Villa mob chased them off with pint pots. We ran them as the Young Guvnors turned and charged back. We give it them at the bottom of Piccadilly Station approach and as we chased more off some knobhead was shouting "come on let's give it them". Pat Berry said "who the fuck are u?" This lad replied "I'm City". He was then told to fuck off which he did. Chappy was seen talking to him later, the police got Pat and searched him then let him go as they were told he had pulled out a blade to the villa thugs which was untrue, he didn't need that shit.

It was at this time that the undercover police were coming out of their shells – making the odd appearance before the uniforms showed up. I brought it to everyone's attention that the raids wouldn't be far off but no one was arsed and others didn't really believe it would happen. It was thought that if it goes off in front of the police, you would get nicked. We never did and more of us Young Guvnors were doing it on a regular basis – smashing up pubs and when the police came they would just film it and move our mob on.

At one game I sneaked into the North Stand and the police chased me. I lost them by running into the St John's Ambulance room and blagged them by saying I had been chased by some lads on the other side of the stand. They told me "keep away from that corner bit as the police are doing an operation on a group of lads over there" so you couldn't have any more proof than that.

BLACKPOOL (A) FA CUP ROUND 4

This was the last game I would attend as a teenager but I never knew it. The day of this game everyone came out: Splodge, my brother, and (Slash neck) Robert Slicker from Oldham. ET and Larry had been up from the night before. We all met at Victoria station that morning and we soon heard that there were groups of United all over the town but they never came near the station. Benny turned up with his mob, Daft Donald with his mob which brought Anthony Worthington out, as the entire older mob arrived on the station the numbers were now swelling.

The early train was almost due and the City mob must have had 400 lads out for the short trip to the seaside. The announcement was soon made over the tannoy that the Blackpool train was arriving on Platform 1, and all the young lot I was with had to wait until some of the older ones got tickets so that we could sneak onto the platform as tickets had to be shown. None of us were paying on and we were planning to also sneak into the ground.

We soon set off when the train made a short stop at Salford Crescent some of the lads got off just in case United had shown as that station was on their patch. There was no sign so we were on our way. There was no police on Victoria or on the train which had eight Carriages and was almost full as there were also passengers on the train. Most of them felt uneasy as there was a lot of singing and swearing. A lot of it was aimed at Man United as the train reached Bolton station. Three of their boys were on there and their main lads were on the opposite platform. We knew it was them as we had a run in with them in the past as I knew one of their lads, Rammy, but he wasn't there. There were two white lads and a mixed race lad with them. As they heard us chanting 'City' they paid no attention until they heard chants of 'shit on The Bolton, shit on the Bolton tonight' they then looked over as everyone started to boo them.

The chants started again and they now echoed around the platform and then the windows on the train nearly went through as the banging on them got louder. People on the station were getting verbally abused as they looked on in horror as for the passengers already on; they looked like zombies as they wouldn't dare say a word. As the train moved off the Bolton lad started to give us all the v signs as lads shouted out of the window 'we will see you lot later' meaning that on our return we would be jumping off the train there to go and look for them in their town centre.

Later in the journey a lad called Mark Dorrian said he had heard the ticket inspector telling someone that the police were being called because of our rowdy behaviour but no one was interested as we were all up for it, happy and buzzing as Blackpool was going to get hit again as it did in 1984 when all sorts went on, including their ticket office getting robbed.

We were nearly there as the train made its final stop at Preston. As the train pulled to a halt and the doors flew open two BTP walked on. As they walked through the carriage and squeezed through all the lads, some of whom were determined not to move out of the way. As the police tried to walk past a lad from Oldham called Clanger he just stood there. The officer, without even saying excuse me, said allreet lads. The whole carriage erupted into laughter at the officer's accent – he wasn't what we expected. Meanwhile as the lads shouted sheep 'sheep sheep shaggers' to the officers, who at this stage looked as if they had wet themselves. As everyone

chanted in their faces they
made their way to the other
end of the train and never
bothered us again but we
knew that there would be
a welcoming party waiting
for us as we arrived.

When the train finally reached Blackpool north station and
came to a halt the officers thought that they had some control and
said 'can we have some kind of order now lads?' everyone just piled
off. As the ticket collector waited at the barrier to collect all the
tickets in with about five BTP officers everyone just rushed through
the barrier with the officers looking stunned. We charged out of the
main entrance shouting 'City, City' then 'Guvnors, Guvnors'. The
mounted officers nearby thought that they were going to escort this
mob to the ground as if we were a bunch of pussies. There were
two of Blackpool's so called Seaside Mafia or the Muckers, outside
the station who managed to take two photos of the mob before
running off through the town centre as City continued their charge.
The police could only watch as the City thugs were now scattered
everywhere on the road which now brought traffic to a complete
halt as chants of 'guvnors, guvnors' reverberated around.

The rowdy behaviour began as shop stalls started to go over, it
was like a mini rampage and, as we got deeper into the town centre,
we saw about twenty of their boys and I gave it one of them as the
rest stuck the boot in. They all ran off… As we were now nearing
the seafront the wind was now getting to be a problem with sand
flying everywhere (I don't know how them desert boys cope in
Ethiopia) and when we finally reached the sea front with most of
the shops shut, we were now going to find somewhere to hang
about.

As the wind was now even stronger on the front we were not
going to walk all the way up to the Manchester pub so we managed
to get to an amusement arcade which was open as everyone piled
in. It wasn't long before the fruit machines went over then about
ten lads lifted a machine up and dropped it on the floor. As the

money went flying all over, the customers looked round before running for the nearest exit. More machines got tipped and some lads who were known to us for popping fruit machines, pulled out a screwdriver and opened the back as they clicked the money out. Then the front got popped open as the tray at the front was now removed and alarms started blaring.

Everyone made their way outside and headed towards the Pleasure Beach which was closed as it was February. There were shops open along the front, some of which sold jackets which looked like leathers. As the mob went past a rail of them went missing as the Indian shop owner came running out but soon did a u-turn when he saw the mob. Half way up the road another stall got took which the contents soon went flying into the middle of the road making a car swerve out of the way. They were all snides anyway all the fake stuff they were selling for some fucked up prices.

We were now not far from the ground as all the thieves ditched their jackets as the police were all over the show, as if they knew that we were on our way. They must have had reports about the amusement arcade and the jackets going missing. As we got nearer they started to get out of all the vans and started taking their dogs out. We all just marched past chanting 'guvnors' to intimidate the police. As we went along a lot of lads stayed at the City end as me, Benny, Slicker and a number of others went for a walk around the ground. We saw Steve Morgan outside the player's entrance so we asked for some tickets which he never had, he lived just up the road from me as he was from Oldham but Slicker knew him better than me as he had more or less grown up with him.

As we continued to talk to Steve a mob of Blackpool came down the hill and we then ran at them leaving Steve at the player's entrance. We chased the Blackpool lot off as the police grabbed hold of us and brought us back round to City's end where our mob had now managed to get hold of some forgeries. While they were sorting out the tickets me and ET went straight out onto the main road with our backs to the mob. We bumped into about 150 of the so called Seaside Mafia as bricks came flying through the air followed by a few racist remarks.

We ran back towards the City end not one of the City thugs saw or heard anything as we got closer shouting. Benny and Splodge now spotted us as we now started to stand. ET's City hat flew off his head and then we just got ran. His hat was now in flames as they set fire to it so we ran back to the car park. They never knew that there were over 400 lads outside the City end and as we chased them, two got caught and got done in. As I carried on running their mob now turned. I picked up a brick and threw it. It bounced off someone's head and hit another one as City's mob started kicking fuck out of them. They then backed off as the Police cars came screeching to a halt.

As we came back off the main road where their mob had scattered I got grabbed by the police who placed me under arrest. As I put up a struggle with the officer a load of City thugs started punching the officer in his head and body and as I got free I got grabbed by another one. I saw my brother get his new jeans ripped by a police dog in the mayhem. Everyone was now fighting with the Police. I got handcuffed and put in the back of a car and I was soon joined by Pete Frith. As the police tried to drive through the crowd a brick came flying through the window and City thugs surrounded the car – banging on the windows and kicking fuck out of it.

We arrived at the police station a few minutes later covered in glass, Pete was taken in a holding room while they searched me in the custody area. Also in there were three other black guys. I then thought that Frith had been released as the police made a mistake as they were only out for the niggers that day. Oliver Browne, Ricky Campbell, and Kevin Mattis from the hood were all in there, they had been nicked for selling forged tickets and later got fined while ten other lads who got nicked that day got three month bans.

Once in the custody area a load of police went running past me as the officer who nicked me said that your lot have gone mad since you got nicked. I then said 'so fucking what'. He didn't like the response as he searched me. The desk sergeant asked me my name address and age as I told him that I was fifteen they looked at each other as the glass came flying out of my jacket in front of the officers. He then told the sergeant that the window in the police car had been put through due to my arrest – he told him that I was under arrest for throwing a brick at rival fans.

I could hear it going off on the police radio as they called for more assistance as officers from Preston were en route to back them up. I was then put in the juvenile cells and taken for interview two hours later. My mum had to come all the way from Oldham to get me out as my brother was still at the ground. I was cautioned and released and as I got to Blackpool North train station with my mum who was kicking off at me as I thought that she had driven there so I could get off and meet up with everyone, there were a lot of City fans there but no thugs as they were still in the town.

There were a load of Manchester Police on the station with a slight grin on their faces as I passed them to board the train. I got another earful about getting nicked on arrival back, at Victoria train Station there was about fifty of United's boys there. They were waiting for City's mob but the only City thug to get off the train was me. I felt a right cunt having to walk through their mob with my mum. From then on I gave them respect as they didn't try or say anything. I went straight home. I heard the day after that it was kicking off until 12 o'clock that night in Manchester city centre with United fans as it was reported on the radio.

THE BATTLE ON PICCADILLY

It was three in the morning when the phone rang. My mum answered and the voice on the other end asked if me and my brother were home which she said yes then the phone went dead. I went to sleep it didn't seem like two minutes that I had closed my eyes than there were two loud bangs at the door. I looked out of the back window and saw a load of police at the back with dogs barking. I woke my brother up and said 'this is it we're getting raided' as about ten police officers ran up the stairs to our bedroom. They told us to keep calm and don't do anything stupid as the house was completely surrounded. They then read the conspiracy charges to us, let us have a wash before taking us to separate police stations

After a long day of questioning I was charged with riots and violent disorder. The sergeant joked 'you don't even look old enough' that didn't stop him charging me though! I was taken to the Central Detention Centre (CDC) above the courts where I met up with the rest who had been nicked. I was surprised to see that certain people were not there and while there were people who should not have been there who had been nicked. As I was a juvenile I was placed in the juvenile cells and in the next door cell was Jamie Roberts. We were the two youngest to be charged. I knew that we would be the only two who would get bail the next day as Jamie was also still in school and was sixteen years old while I was still only fifteen. Everyone was shouting to one another all night and singing City songs.

The next morning we were taken in threes to court – me, my brother and Jimmy G were taken up once in the court after confirming our names and ages. We sat down as I was handcuffed to my brother and Jimmy G was handcuffed to a screw. Once bail was mentioned the prosecution then read out our previous convictions. As they read out Jimmy's saying that he was locked up for the Moss Side riots, it made the magistrates raise their eyebrows.

They sat staring at me and my brother because we were both black even though they had just been told that we were the Rhoden brothers they then said 'could Mr. Gittens stand'. As Jimmy did their heads went back and they then repeated it again 'can Mr. G please stand up' as jimmy said 'I am Mr. G ' I then said 'the cheeky cunts'. My solicitor leant over and told me to be quiet. I said 'they are surprised that jimmy is white and been to jail for the riots, all the rioters were not all black'.

Jimmy and my brother got remanded with 22 others, me and Jamie got bail with conditions that we had to sign on at the police station three times a week Monday, Wednesday and Saturdays at three o clock with a 7pm curfew. Also we were not to go within half a mile of any football ground (not forgetting that I lived less than five minutes from Boundary Park). I would have rather taken remand instead of all that shit but I was now starting to revise for my school exams and after all that's what we all went to school for, so I didn't fancy missing them.

As the days went by the police were on constant watch outside my house after seven at night to see if I went out. They soon got fed up and as a complete pisstake the police were all over every news station possible saying how they had now broken the backbone of the Guvnors and Young Guvnors. So all week they were on the TV and in the news papers and on the local radio stations boasting how they smashed us and that they had rooted out all the trouble makers.

They were soon left with egg on their faces as all the 22 were still locked up in Strangeways and with the exception of me and Jamie they said their were no more trouble makers and that the rest would go underground. The Police searched for more but in truth they had no more to arrest for the Operation Omega case that was just to make out to the public and other people higher up think that they had it well under control. But it wasn't to be as on the 20th February 1988 the City fans met in the City centre and had a chat about a few things as they wanted to get the Guvnors name back on the map and not let the police raid think that they had scared anyone away. In total they had arrested 26 people and charged 22 but where do they think the other three to four hundred went?

It was now two o'clock on Saturday afternoon and as everyone left Brannigans in the Royal Exchange to go to the home game against Plymouth, which was the FA cup Fifth Round, I went to get the 182 bus to Chadderton police station in Oldham to sign on for three o clock. I came straight back to town and waited with a few lads until the game finished – it was six o clock before the City mob came back and they said that they had just kicked it off with Plymouth's Central Element mob at the ground and that some of their lads had been nicked and some of City's too.

We all went to Shudehill where we stayed in a pub called the Lower Turks Head. As we waited there for an hour we were all going to give it the United fans when they came back. As we were talking about them the landlord kept on walking past us all and trying to listen to what we were saying so we decided to leave and then we all marched towards Piccadilly. The mob we had was about 80–100 lads – it was a big difference to what the police were saying a week a go. We walked through the city centre unnoticed. As we went down back streets after splitting up into different groups so the police didn't get onto us, even though they were saying all week that basically the problem had gone away, we reached Nicklebys pub near Piccadilly.

This was an easy way to get near the station without using London Road so we could avoid detection. It was now well after 7pm and my curfew had started but I didn't give a shit – I was now already on two charges so another one would make no difference. I was still pissed off about the fact that the City lads who were in jail shouldn't have been there – they had been stitched up as the case hadn't even started so it was like everyone was presumed guilty.

So as we were in Nicklebys I made a phone call to one of the Arsenal mob. I rang a payphone which was in the Lion and Lamb pub which was near Euston station. One of the Gooners answered and said that they had just had it with United an hour and a half before so they were on their way back. So that was it – it was time to leave as twenty of us made our way up to Piccadilly station and then split up into fives. I then made it my business to look up at the CCTV Camera and give a wave and a smile – it was way after curfew but that's life. City came first at this stage! We were now on the station all bunched together.

As we checked the time table the train was due in half an hour so two of the other lads ran back to the pub to get the rest but five minutes later the train arrived so as we bunched together a load of fans came off shouting 'United'. This lot all had hats and scarves so we waited as we now saw some police coming our way with a Mob which was their boys. The ticket office where we were was now packed with United boys who now spotted us and they were now chanting 'you're supposed to be in jail'. I took it that they aimed it at me.

As we tried to stand and with the police still by their side they ran at us. As we stood fighting by the station doors it's as if they all came for me as one of the City lads flattened one of them, the police then went for him as the United thugs chased us down the Station Approach with the police as always. I had a near miss with a black cab I shouted to the City lads 'everyone stick together and head back to the pub', as I didn't think that City's mob would be out of the pub yet. On other occasions when they were told that a mob was coming it would be me and the young guvnors doing the business first as they would never believe us and stay in the pub drinking but this time they were now on their way up as we were getting chased down.

We turned and about 80-100 City thugs went charging back up at them. As they ran back onto the station the police chased us back down but on the way the police tripped up one of the lads and as he went flying along the floor. Three of them started hitting him with truncheons as some City lads shouted 'stand they have got J_____ V_____'. As everyone turned we went back as the lad was still getting hit they came at us and I could see about twenty lads surround him and one of the lads punched him right in the eye. He went stumbling backwards as the rest of the mob now got the other lad free another officer came at them but got a bottle smashed over his head and about ten lads now tried to throw him through the plate glass shop window. He didn't go through as a third officer came lashing out at everyone. He got surrounded and everyone steamed into him as a hammer was produced and smashed over his head he went down. As he did so he was punched and kicked as the other two now backed off and talked into their radios.

Everyone then scattered from the scene. About twenty of us ran through the city centre as police sirens were sounding from all directions and jumped on a bus to Oldham. That was it for City – now there would be more doors coming off but not mine as I was at home all night on a curfew unless they looked at the station CCTV!

The next day it was all over the news as the police said on the TV that a large group of Guvnors and Young Guvnors connected to Manchester City were believed to have been involved and that the police were studying video films shot for Operation Omega. They suspect that most of the 80 or so thugs might appear on the film used to smash them.

The police were now well pissed off with City's mob and they were now on the news and in the papers everyday appealing for witnesses as the City thugs hit the headlines. The lads who were on remand in Strangeways must now have thought that they were never getting out as this was to affect their possible release on the Friday when we all went back up. But on the Thursday morning the Police had to move quick as they never wanted the other City thugs in Strangeways out while the ones they were looking for were still on the loose, so they started taking doors off.

Ten of them were in Oldham (thankfully not mine again!) as they arrested 27 more City hooligans for their part in what they were now calling 'The Battle of Piccadilly'. I attended court on the Friday everyone was also looking to get bail. There were 26 up together for the Operation Omega case, 27 more were also up for the Piccadilly case. There must have been at least 53 defendants up and 40 other thugs outside the court room who came to support them, it looked good. As the Omega lot got bailed, the Piccadilly

Top: City's lads outside Maine Rd in the early 1990's

Middle Left: City at the Whalley Hotel before the 1986 FA Cup match against United

Middle Right: United's boys head towards Maine Rd before the 1986 league derby

Left: Me and the lads on the way to the Whalley Hotel 1986 FA CUP before United boys turned up.

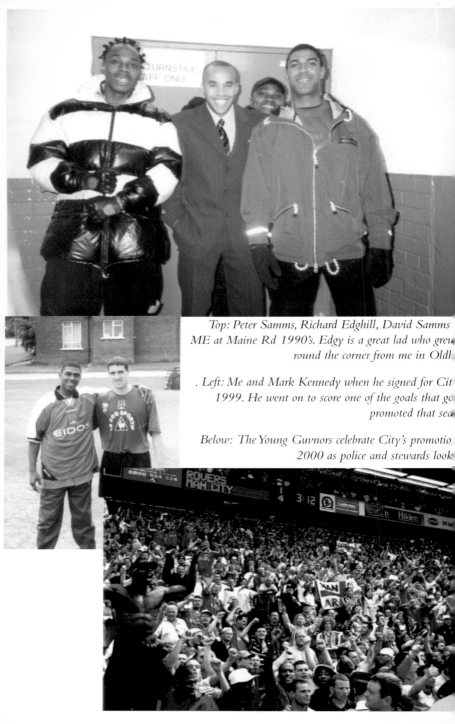

Top: Peter Samms, Richard Edghill, David Samms
ME at Maine Rd 1990's. Edgy is a great lad who grew
round the corner from me in Oldh

. Left: Me and Mark Kennedy when he signed for Cit
1999. He went on to score one of the goals that go
promoted that sea

Below: The Young Guvnors celebrate City's promotio
2000 as police and stewards look

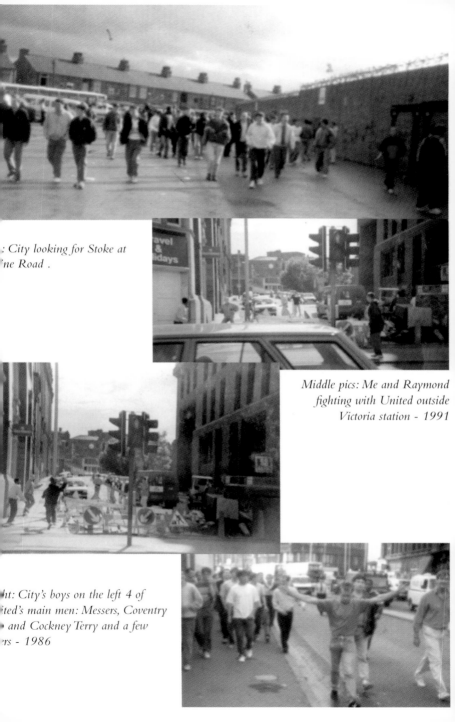

: City looking for Stoke at
'ne Road .

Middle pics: Me and Raymond
fighting with United outside
Victoria station - 1991

ht: City's boys on the left 4 of
'ted's main men: Messers, Coventry
 and Cockney Terry and a few
rs - 1986

Top: City's Mob b[...]
escorted to the new Cit[...]
Manchester stadium 2[...]

Middle: Riot police kee[...]
watch on City outside [...]
Clar[...]

Left: GMP underc[...]
detectives keep an eye [...]
brother - the moust[...]
and the sheepskin coat [...]
give-a[...]

This is what I have to put up with - police harassment at Rotherham . I had only nipped out of the pub to get some cash and the fuckers were filming me, so I filmed them right back…

Middle: My girlfriend Anastasia, me and the lads in Copenhagen.

Bottom left: Me and the lads at Villarreal before City's Champions League tie

Bottome: right: Me and the lads in a pre-match boozer before the FA Cup derby 2012.

*Top: Me involved in a demonstration at Maine Rd following City's defeat to Luton. We h[a]
endure some shit football in this period culminating in our relegation to Division Two.*

Below: Me and the lads in Blackburn which is always a good trip.

*Right: A Collection of cuttings concerning the rise and fall of The Guvnors and Young Gu[v]
Needless to say we were headline news for a few years…*

Soccer terror: 21 face court

...NTY-ONE Man-
...er City fans,
...ted following a
...e probe into organ-
... soccer violence,
...ared at the city
...strates court today,
...but two face charges
...nspiring to riot or
... public disorder at
...ees.

...et are also accused of
...ng riots at matches in
...ester and West Brom-
...last November and in
...ry.

...the court were: James
..., aged 24, catering

assistant, of Sandyshot Walk,
Peel Hall, Wythenshawe; Mark
Chapman, 26, unemployed, of
Withnell Road, Burnage; Errol
Rhoden, 19, unemployed of
Margate, Chadderton Way,
Oldham; David Foulkes, 24,
labourer, of Clinton Avenue,
Fallowfield; Mark Martin, 21,
railman, of Judy Street,
Moston.

David Goodall, 22, ware-
houseman, of Beckton Gardens,
Benchill, Wythenshawe; Mark
Herman, 23, unemployed, of
Aston Avenue, Fallowfield;
Steven Stanton, 21, window
cleaner, of Melvin Avenue,
Crossacres, Wythenshawe;
Anthony Worthington, 20,

labourer, of Hopwood Road,
Hollins, Middleton.

Patrick Berry, 24, unem-
ployed, of Bickerdike Court
Longsight; Mark Fiorini, 19,
unemployed, of Ashton Old
Road, Openshaw; Michael
Francis, 27, scaffolder, of
Edenfield Road, Prestwich;
Paul Berry, aged 25, unem-
ployed, of Fortuna Grove,
Levenshulme; Brendan Murray,
19, unemployed, of Broadfield
Road, Moss Side; Christopher
Francis, 26, cellarman, of
Acomb Street, Moss Side;
Michael Ossai, 18, general
cleaner, of Collyhurst Street,
Collyhurst; Paul Gunning, 17,
unemployed, of Bletchley

Close, Longsight; and two
juveniles, aged 16 and 15.

All charged that, between
August last year and this
month, in Greater Manchester
and elsewhere, they conspired
to cause riot at matches.

Karl Valentine, aged 25, a
youth development officer, of
Greenend Haughton Green,
Denton, was charged with im-
personating a police officer.

Stephen Montagne, aged 23, a
driver, of Lowther Road,
Queens Promenade, Blackpool,
is alleged to have unlawfully
and maliciously wounded football referee John Deakin.

(Proceeding)

'SOCCER THUGS' '90 YEAR BAN

...ENTY-five soccer thugs who waged a war of
...red on rival fans were banned from football
...unds for a total of 190 years yesterday.

Undercover cops infiltrated the Manchester City sup-
...ters, using hi-tech surveillance gadgets to bust their
...n of terror.

Known as Guvnors, they were aged between 20 and
... Young Guvnors — aged from 14 — were incited by
...r elder tutors.

...one match, 30 of them
... two innocent men to a
..., purely to satisfy their
...od-lust, Liverpool
...wn Court heard.

...e accused, all from
...chester, admitted con-
...ng to cause violent
...rder at grounds across
... country during the
...-88 season.

...ngleader Michael
...cis, 29, of Edenfield
...d, Prestwich, was
...d for 21 months and
...ed from grounds for
... rs.

...rs were banned for
...een five and 15 years.

Guvnor busters praised

A JUDGE yesterday
praised Operation
Omega which resulted in
25 soccer hooligans being
banned for a total of 190
years.

"Everyone involved
should be highly praised
and applauded", said
Judge Dennis Clark at Li-
verpool Crown Court.

How Guvnors were smashed

Police curb on soccer yobs' pub 'HQ'

BY NICOLA DOWLING

THREAT Afternoons will close on Saturdays

Bar must close on Saturdays

A CITY centre bar said to be
used as a headquarters for
Manchester City football hooligans has been forced to close
on Saturdays.

For the first time in Greater
Manchester, police have used
new legislation to ask magistrates to grant a temporary
closure order at the Athenaeum
in King Street because it has
attracted large gangs of football
fans intent on causing trouble.

The move is one of a number of

techniques used by police to stamp
out football hooliganism in Manchester.

It comes as 14 Manchester City and
Stockport County fans wait to be
sentenced for their part in a brawl
last month, which led to Grand Street
in the city centre, following a match
in October 2002.

City prosecutor Barry Horne
from Boddie Street police station
said: "This newspaper has told of
that the bar is used by Manchester

City hooligans and on Saturday we
attended to see a group of about 30
men in the bar in carrying weapons
after we had received information
that there was to be a fight in the city
centre between City and United fans.

"Officers dispersed the crowds
before any trouble could take place.

"We have also been called at least
four times in the last month about
large numbers of Manchester City
fans who have been helping themselves to
alcohol from behind the bar or at

our windows, trying to avoid music
from the bill.

"We want to send out a clear mess-
age that we will not tolerate this kind
of behaviour and are determined
to ensure the city centre is a safe
place for people to come and try to
make a night out."

Spokesman for the Athenaeum
Snooker Club said the music club were
helping to the police help resolve the
problems.

The closure order will remain in
place until March 31 when the order
ends. The police and magistrates will
then assess the situation and decide
whether a new order should be

GUVNORS BANNED FOR 75 YEARS

... soccer thugs who ambushed and
...ered rival fans throughout the coun-
...were yesterday banned from attend-
...for a total of 75 years.

...ey were among 25 Manchester City

Michael Francis, 22, of Prestwich

'CCER MOB 'GOT KIDS TO SPY ON VICTIMS'

Fans picked out for a battering

Monster' gang
... soccer aggro

Fan cracked skull of PC with hammer

A HAMMER-WIELDING Manchester City fan fractured a police officer's
skull in a carefully-planned mob attack, Oldham Crown Court heard
yesterday. David Clayton, of Copster Place, Oldham, admitted causing
grievous bodily harm and conspiring to cause violent disorder. Seven other
City fans pleaded guilty to the charge of conspiring to cause violent
disorder.

Mr. Peter Wright, prosecuting, told the court that the eight men were among 70 to
80 who met up in pre-arranged city-centre pubs in the early evening of February 20,
last year, with the intention of meeting Manchester United fans at Piccadilly Station
and fighting them.

About 70 youths gathered in
the Lower Turks' head,
Shudehill, where the landlord
overheard a conversation
about the arrival of Man-
chester United supporters on
a football special after their
game with Arsenal.

The group then assembled
in Ricklebys, near Piccadilly
Station, not by coincidence
... in order to go to the
...tion without using London
...el, to avoid detection, Mr.

USHERED

...r. Wright added that it
...s quite clear that the ring-
...ers were not in the dock
... had directed operations
...m a safe distance and that
...one degree of sophistica-
... was employed.

The group left the pub
...d the way to the station.

returned to full uniformed
duty, as a result of his injury.

Another of the men, James
Wilde, of Bexhill Walk,
Chadderton, told the police
that he had had no choice but
to be involved because he did
not want to be seen running
away because "he was scared
of the older blokes".

Judge Anthony Hammond
told Clayton: "There is no
need to tell you what this
public at large think of
thugs. He described the
offence as "wicked and
cowardly."

He sentenced Clayton to
three years in a young
offenders' institution for
causing grievous bodily harm
and a further nine months, to
run concurrently, for conspiring to cause violent disorder.

MOB AMBUSH WAS 'WELL PLANNED'

Thirty to 50 waited at the
bottom of the approach under
an archway and a "sort of
skirmish party" of between 10
and 25 went into the station.

The prosecution pointed
out that by the time this
group had made its way to the
platform, only a few United
fans remained and a police
officer ushered the City fans
back, an effort which met with
very little resistance.

Outside the station PC
Duffy was joined by two other
police officers, who attempted
to usher them down the
approach. Mr. Wright said
that civilian observers got the
impression that the police
officers were being lured away
from the station.

One of the officers, PC
Martin, was hit on the nose
after an order to stand and
was given to the mob, PC

Top: The Guvnors at Wembley 2011 before we smashed United
on the way to winning the FA Cup

Below: With lads at my engagement party at City's stadium - January 2012.

Hero victim of the thug fans

Pc Darren Yates (left) and Pc Steve Martin ... attacked by thugs.

By Peter Sharples

HERO JOHN DUFFY had a bedside visit from his police colleagues today as he recovered from his beating in the Battle of Piccadilly.

The 37-year-old railway policeman's skull was fractured as he was kicked and battered by a mob of marauding yobbos in an ambush on the Manchester station approach.

Pc Duffy was one of three officers escorting a trainload of Manchester United supporters who returned from their team's FA Cup defeat at Arsenal.

The former Army corporal waded in in ward off attacks on his colleagues.

Pcs Steve Martin, aged 30, and Darren

Comment: P6

Pc John Duffy ... defended his colleagues.

lot got remanded, the police were pissed off.

The next time we all went back to court the bail conditions got from bad to worse and as the lads in the Piccadilly case also now got bail the police were on high alert as there were rumours going around that there was going to be a big kick off at Maine Road with the police and the scousers as part of even more revenge. The scousers came down for an FA Cup game that was moved to a Sunday which did not coincide with the Saturday bail conditions. So it was a free day for all at the ground – it went off in the North Stand near to the main stand with Liverpool fans who thought that they could take it over as they thought that there were no Young Guvnors about. But we ended up fighting until the police got in the middle then took the Scousers back to the Kippax and Platt Lane stands.

We managed to sneak to the Platt Lane end of the ground as some of us were now on bail condition not to go anywhere near. Well we did and a load of bricks started to fly over the wall towards the scousers before we all got off back to town. But on the way some of the lads wanted to get everyone back to town but were not sure if everyone would go back after the game so we came up with a story that I had got slashed by the Mickey's and the word soon spread. The rumour brought a few Rastas out, who were always up for the scousers and knew me and knew that I would be backing them up no matter what.

In town we didn't expect anyone to buy it but as I was in Burger King in Piccadilly with a few lads about 80 more turned up. Yeah they bought it alright, as about 20 Rastas came leading the mob. We came out as I then told them it was a blag and they were not happy at all but they stayed in town as the scousers came later on into the gardens. A few scuffles started and the police were on the scene within seconds as they were watching the scousers all the way from the ground. Everyone scattered as the police soon rounded me and ten others up at the 182 bus stop in Stevenson Square where they lined us up against the wall and took our pictures and told us to fuck off from the city centre or we would be nicked so we did.

ARTHUR ALBISTON TESTIMONIAL
MAY 8th 1988 - CHESTER ROAD

It was the day after the football season had ended. The City team had to travel back to Manchester for this Sunday game as they had just played Crystal Palace in London the day before and as most of the City thugs were still in London we had to get a mob together and quickly. We all met on Great Western Street in Moss Side outside a club which was there at the time. There was only ten of us so we decided to go to the city centre as we knew that some of the lads would go their first. We made our way by bus to town and we reached Piccadilly bus station where we saw about 50 City lads at the other bus stop across the road. As we met up there was word that United's young ones were in the Merchants Pub so we went through the gardens and onto Oldham Street.

As we approached the pub doors suddenly shut as they saw us from the window. We were now outside the pub and I saw Matthew Fitton aka (Pratt) who lived near me and who went around with us up there but he was United through and through. He was inside the pub talking to me from the window when some knob head came giving it the nigger shit. They must have known by now that that shit didn't bother me in the slightest. I told him to open the door so me and him could have a one on one. He shit it as Pratt told him to shut up. The door wouldn't open so I told him I would see him at their ground. He put two fingers up and suddenly a brick went flying through the window as glass shattered all over me - they could have waited until I moved out of the way.

The United mob backed off inside the pub as chairs and tables then came out followed by their mob but as they finished throwing everything at us they then backed us off as now they had no tools left. We charged back with half of their tools as they ran in the pub and down the side alleyways. We then got off for the bus before the police got there. We then went back to the same spot in Moss Side on Great Western Street where more lads had now gathered. The turnout was about 100 but as we marched through Doddington and Gooch we came to the Whalley Hotel. As we were there it was clear that certain people were shitting it to go to United's ground with 100.

"What 100" I said, "if you all look around there are about 70 lads left unless the other 30 got kidnapped when walking through the estates or they just shit it". It was all the Young Guvnors that I was with and I said, "if anyone else wants to fuck off, go now as I don't need people sneaking off" but no one else went so we marched through Hulme then onto Chester Road.

Lloydy from Oldham said "Rodney, look behind you" as I did I nearly fainted as the mob had almost disappeared at the back. I could see ginger Shaun from Miles Platting and Slicker calling some lads back then a car drove past us with some of United's main men in it - Binnsy and Coco. One of them shouted "you are all going to get done when you get down there" and drove off as Padina and George tried to brick their car. It was a joke there were 100 lads to start with and there were now 50 of us left. We were all good lads - Steve and his Bury boys, ET, Crawford, Maynard, Carl Stewart, Cat, Slicker and a load of game lads that wouldn't run. I said "fuck it, we will do it with this".

They knew I wasn't allowed in the ground or within half a mile of the ground but I was now around the corner and approaching the Trafford pub on the corner when the Munich's attacked us with sticks and bottles. We had fuck all and just ran at them, McKeague and Belly from United ran at us as, McKeague threw a stone at me as I was right at the front. I jumped out of the way of it as other City lads ran at him and then Belly who was also making his way to me with a stick soon dropped it as I approached him. We chased them all back as one United lad who was a lot older than us got caught and he got the worst kicking yet, his head and body were stamped on as the United mob just stood and watched. Then Steve from Bury came running through City's mob chasing the United mob. As I threw a stone at one of them we then turned to go. The United fan was still on the ground getting kicked I just ran over and done the hop, skip and jump or the triple jump on his head as the Police vans arrived.

As we fucked off Brian Padina got nicked at the scene as the police took names from the United mob. One of them gave my name to the police as we went to town and waited for the United mob. Our older mob had just arrived back from London to join up as United's mob came into Piccadilly bus station thinking that we still only had the fifty.

As Brazedale, Timmy and the older firm of City chased United through town, I jumped on the nearest bus home. Later that night I heard that United were going round saying that they had done us at their ground. Only time would tell. A month later I was arrested and I admitted what I did as the video was shown to me and I said no more. I could see on the full video when the police arrived and we had long gone. It shows some of their boys still chatting to the police and pointing. Three weeks later I appeared in court. Also up with me was Brian Padina, Vinny George and Tony McKeague.

As I sat outside the court room with my dad talking to Conrad Dunkley and Che Cole from Moss Side, the police arrived who had charged me and called me to the court room door. They said that I was also being charged so I would have to come with them. I said 'yeah, when my solicitor gets here'. 'No,' they said 'you're coming with us now as they both grabbed me'. My dad came over and said 'what the fuck are you doing to my son'. As one let me go, the other had hold of my throat. I head-butted him in his face, he soon let go. As a scuffle started police, court officials and other solicitors came running over to stop it as the officer was still dazed. The other one placed me under arrest for police assault.

As we got round the corner near the lifts the police tried to attack me again as some little Black guy from Old Trafford jumped on the back of the officer. As he hung onto his neck he also got nicked. As we reached the lifts with the two of us now handcuffed with my dad there as an on looker, the police tried it on again. When the lift door opened two detectives who were called to the scene saw the officers try to punch me and told the officer about his conduct and said he would report them if they put their hands on us.

The two detectives now followed onto Bootle Street police station where they mentioned it to the desk sergeant. All I can say is respect to them as there are few who were keeping it real. I was later charged. It was a bad day all round as I went into court with one charge that day and came out with three plus the two conspiracy charges. It was now five altogether and the charges were building up. I knew then that I was going to jail for one of them, so I just thought to myself I might as well go all out. Just two days later I was nicked again, this time for when I got nicked at the Blackpool game and got cautioned.

They now got me up there and charged me with violent disorder for throwing a brick at rival Blackpool fans – that was charge number six! The fuckers were now on my case.

STOCKPORT COUNTY (A) FRIENDLY

By now I had left school and it was time to get a job, so I sent off an Application form for a trainee at British Gas. As I was waiting to hear I got a warehouse job at Hays in Cheetham Hill where I saw a City thug there called Anthony Rowan who was a driver for them. He told me it was a good firm to work for and not to fuck about in there so I took his advice. The job did me a world of good. I rang my solicitors to tell them so they could get my curfew lifted and signing on at the police station lifted to just the Saturday so as good as Burton Copeland are, they got it lifted for me within hours thanks to Mr. Mike Mackie and Mr. Nick Freeman, Mr Gwyn Lewis and the rest of the team

But two days into the job I let them and myself down as I was influenced by the City thugs who didn't honestly realise that I was no longer allowed within half a mile of any grounds. I went to the Stockport game - as I met the Young Guvnors in Stockport town centre it's as if they were all waiting for me but I wasn't going to let a few charge sheets stop me as the fifty of us marched to the ground. The Fallowfield lot had made an appearance -John Sheehan, Franny Charles and Neil Crawford turned up as well as David Bandapara aka (Scooby). We were not going to run as we reached the first roundabout. The mounted police got onto us and started monitoring us - I knew then that I had got clocked and that I was just two minutes away from the ground but I just carried on leading the mob to the second roundabout. We got totally surrounded by their mob- there must have been 100 of them and we were well outnumbered. As I was at the front I got targeted first as some big fat guy with a skinhead who was said to be one of the main hooligans with England mob said 'come on nigger'.

There were ten of us but as I was the nearest he said it to me. I said 'come on then you fat bastard' and it erupted. I kicked him between his legs causing him to go down as fighting broke out all over the street. City's mob then backed the Stockport mob off onto a grass verge as it was still going off. I got nicked, handcuffed and slung into the back of a van. As the officer left the door open, I jumped back out still handcuffed in an attempt to escape. I was soon re-arrested and at the police station they blamed me for starting all the fighting and as I had a Public Enemy hat on which I borrowed off Franny Charles, he was well into his gangster rap shit at the time but it didn't save me .

I was later charged with public order and breach of bail so that was now charge number eight and counting! After I had my fingerprints taken and was washing my hands one of the older Stockport thugs said 'Rodney you black bastard' so I just made out that I didn't hear him as he still had his head out of the hatch I ran up and punched him in the face as the arresting officer pulled me to one side he opened the door and grabbed him and said if 'I hear you saying that shit again I will let that sixteen year old in here to do you in'.

The next morning I was on the way to court handcuffed to Neil Holland who is their main man. I get on alright with him as he had been to a few City games. As we spoke, the drunken thug who I had punched the night before was now in the queue and said he was sorry. As I was in court with the ten Stockport lads who got nicked I got remanded in to the care of the local authority which was Oldham at the time. They were ok with me, they let me go home at night but I had to go back there in the morning so they could keep me out of trouble until February as I had lost my very first job and it wasn't worth getting another one as I knew I was going to jail soon

I was wrong. I soon got pissed off with going to the care centre everyday so I decided to go to the job centre that day and I found just what I was looking for in a warehouse the next day. I had to go to Cheetham Hill for the interview – it was just a small unit where I met Mr. Max Hameed who was the owner. It was a slipper warehouse. I never expected that he wanted me to be a slipper maker which I didn't think I could do at first but I soon get the hang of it. After twenty minutes he was impressed so it was back in his office where he asked what I thought and if I wanted the job. I said yes and for £80 a week Monday to Friday as it would be better than the last job I had for three days which was down the road. I told my new boss that I was in court for certain football offences and that I might be going to prison in seven months time. He said 'no matter what I would still get to keep my job'.

I finally started my job and the time soon went by and before I knew it the football season had started, so even though I was not in work on Saturdays it was tempting to go but I steered clear. I kept my head down and went in work on a Saturday to pass the time and keep my mind off the match. That was when I knew I had to keep away because if I didn't there was always a chance that I would get nicked if I went anywhere near the ground or in the city centre.

I still had to go to Chadderton police station now and again to sign on. The months went by and before long it was now well into 1989 and it was only a week of so before the court case. My boss wrote me a letter which basically said that the job was still there for me no matter the outcome of the case. A few days later I had to go and see the solicitor and barrister and shown them the letter. They said they would mention it in court but I had to come to terms with the fact that I was looking at a custodial sentence.

THE CHESTER RD CASE & Y O I

It was now February 1989 and it was sentencing day at Manchester Crown Court as Vinny, George, me, Brian Padina, and Anthony McKeague were all up. As the details were read out to the judge our background as we all pleaded guilty from the start. The letter from my boss was read out as the barrister tried his best for me as the other barristers did for the other lads. I really thought that I was going to get slammed as I was on eight charges.

I was buzzing when the judge gave me six months as he said that his powers were limited – if I had been older he would have given me the maximum sentence of twelve months for jumping on the head of a rival fan and we all got a five year banning order from attending matches which the BBC reporter and the news paper journalists forgot to mention in their broadcasts. I was then taken to Werrington House Young Offenders Institution which was in Stoke on Trent near to Alton Towers.

I arrived by taxi and after I was booked in I had a shower. I was taken to the canteen area where everyone was and watching the TV with lads in there my age and younger, a lad called Sykes from Oldham was in there who I knew. As I sat with him he said 'you have just been on the news' very loud so everyone could hear – as he turned it over to the other news channel so I could see it again so everyone could watch. It felt good as my name was broadcast all over the national news. I was a bit gutted to hear a few lies as they said that the fight was arranged over the phone two weeks in advance and that a month after the incident members of these same gangs were combining forces to attack German fans during the

European championships which was a load of shit as no one joined up with United and none of the City lot went to Germany either as they were too young

I like the way they made sure that they didn't mention that we all got banned for five years from all football grounds. They knew it was a piss take getting that ban just for what went on. I had been in far worse battles at grounds than that and didn't get banned, the court was told that we never had intended to watch the game, which was a load of shit because the reason I wasn't going to the game was because I wasn't allowed near the ground which was why we turned up at half-time.

THUGS CAUGHT IN VIDEO TRAP

Four soccer thugs were trapped by a police undercover surveillance squad filming street violence outside Old Trafford. One 16-year-old youth was spotted throwing a missile at other fans before he jumped twice on the body of a man lying motionless on the ground. At Manchester Crown Court this week the four hooligans were all sent to HM YOI, for offences of violent disorder. McKeague 12 months, Padina 9 months, George 3 months and Rhoden 6 months.

Mr. Peter Wright, prosecuting, said the clash between rival groups of United and City fans occurred during the game but the scene was captured by surveillance equipment and the three minute 20 second clip from a video film of the ugly scenes. Rhoden, Padina and George were among a group of youths known as the Young Guvnors who claimed to be Man City supporters.

When the gangs clashed various scuffles started then the City fans chased the United fans. As one United fan fell he was attacked by several youths and kicked. Padina was seen to kick the man twice as he lay on the ground and then Rhoden ran across and jumped on his body.

When McKeague was arrested he claimed he had been to the game but left at half time, he said he had seen the incident in the street and said he was acting as a good Samaritan, but when the video was shown to him he

admitted he had been fighting. Padina claimed he had never met the City fans before that day and said that he had fallen on the man lying on the floor. When Rhoden was arrested the video was shown to him, he admitted arming himself and throwing a missile, but refused to say if the fight was pre- arranged.

AT HER MAJESTY'S PLEASURE

That first night in jail was ok – I wasn't bothered one bit about going as I knew from the year before that my time was not long away as the charges piled up. The only thing I was gutted about was the fact that I got a five year ban from all football grounds. I was the first at City to get that long – it was a joke! Now, aged sixteen, I got slammed like that! I soon got over it after a few weeks as I just kept my mind occupied on my prison sentence. It was a laugh in there – I met up with lads from all over including three Plymouth Argyle hooligans from the Central Element. One of the older ones who was downstairs in the prison with the 17 – 21 Year olds was in there for fighting at Maine Road when they played us in the F.A cup and the other two who were upstairs in the prison in the dormitory where I was, they were only 16 too, so they got locked up for fighting at a Shrewsbury Town game. They were Mark (Charlky) Watson and Paul Poleglass. They were good lads and had been in there for a bit but got let out a month after I arrived. I met up with some of the Central Element in Hamburg when City were playing a friendly there the other year, I had a chat with a few of them as their mob were still going strong. They said that they were over there on a stag do, they should have joined up with us as they were much welcome. I never saw Poleglass or Watson.

Another thug I met in there was one of Burnley's Suicide Squad boys, Lee Entwistle. Me and him were like best mates in there. He was a good footballer. We were on the prison team. Some Scousers also played including two Toxteth lads Mark Osu and a white lad Lee Parry who was also a mate. I was to meet up with Lee again in my next prison sentence. There were some good days and some bad days in Jail. When we had PE it was hard at first as we had to do circuit training then a mile run around the perimeter fence as we had to do six laps around the field but in the end it was all worth it as it made me a lot fitter.

I soon got myself a job in their works department going around the prison doing odd jobs. It was easy and there were five other lads who were in my group, so we all had a laugh but when it was raining it was shit. We had to stay in one building all day and that was when it started to drag like fuck and if it rained all week every one of us would get depressed as we couldn't go out and would have to stay in and clean the prison.

Three of us would have to clean the two big dormitories and two small ones which was just one floor upstairs. To make matters worse when the weekends came it would go quick but there was no association in the afternoons so when we all had visits, and then something to eat two hours later it was then back upstairs for six o clock in the dormitories for everyone to have a wash and a shower and chill out. Then there would be two more hours playing cards or whatever or just having a laugh with the screws who were all 100% ok but when it was getting on to eight o'clock everyone had to go to sleep as the lights were about to go out, even though it was still daylight outside. But they were the rules as we were still classed as kids but the lads down stairs in their bit who were 18 and over could stay up most of the night as they had a TV. A few weeks after my sentence I had to go back to Manchester juvenile court for the police assault.

When I arrived back, I wished that I was out and free but it didn't affect my time in prison, as I could handle my bird just fine as I was taken into the court room my solicitor from Burton Copeland told me that I had about five witnesses, which I never even knew about, but I soon came to the decision that even though I had a good chance of getting off with it I couldn't be arsed chancing running a trial because if I was found guilty there would have been only one sentence that I could get and that would be more time inside and I just didn't want that as I still had to go to court in Blackpool for throwing a brick and fighting with their mob. That would be followed by the case in Stockport for fighting when City went there and then after that would be the big one which was the Operation Omega case at Liverpool Crown Court with the other 25 lads, so if I didn't get more time I would be out three weeks before that case.

So in Manchester I went guilty to police assault and got 28 days concurrent so it just ran along with my sentence with no time lost so I was ok with that and for some good talking by Mr. Mackie on my behalf to keep my sentence on track. I trusted in Burton Copeland solicitors as I was to use them again for my other cases. A week after going back to Werrington House Y O I, I was on the road again as I now received three letters for more court dates as they were now coming thick andd fast. I was now into the second month so next stop was Stockport magistrates court for fighting at that game when City played.

Again Burton Copeland Solicitors were representing me and they sent the hot shot Mr Gwyn Lewis – he's one of the best you can ask for as he represents all the criminal gangs as well as murderers and football players who were totally innocent. When he's about there is no doubt that justice will be served but if you're guilty he knows how to get you a fair deal. As that was the case with Stockport, his firm and I knew that I had no chance of getting off as I was basically bang to rights as all the attention was on me and a few other City thugs that day as I was in there first kicking it off because I knew that the nearer I got to the ground whilst under that banning order, I was going to get nicked.

I would have been stitched up even if I wasn't fighting and the way the police were with City's mob and at what had happened in the past anything was possible so with all the police statements I was fucked. The witnesses I had from the City mob were non-existent from the minute I got nicked as I didn't see any of them coming to the police station when I got nicked or coming forward with a statement for me (talk about sticking together!). So in the end I went guilty but the solicitor knew I was going to at least get another two months or so inside as the police statements were spot on for a change.

After Mr. Lewis did all his hard work and tough talking he got me a very good result and I ended up getting 28 days consecutive so in the end – a matter of days instead of months. I thanked him for all his hard work at getting me a light sentence before I left and went back to the Y O I. At least all the court appearances broke up my time inside as these days out were ok and better than looking at fences and fields all the time. As I was on the move my job in the prison was now taken so I was put on a home maintenance course for which I was taking a City and Guilds. I soon passed and received a certificate from Stoke Technical College after that three week course – I was glad to finish it in time for my next court case which was now at Blackpool juvenile court for throwing a brick at their mob and fighting .

I was woken up at 6am by one of the night screws as I had a long way to go. I got washed and changed into my normal clothes and set off by seven for the early morning drive to the seaside. We arrived at 9.15 and I was then put into a holding cell and I asked if anyone from Burton Copeland solicitors had arrived yet. They did this time and another well known name came to my rescue a Mr Nick Freeman (now famously known as Mr. Loophole). I asked if he thought that I would get more time and he laughed and said 'why do you want more?' I said no and knew then it was time for me to shut up and let him do his job as he knew it better than me.

I was directed to throw in a guilty plea and Mr Freeman argued my case as to why and when I was arrested on the day of the match and then later cautioned and no more was said of it. I was re-arrested a month later after I had been arrested in the dawn raids and he noted the coincidence that the Police did that. I was then given another concurrent sentence which was this time only 14 days in prison and a 12 month banning order from all sporting events including Wembley stadium which I wasn't bothered about as it was just another year added onto the five years ban I got two months earlier.

So still at 16 it was now looking like I was not going back inside a football ground until I hit 24. Well at least another case and more charges were out of the way - it was just the Liverpool Crown

Court case left. In a way it was a good thing I got locked up when I did because if I had still been out on the street I would have got slammed with all these violent disorder, police assault and public order charges and maybe the courts wouldn't have been so lenient. But I still had the conspiracy to violent disorder charges to go up for. After all the cases including the Blackpool case.

I settled back into the prison sentence again and with only a few weeks left until I finished my sentence I got nicked in there with four other lads for pillow fighting and tipping over people's beds while they were asleep in them. The night screw walked into our dormitory when we all thought that he was downstairs clocking in. The smart cunt doubled back up the stairs and clocked us all tipping over a bed and when the lad got off the floor we all laid into him with our pillow cases.

The old cunt thought that he was getting promoted the next day the way he was going on in front of the prison governor as he added a few lies to his story to make him look like the hero. If we had known that he was also going to lie about what had happened we all would have done him in and held the cunt hostage until the next morning! The governors weren't interested in what we all had to say as we all got found guilty, we got seven days suspended, so that wasn't too bad but after that I just kept my head down so I didn't get nicked in there again.

When it came to Sundays it was always a shit day as everyone had to go to church in there, as we all had to put on our best prison clothes including our grey jackets. It was also cleaning day for everyone then just before dinner time we all had a Governor's inspection, he was ok to get on with most of the time and when on inspection when he came to me he always said 'you're the City fan aren't you?' then he would look at the picture of Natalie what she had sent me and say 'she's a nice girl' as if he was jealous.

He told me that he was a United fan, there was another United fan in there who was a Prison Officer called Mr. Scofield who was from Miles Platting or Collyhurst and a works officer called Mr. Flood, they would walk with the governor sometimes when he checked that all our lockers and bed packs were neat and tidy and that our tight prison slip on shoes were polished and shiny. If anything was out of place we would be put on report and lose our association for two days, that was the only time they were strict in there, everyone really hated the weekends apart from the visits.

My prison sentence was almost over as I had just under two weeks until my release date which was going to be the 25th May. I was buzzing as everyone would be when they are due for release. I had missed the streets so much but it wasn't to be because by the end of the week I had a letter from my solicitors saying that the judge has remanded me into custody for a further two weeks after my sentence has finished. I had thrown a guilty plea in for the riot and violent disorder charges at Liverpool Crown Court a month earlier, I was a bit gutted but I knew I was going home either way when I finally got to court. A week later it was my release date and I was also being moved to a prison which was near home and near Liverpool, I was taken by taxi again from Stoke on Trent where I had lived for three months to Hindley Prison in Wigan. I was glad in a way as there would always be people in there who I knew as all the Manchester lads got sent there who were my age and now going to a real prison meant that it was no more dormitories and straight into a prison cell and banged up for 23 hours.

As one of the new ones they were ok in there and the cell was cleaner than I thought it would be. After a day or so I got used to the rules and at night it was a bit noisy as there were people shouting out of the windows and the odd few who couldn't handle their bird were singing out of the windows for most of the night.

LIVERPOOL CROWN COURT (1989)

The two weeks soon went quickly in there and before I knew it I was on the way to Liverpool's Q E 2 crown courts in a sweatbox. Once in there I met up with a few City lads who I was going to be up with. One of them was Pat Berry who I kept in touch with by letter while doing my sentence. We had a short chat before going up in front of the packed court as all 26 of our families were there except for mine as my brother was also in the dock too. The judge said to the friends and families in the public gallery's that before he started sentencing that he didn't want to hear any outbursts or they would be removed from the court and then asked me to stand up and explained why he had remanded me for the two weeks as he didn't want me to get into anymore trouble because the first time I appeared with the others and the time after that I received another charge which I was captured on video jumping on a United fan's head.

Everyone in the court started to laugh as the judge asked for silence. As I was laughing also, I soon sat down as he started sentencing. There were about eleven of us that day who got dealt with as seven got locked up who were Chris and Mickey Francis, Mark Dorrian, Steve Kinsey, Dave Goodall, Micheal Ossai, Brendan Murray, Steve Stanton (RIP) and David Foulkes. They all got between six and twenty one months which was a good result for them in the end.

Then it was our turn; me, Adrian Gunning and Jamie Roberts, were up next as the judge gave us all community service. As I went up I wasn't arsed as the judge had told us all before the trial that a deal was struck and that everyone under the age of twenty one would get community service – so that is why nearly everyone went guilty from the start.

It was totally different from what the police reports were after the case. They had said that they had concrete evidence against everyone and that was why they got convictions out of all twenty-six defendants. That was untrue as everyone just wanted it over as it was going on for over a year. When I went up I was hoping to get a jail sentence again as I didn't really want to be getting out of jail that day and doing what I would call more prison work and I knew if I did get more bird it would only be a month or two but it wasn't to be and I got 100 hours CS and a seven year ban from the games to go on top of the five I got back in February.

So that was that – all my troubles with the courts and the police were over and we all knew that the police were gutted as they wanted everyone to go to prison. Outside the court some senior police officers were there who were involved in the case and were been interviewed by the TV Cameras and newspaper reporters as we walked past with our coats over our heads, we were also expecting a few Scousers to arrive as when the case very first came to Liverpool there was talk of hooligans from both Everton and Liverpool to come and have a go. They never came – I think if it was United they would have shown up!

As I made my way through Liverpool city centre with Jamie Roberts and the others who were lucky to be set free, we were always on the look out just in case there were any attacks but nothing happened and we got to Lime street station and soon set off back to Manchester. It was good to be free smelling all that fresh air and seeing new sights as the only thing I ever saw inside were fields and the smell of shit from the farm outside the prison. The train trip was taking ages to get back and seemed to stop at every station but eventually it arrived back in Piccadilly and we all said our goodbyes. As I walked through Piccadilly the place looked bigger, busy and different and as I strolled to the bus stop so I could make my way to Oldham.

FREEDOM

On my first day of freedom I woke up at 6.30 am still thinking that I was still inside. It was quieter – there were no keys banging or screws shouting, just nice and peaceful until I realised that I was out at home and free. My brother was getting ready to go back to Liverpool Crown Court as him and fourteen more were to be sentenced and most of them who went up that day were aged 21 and just over and they had nothing to worry about as they knew that they were getting community service as part of the deal which everyone made and pleaded guilty, although Pat Berry got slammed that day with a 15 year ban and 15 months inside. I think he was not arsed about the sentence as he was already doing bird but he was more pissed off at the length of the ban but how did he think I felt? He was 25 years old and at least he had enjoyed a good run at the football. Not like me, I was still classed as a kid and only been going with the mob for a few years and not really had my so called 'buzz' yet as I was only 15 when I got arrested in the dawn raids, 16 when sentenced and then banned for 12 years altogether so all my teenage years I would be sitting out a ban! A year later I got the 12 year ban lifted and reduced to the original 7 years with 5 to run concurrent. Pat couldn't get his lifted so he had to wait until he was 40 before he set foot in any football ground.

As everyone that day got CS they all made their way back to Manchester and to a pub. I was about to make my way down but had to first meet Natalie Guest only for her to tell me she didn't want to see me again which I couldn't do anything about. So we went our separate ways but I respected her for writing and staying in touch with letters while I was in there. Apart from my family who visited and wrote there was no one else. I did write to my old boss, he was sound and down to earth and he knew the score. He wrote back and told me that he had someone working with him but to give him a call when I got out.

None of my so-called friends wanted to know - when I was in prison they were nowhere to be seen. As usual when you get out they all want to know you - now when most of them get locked up these days they feel as if half of us have some sort of right to visit them, as if they have had a short memory loss. Not me! I don't forget fuck all like that.

I saw Natalie G about nine years ago while I was on the bus in Oldham on the way to work in Manchester. She got on but didn't recognise me and I left it at that but if she did recognise me she probably thought fuck talking to him as he is probably on his way back to prison as I had been locked up again from when we last met on my release two years after the Omega trial at Liverpool crown court. I got two years for conspiracy to riot that was to do with fighting at a derby match with United. I eventually got to Manchester to meet up with all the convicted City thugs having had a Dear John letter by Natalie - all I could say is 'you win some you lose some' but I won't lie, my head was fucked.

It might have been worse if I had still been inside when we finished, some guys when they're inside hang themselves but not me - I would just have taken it out on people and kicked it off and then ended up losing a lot of days which was normal practice from some of the lads in there. As all the lads were now in a pub in Piccadilly and we had been informed about the middle page of the Manchester Evening News which we all soon went outside and bought. There were a lot of faces in the paper - mine wasn't in it as they were not allowed to take or put my picture in the paper for legal reasons as I was still only 16 at the time. I was a bit gutted but I did have my stardom back in February when I was all over the television news fighting on Chester Road with United. We all had a good chat in the pub that day and the word football match was mentioned. Everyone went quiet - they all knew because of my age and everything else I wasn't going to keep away. No one was interested and just wanted to start their lives back with their families and get jobs again. I didn't want to hear all that shit so I fucked off out of the pub and back home to the hills in Oldham. As I was on the bus I just started to read the newspaper:

How Guvnors were smashed

INSIDE STORY OF THE HUNTING AND CAPTURE OF SOME OF BRITAIN'S WORST SOCCER THUGS.

The capture and conviction of 25 soccer louts in Operation Omega has been hailed as the best police crackdown on some of Britain's worst Football thugs.

Other forces have now contacted Greater Manchester Police for advice and assistance in setting up similar operations at clubs with a hooligan problem.

Sensitive details about how undercover detectives infiltrated the Manchester City louts known as the Guvnors and the Young Guvnors so well that they were accepted as thugs themselves, have been passed on.

It was the first successful mass arrest court case where police set out to target organised gangs. Last year, three major London court cases against fans from West Ham, Chelsea and Millwall, collapsed amid allegations that police evidence was unsafe.

Chief Supt Frank Halligan, who organised the GMP'S secret Surveillance operation, said: "The evidence given by our officers was corroborated by members of the public, and we had back-up evidence of video film showing some of the hooligan incidents and the people involved.

"In many cases we were able to tip off other police forces to expect trouble, acting from information from our men. The fact that so many of the defendants pleaded guilty at such an early stage indicates the weight of evidence we had against them.

"I am confident that at Manchester City, we have removed the hard core of troublemakers, these people were highly organised and intent on only one thing - violence.

"There's no way the current good humoured fad of taking inflatable Bananas to Maine Road could have developed before these hooligans were locked up."

Liverpool Crown Court heard how a small group of undercover Detectives infiltrated the gangs by donning disguises and writing up their notes at safe houses after each match.

One officer told how he even drove the thugs to away matches and followed them around as they caused mayhem.

HIS DIARY OF HATRED

Teenager Vinny George kept a detailed diary of his part in savage attacks by the notorious Manchester City "firm" of soccer hooligans nicknamed the Guvnors and the Young Guvnors.

He wrote page after page of his own hooligan reports, often misspelt, bragging about his role in the attacks and explaining in detail how they were carried out, including drawing sketches.

In poor grammar he explains how the Guvnors arrived in Manchester city centre near to the Arndale awaiting the arrival of the Oldham fans. He wrote: "Ordinary people were standing about near the cash point machine and then suddenly out of the blue there was a cry of 'war, war' and 'Guvnors, Guvnors' and then we all started running into each other, rowing (fighting) for about two minutes none stop until the police came and spoiled it for us.

"I jumped into the cue of people watching on in horror and amusement that no police were in sight until it all finished. I was stood behind a boy and his parents. The boy aged about six years old was crying. He had received a punch off somebody and when I heard about it I felt sorry about what had happened to him but I didn't let on that I was one of those vicious soccer thugs"

Later, the City gang went to Oldham town centre and "rowed" with

The Fine Young Casuals: Then we wrecked the town centre and then went home and went to bed, cool as fuck."

George took clippings out of newspaper reports of the dawn raids by the police when the thugs were captured. He claimed the Guvnors knew that the raids were coming but they didn't care because "most of the Young Guvnors are only juveniles and nothing much could happen to us." He added: "so if I get caught and I get found guilty in a court room I would just like the magistrate to read this and they would all know the newspapers, news programmes and the police are all telling lies.

His most detailed account of an ambush was written after City played Plymouth Argyle on February 20 last year. He explained how the Guvnors and the Young Guvnors beat up six Plymouth fans and then split into three small "firms," each ten strong, ready to attack another group of fans. George wrote:"I was the first to go in. we used weapons which we found lying about near the town hall and then we organised the ambush.

"When we went in and started it off (we were the ones who always go in first to get the ambush started) by now we were tooled up with sticks, bottles and metal insides of bins and cobblestones which were being pulled up by the workmen.

"When my firm went in at them we threw the bottles and stones and then ran in while they were still surprised with our actions. Then they started back at us. It was then the other two firms sprang the ambush. It went like clockwork."

*

The next day, after everyone had been sentenced and the case was now at long last finished and after all the police interviews on TV, the national newspapers took over with all their headlines and reports on the case. In their eyes it was the biggest conviction and success as the other hooligan cases up and the country had all collapsed due to unsafe police evidence but the Greater Manchester Police made it almost impossible for that to happen in this case.

Headlines which read:

VIOLENT WORLD OF THE SOCCER GUVNORS
&

SOCCER MOB 'GOT KIDS TO SPY ON VICTIMS'

The papers made everything they could out of this police result. It was in every paper up until the Sunday but that weekend there was trouble in Manchester's Chorlton Street coach station even though the season had finished as City and United thugs bumped into one another on their way to a local pub. There were plain clothes police on the roof of the coach station car park watching the trouble as they radioed for assistance as fans from both sides were arrested. I fucked off as I couldn't be arsed with it all – the plain clothes police were on the roof of the car park only by coincidence as they were looking out for car thieves.

That was it for me, it was time to leave all that shit behind. At this stage it made me think how lucky I was to be out and free and it was approaching summertime it was getting hot and it wasn't worth it being locked away in a cell while the sun was beating down, it was nice to get my freedom back and I just wanted a break from all that shit and to sort my head out as there would be no football matches for me to attend for another seven years.

Two months later I managed to get my old job back as I had been in touch with the old boss so that wasn't so bad. I stuck at the job for a whole year until I decided to move on and try and get a trade at something. I enjoyed my time at the slipper factory and had a few good laughs with the rest of the lads but I was now 17 and I felt a lot more mature. The boss didn't mind me moving on and I thanked him for keeping my job open and having me back to which he said 'it was a pleasure' as we had a good little team of workers.

The next job I got was nearer to home in Oldham at the Oldham Youth Training Workshop on Arkwright Street. There I started my YTS course as a trainee joiner – the money was now £35 a week but I had to do the job just so that I could get a trade in something. I learnt a lot, it was sometimes like being back at school in that place as some people never got on with each other in there and it was getting to a stage that the training staff their knew there was a lot of friction among the youths. They decided to sort it out and try and bring everyone together as a group so they organised a trip to Cumbria for about 20 of us. We went to a place called Bendrigg Lodge in Kendal where we all stayed for a week doing allsorts of out door activities like abseiling and canoeing. We all had a good time and got to know each other – it was like being back in prison while I was there for that week but overall it was ok and a nice break away from everyone and everything.

As the time went by on the YTS, time in general was moving and my pocket was getting empty and beyond a joke I had to find another job even though I had been there seven months and I had another nine months until I could complete my training but I soon found another job as an administration clerk for a company called Info Link in Manchester city centre.

It was a step up in the world for me but the job was only temporary for six months then they would lay you off for four months before taking people back on. That was the chance I had to take, whilst working there I met up with a City hooligan David Samms who started at the same time as me, so it was to be ok after all. I knew people because whenever I started a new job I was always a bit nervous as anyone would be, so it was good to know someone.

I had known David for some years and he was a good friend even though I didn't hang around with him as he was older and busy dancing with his brother in there dance group Foot Patrol. However we did finally knock around together when we met up at the football matches years later and he was a thug but he wasn't as active as me at the matches so he was one of the lucky ones who escaped the dawn raids. Hs brother Sampson also was in the Young Guvnors, it's like when most people got banned after the court case most of the City mob went underground for a bit until the mob, resurfaced and got it back together but before then I heard that teams we played were taking the piss with what was left of the City mob even though there was still a bit of a mob.

Not everyone got involved as they thought that they would still be targets for the police as the police said after the case that the operation was still ongoing, but it was just to scare people from coming back and fighting. But it wasn't and that was just to scare off any more would be trouble makers. Man United were still on top of it as the police didn't bother them so their mob was still all intact and still doing it everywhere they went, there wasn't any trouble with them or City as City were in the old second division then and after games home or away, the two teams never met up in the City centre because of the heavy police presence all the time.

The two firms didn't meet head to head because most of the thugs from both City and United were on talking terms as they sometimes met up in certain nightclubs in the city centre and it was always trouble free, but the funny thing about it was that we would always get on well in clubs mostly on a Friday night when there was more than enough lads on both sides to kick it off but we all had a good laugh and the next day it would be different.

A week before the long awaited Manchester derby, City hooligans were in the headlines again this time for sentencing at Oldham Crown Court for the so-called Battle of Piccadilly almost a year before; me and Daft Donald went to Court to give the lads a bit of support but the police didn't like it and tried to get us kicked out of the courtroom for fuck all. The City lads were going to get stitched up as they had the same prosecutor that I had the year before for the Chester Road trial. Most were dealt with that day and hit the headlines on the local Oldham Chronicle News Paper;

Fan cracked skull of PC with hammer

A HAMMER-WELDING Manchester City fan fractured a police officer's skull in a carefully-planned mob attack, Oldham Crown Court heard yesterday, David Clayton, of Oldham, admitted causing grievous bodily harm and conspiracy to cause violent disorder.

Mr. Peter Wright, Prosecuting told the court that the eight men were among 70 to 100 who met up in a pre-arranged city centre pubs in the early evening of February 20th, last year 1989, with the intention of meeting Manchester United fans at Piccadilly Station and fighting them.

About 80 youths gathered in the Lower Turks head, Shudehill, where the landlord overheard a conversation about the arrival of Manchester United football special after their game with Arsenal.

"The group then assembled in Nicklebys, near Piccadilly Station, not by coincidence, but in order to go to the station without using London road, to avoid detection," he said.

USHERED

Mr. Wright added that it was quiet clear that the ring-leaders were not in the dock and had directed operations from a safe distance and that "some degree of sophistication" was employed. The group left the pub and made its way to the station.

Thirty to 50 waited at the bottom of the approach under an archway and a "sort of skirmish party" of between 10 to 20 went into the station. The prosecution pointed out that by the time this group made its way to the platform, only a few United fans remained and a police officer ushered the City fans back, in an effort which was met with little resistance.

Outside the station PC Duffy was joined by two other police officers, who attempted to usher them down the approach. Mr Wright said that civilian observers got the impression that the police officers were being lured away from the station.

One of the officers PC Martin was hit on the nose after an order to stand and turn was given to the mob. PC Duffy ran past and attempted, by using his truncheon, to create a safe distance between the group and the arrest. The officers were then encircled by the mob, which initially verbally attempted to free the prisoner and then attacked the police officers.

DROPPED

Mr Wright said that PC Duffy tried to fend them off with a truncheon in one hand and his helmet in the other. Clayton produced a hammer and struck him on his head, fracturing his skull. As a result of police inquiries after the incident, 17 people were arrested. Proceedings were dropped in the other cases and the eight fans' candour led them to be in the dock today, Mr Wright said.

He acknowledged that Clayton had expressed some regret about his action and had later realised that he could have killed the police officer, who spent four days in hospital and eight months off work. He has still not been returned to full uniformed duty, as a result of his injury. Another of the men James Wilde from Oldham told the police that he had no choice but to be involved as he didn't want to be seen running away because "he was scared of the older blokes".

Judge Anthony Hammond told Clayton; "There is no need to tell you what the public at large think of thugs." He described the offence as "wicked and cowardly".

He sentenced Clayton to three and a half years in a Young Offenders' Institution for causing grievous bodily harm and a further nine months, to run concurrently, for conspiring to cause violent disorder.

BAIL

Andrew Bennion of Wythenshawe was sentenced to nine months in prison for conspiring to cause violent disorder and for breach of bail, one month to run consecutively.

Larry Philips of Edmonton London, Lee Fiorini of Wythenshawe, Kenny Simpson of Oldham, Scott McCallum of Oldham, Jimmy Wilde of Oldham, were all granted bail while social inquiry reports were prepared. Another Oldham man was remanded in custody for reports.

Another man Mark Timperly of Oldham, who took no part in the disturbance but looked after the hammer for Clayton after the attack was fined £100 and warned that if he defaulted on this payment, he would be sent to a young offenders' institution for 14 days.

THE WORST DERBY IN YEARS

I was now well into my new job which I enjoyed. I met a lot of friends male and female so it was in a way like being back at school the only difference was that we were all getting paid £190 a week and having a laugh in the meantime. Every dinner time we were all in the canteen on a Friday me and David used to sit with all the girls but on the boys table all the talk was about football and I really didn't want to hear all that, so as we sat chatting to the girls one of the lads called Jimmy C, who was a Man City fan, could always be heard or I think he wanted to as he argued with all the United fans.

Then he would shout across the room (as it was a big canteen with about 40 people in it which was mixed with both City and United fans) if you hate man United clap your hands and repeated to sing it until all the City fans including me started clapping then he followed that with chants of MUNICH, MUNICH, as we all then went quiet as we were surprised what he had said as the clapping of the hands was just natural banter but he was then out of order shouting that and he knew it as he then tried to style it out by shouting to me across the room saying 'You hate Man U don't you Rodney'. I looked at David as if to say 'what have you been saying to that knob head?' as he only knew me to say hello to and that only David knew that I had troubles with United in the past, so because he called out my name it was obvious that he was told something.

I never spoke to that guy Jimmy C again, every time I saw him in work I wanted to do him in and he knew it. He was one of those loud mouth pricks that was louder than everyone else and thought he was some kind of main man about the place but everybody knew he was a prick. He never went to a City game as his excuse was that he had a Saturday job to do however a week before I left I did talk to him and as I called him over he was buzzing just like a little kid. The fact that he thought I was going to be his friend, he was a lot older than me and I said to him as it was soon to be derby day again, if I ever see him at any City games if I'm on my own or with a mob I would do him in.

He was in shock as I walked off and he later started bitching to David about what I had said but he just told him to do one. It was only a matter of days to go until it was the 112th Manchester derby and it was at Old Trafford. I had not shown my face at any other games until then apart from the 5-1 game at Maine Road only four and a half months ago but I was only there for a short time on that occasion. This game was tempting as everyone was talking about it and every time I walked into Piccadilly to the bus stop after work I always saw a few City thugs. It's like they were stalking me as they chatted about the game to come as City had not been to Old Trafford since March 1987. It was a long time a go as City were in Division Two. As I got home that night to Oldham I went to the park in Chadderton to see some of the Young Guvnors who I knew were still at it but not on a regular basis. I had a good chat with them and I told them that I had a funny feeling that this game was going to be explosive as the City supporters only got 4000 tickets. Not that I was arsed about that because I was now into my ban, but I knew that as there was good support at City and that they had many more season ticket holders there was no chance of all the mob getting into the ground.

There would be trouble before during and after the match so in the end I thought fuck it I'm coming out of retirement. I didn't waste anytime phoning around to find out a few things; I met up with Benny, David Maynard, Crawford, Stefan and Danny Gaye, Carl Stewart for a good chat and I also met up with Pratt who lived in Oldham but was a United hooligan to tell him that City were meeting in town the next morning and to make sure he got all United's mob to St Peters Square before the match.

The next morning which was Derby day I travelled down to Manchester early that morning by bus and made my way straight to

Moss Side to go and meet up with Maynard and Stefan but as I was passing through town on the 101 bus to Moss Side I saw about 70 lads walking through and they had just obviously got off the train and as it was only 10am. I knew then that it was the cockney Reds as I checked the fixtures in the morning paper I had and it didn't look as though there was any other team cutting through town and not that early.

As I got off the bus in Moss Side there was a sense of calm about the place as the streets were quiet. As I walked down Claremont Road towards the Claremont pub where most of the City mob from that half of Manchester were meeting, I was stopped by some pisshead trying to sell me a sticker with support the ambulance drivers on it. I said to him 'are you pissed? I know your game, I'm not contributing to no drink' as I don't even drink my self. That cunt would have been better coming with us as I knew that a lot of people would be sat in a pub for most of the day drinking getting pissed up as always!

As I arrived at the Claremont there were about fifty lads there. The doors were shut as everyone was on the streets but no one phoned the police to tell them as everyone was in bed. I told the lads that the main bulk of City's mob were meeting in Piccadilly at 11.30am and everyone needed to get there before United did. I Pete Frith that I had told one of the United boys that we were meeting in town at 12.30 so it would give us time to get there.

As everyone was leaving I saw an old City lad called Pinky driving past. As I waved him back I told the City mob that I was getting a lift to Hulme to see if United's mob were at the Grey Parrot pub where they were mainly based when meeting away from town. As I got there with Maynard, Carl and Benny, we spotted them outside the pub. There were about 400 lads outside on the big car park and as Pinky spun the the car round and drove back past the pub, the United mob were now on the move and it looked as if they were making their way to town.

I asked Pinky if he would drop us off in town on Oldham Street which was where the Merchant's pub was which was also a United pub but it would be ours for today. As we got there Pinky said 'make sure you do them today' and he told me to watch myself as I was still on the hot list with the GMP. Pinky was a safe guy and I had known him for a number of years through Paul Gaye who had two kids to his daughter and who brought me to City in the first place. Paul is Danny and Stefan Gaye's brother.

On arrival at the Merchants, the pub was packed out and outside there was a good mob as everyone who I could mention was there. As I squeezed through the fans to get into the pub I got to a lad called Martin Townsend and told him and some of the lads at the bar to drink up as we were on the move in a few minutes as United's mob were on their way to town and that the landlord of the Merchants might tip off the police or anyone from United's mob that we were in there as we were not liked as in recent years it was us lot who smashed his pub up. He was a red and he would have been thinking that we might smash it again just to be spiteful we were now making a move out with Daft Donald and Stefan Nolan arrived, Not far behind them was Larry and ET who had just came off the train from London – they were lucky not to meet up with the cockney reds as they had bumped into them in the past.

We all started to move through Piccadilly Gardens. Looking behind us, the mob was long as fuck – there must have been about 400 lads now as all the shoppers stood and stared at us. We started chanting 'City were from Manchester' followed by 'Ooh – ah, 'Ooh – ah, Ooh to be a Guvnor'. They all wanted the shoppers to know who we were but all that noise was just going to bring it on top with the police but they were nowhere to be seen. As we walked down Mosley Street surrounded with buildings on both sides the chanting started again and this time it was aimed at United as they chanted 'MUNICH, MUNICH' – the sound reverberated off the walls. It was loud as fuck as everyone was getting all geared up for it.

We were now approaching the Manchester Art gallery, as we carried on there was a silence as we could hear something like a roar and saw about 600-700 United thugs running towards us. We were well out numbered as we charged at one another. One of the City lads knocked out two of Man U's boys as fighting broke out all around. Car horns were heard as the fighting continued.

As I looked up I saw a traffic camera pointing down to the fighting as my hood went up. The fighting carried on as a United thug ran off with blood purring from his face as he had been slashed, the main United thugs were at the front. They all had southern accents as they shouted out 'come on niggers' and the rest of the shit. They got weighed in and, as they tried to run, we could see the United hooligans from Manchester pushing the cockney reds forward as they tried to get at us.

Eventually the police arrived in force and everyone started to scatter in all directions Bootle Street police station was only yards away now. No one got done there as it was just toe to toe fighting and it was all happening only 500 yards away from Bootle Street police station. As the City mob I was with ran past, the police were chasing everyone in all directions towards Deansgate train station. As we reached the station we decided to get the train but the United mob got on and they spotted us. That was it – the bins were out and the windows on the train went through as we made our way back out of the station and onto City Road.

By now more police had arrived. Me and Maynard made it look as if we had been attacked by kneeling on the floor like we were throwing up. A police van slowed down next to us then speeded up after the United thugs who brought themselves on top as they carried on running away instead of walking. That was it for us; we got off straight to Moss Side.

After the match, which finished 1 –1, we all made our way to the Bowling Green pub which was right next to the Manchester Royal Infirmary. There I saw a banner up saying ambulance strike so I knew from then on that if any damage was caused, no ambulance would be taking anyone anywhere. As most of the lads started gathering at the pub waiting for the rest to get back from Old Trafford; me, Maynard, Carl Stewart, Stefan Gaye and Benny made our way in the opposite direction to Hulme and to the flats which faced the Grey Parrot.

As we hid there we watched United's mob gathering outside and we also saw a black ford Sherpa police van parked up down the road but not in view of the pub. Two guys got out who were not in uniform so as I ran down balcony I shouted Benny to come and have a look at the two guys. They were undercover police officers who were involved in the Operation Omega case against us, so it was all making sense now as to why the police were always chasing City off every time they got near the United mob as they knew that we would spot them. I thought, fuck it I'm going to get word to them who I knew and tell him that there was undercover police in their mob.

As we waited in the flats for a good hour, United's mob was on the move and two cars sped out of the car park to find where City's mobs were. We followed behind them most of the way and we managed to get into the back of United's firm without being clocked as all their main boys who could identify us, especially me and Benny, even though they had spotted Maynard and Anthony Wilkinson in their mob after their FA Cup match with QPR when United's mob rushed into Moss Side precinct and give it pure black guys. Maynard and Wilkinson thought it was City's mob as we were also at home to Leicester City that they got ran by about 200 lads.

As we got in-between the Dental Hospital and the Manchester Museum near Oxford Road our hoods went up as we spotted Shawn Towmey from United's mob. As we walked we saw the two undercover police officers and I shouted out 'there they are'. As everyone looked around we ran for our lives out of their mob as we now had been clocked but Shawn and directed them to the two undercover and we saw everyone surround them. I don't know what happened to them though as we got off to the Falcon pub in Chorlton on Medlock.

With United only minutes away we told the City lot that there was about 700 man United thugs making their way over. Only a few believed us and came out and as we got onto Upper Brook street the 700 United thugs came out of the bushes in one long line and charged at us – we ran to the pub as City now decided to come out. The pub got smashed, City chased them back to the road and now armed with pool balls and chair legs we attacked them. Only

Riot fan in fight for life

200 of United's main boys stood fighting – it was going on for five minutes as traffic was now at a standstill. The police were on their way but before that the eye in the sky arrived on the scene (the police helicopter) its lights were now pointed on all us fighting as the police tactical aid unit arrived.

Everyone dispersed but Carl Stewart was unlucky and got nicked – it was as good result for United. We made our way to the city centre where we re -grouped in the Bierkeller pub on Rochdale Road but we were soon on the move as the fruit machine got drilled with a screw driver as Daft Donald said that one of the pub staff got onto us. So we made off out of there and took a short walk to the Crown and Kettle where we stayed until we were told that United were only down the road at Wetherby's on Port Street.

So we marched round about 200 strong and all tooled up. We had to move quickly as the landlord in the Crown and Kettle pub was on the phone, no doubt to the police as his furniture was broken up and taken out. We soon got to Wetherby's and me and a few others started to brick the windows. As everyone else shouted 'come on Munich' – they came out with their tools. The ones at the front started shouting to us saying 'come on niggers' as there was a load of blacks there.

I saw a City lad put one of the bar stools over the head of one of United boys but he now fell to the ground as United's mob closed the door on him he was getting kicked to fuck as someone stabbed the tip of a golfer umbrella into his head. The attack on the pub was going on for ever as 300 plus man United hooligans came out of the Crown and Anchor public house and gave chase. We knew there were more but never knew that they were that close by. They chased us to Great Ancoats Street and as we turned at the Land O'Cakes pub fighting with them as more and more came we were outnumbered as there was too many of them

We got ran to the Crown and Kettle and told no one to run in there and stay on the road, so we could find some weapons. About 50 ran into the pub and as United got there they smashed all the windows which were those Victoria stained glass ones as some of the City mob came out with bottles and more chair legs. The police arrived me and (Smiler) Jason Miles from Longsight ran down Oldham road towards the Thunderdome as the police came from everywhere. That was it for me.

The next day which was on a Sunday it was all over the radio news and TV, and in the Manchester Evening News on the Monday with the headlines which read.

'Monster' gang in soccer aggro

Soccer fan Gerard Conner was fighting for his life today after Manchester's worst derby game in years.

He was rushed to hospital in a police van as the ambulances were on strike to an intensive care ward at Manchester Royal Infirmary after being savagely attacked in the street by a mob of Manchester City hooligans, known as the Guvnors and Young Guvnors.

Hundreds of United and City hooligan's battled during the night following the 1-1 draw at Old Trafford. Throughout the day there had been fears of reprisals after City were allocated only 5,000 of the 40,000 tickets because of segregation problems at Old Trafford.

Police called in a helicopter to light up the scene as the two mobs fought with bricks, bottles, sticks, iron bars and chair legs. Six hundred hooligans

clashed near the Falcon pub, in Kincardine Road, Chorlton on Medlock. Two men were arrested.

Hundreds more City fans roamed the city centre, wrecking pubs and terrorising drinkers.

Mr Conner who is 25 was attacked as City fans laid siege to Wetherby's Club on Port Street.

He was today lying critically ill on a life support machine at the Manchester Royal Infirmary. He underwent an emergency operation after a blood clot formed in his brain when his skull was fractured. He is also suffering from a punctured lung caused by a broken rib.

His family said that "He has never been involved in any football trouble before.

"He told us that he had been going so long he could sense trouble starting and get out of the way before it began"

During the battles more than £30,000 of damage was caused in fighting at the Crown and Kettle pub at the corner of Oldham Road and Great Ancoats Street.

At Wetherby's Club there was more than £20,000 of damage caused as 200 Man City hooligans "bombed" the premises with missiles. Licensee Thomas Blake said that the City hooligans attacked as the United supporters were drinking inside.

They battered the injured lad outside. There were about 40 fans inside and 200 outside attacking the place.

"Windows were smashed with bricks and billiard balls. The United fans were terrified and they broke up the furniture for weapons to defend themselves."

Twenty-five other fights were reported to police later on that night as they made nine arrests.

Police have issued a special "hotline" number for information about the attack.

(No doubt we all got grassed up again.)

*

That was all we needed to hear as we all knew that the police would be out for us (WOGS) as they had not witnessed anything like it for years. As they thought that City's hooligan element had finished, but they were going to have a field day over this as the day after the paper headlines said someone from the City mob who I now know went to the papers to give an interview weeks later before we all got nicked and charged .

Carl Stewart, Tony Walker, Paul Derry (who got done with me on the Guvnors case), Tony Hughes and Daft Donald all got their charges kicked out at the Magistrates court. Carl, who got nicked at the Falcon pub that night, was soon charged and let out so the police couldn't prove where he was and as for Daft Donald, when he got nicked he said to the police who claimed he was there at the scene that 'I wish I was as you all know I'm one of the Guvnors and love a fight but I'm sorry as this time I wasn't there because if I was I would have been kicking it off'.

That statement cleared him, so in the end Me, David Maynard, Larry Philips, ET, Martin Townsend, Stefan Nolan, Brian Screeton, Rodney Sloan, Ian Parker, and Paul Morris all got sent for trial at Bolton crown court.

The newspaper interview from the so called City thug days later didn't help as it read.

The Soccer hooligan rampage through Manchester after Saturday's derby match which left a young fan critically injured was planned in advance.

It was a military-style operation by Manchester City yobs designed to cause maximum damage to their United rivals, it was claimed today. The information was supplied to the Manchester Evening News in a secret meeting with "Frank" a self-confessed member of City's "hardcore" hooligans.

Meanwhile, police are meeting a wall of silence in their hunt for the attacker of Gerard Conner outside Wetherby's club in the city centre. They have set up a special hotline number for anyone with information. The paper was told by Frank that he was breaking the group's mafia-style code of silence because of the appalling escalation of violence.

"Fighting is one thing" he said "but it is getting out of hand. They take shooters with them now and before long someone is going to get killed."

The former soldier said the main group of yobs called itself the Beer Monsters. They are older, usually in their 30s, and got the nickname because of their beer guts. He claimed most of the City gang are protestant and many belong to the orange lodge. United sided more with the catholics, he said.

They have not met head -to- head for some time because City went into the Second Division, but violence was inevitable once the teams were facing one another again.

Frank explained; 'A plan is put together by 10 men. They decide where and when it is going to happen and how many troops they will need. Scouts are put out all over.

CRIMINALS

"We know for instance, that the hardcore of visiting clubs will always arrive the night before and never come straight into Manchester. If they are coming from London, they will usually come to Stockport first. "The "aggro" has little to do with the playing of football. The clubs are used as 'flags' for rival street gangs who want to show they are top dogs.

"There is a Mafia in every town which runs the place. Then there are the gangs."

"It will never be stopped, it is part of life." The Beer Monsters, he claimed, was 150-strong and made up of individuals from all walks of life. Most, however, are unemployed and habitual criminals who go to away matches on stolen credit cards. He listed a number of pubs used by the gang. This has been passed on to the police.

The Young Guvnors, a well-known gang of teenage thugs who have attached themselves to Manchester City are used as a diversion to get opposition "hardcore."

"The kids start it and corner the opposition, and then we move in and finish them off," said Frank. He has been stabbed severely in the back and believes it's only a matter of time before shotguns are used.

*

Not long after that all the charges came, it was time for me to take a back seat for a while as the police were always on my case at the matches as they didn't get me for the battle on Piccadilly court case which had just finished. They were pissed off about that, and they didn't like seeing me at home or away games. They knew that I wasn't allowed in the grounds but couldn't stop me from travelling but they would always bring a photo album with them to games and hot me up with other police forces pointing me out as they only knew I wasn't there for the game as I would sit in pubs with a few lads or sometimes just roam the streets with a few lads at away matches like at Liverpool away one season when we were under police escort to Anfield.

As we approached the ground most of the mob said that they didn't have tickets but as soon as it went off tickets came out from everywhere. The shitheads fucked off into the ground and left me, Carl, Stefan and about twenty more outside to kick it off with the Scousers. We soon got ran as they came only for the niggers again as the white lads we were with just easily mingled in with the crowd outside the ground.

We had to jump into a nearby black cab and out of there that was it for me I gave it a break and stopped going in the end. I just concentrated on my work and kept away as my court case at Bolton crown court wasn't far off. When the case did finally go ahead weeks into the trial Me and Maynard got into trouble off my barrister one morning because one night which we left Bolton crown court and went back to Oldham we bumped into Oldham's FYC mob who were playing Middlesbrough that night at Boundary Park. We joined up with them yet again and had it out with the Boro Casuals on Rochdale Road and on the corner of Crompton Street where I was living at the time. No one ran as it was toe to toe fighting and no tools. The police finally came and split us up. The police got me and Maynard straight away but as we had an alibi, they let us go and followed us straight to my front door.

The barrister, who we were trying to convince half way through the case, saw us kicking off and told us it was in our best interests to plead guilty. We never and just took the piss for the rest of the trial as ET was also making us laugh in the dock as the Asian dock screw wouldn't let him go to the toilet. He put his hand up to the judge and said 'this fucking prick won't let me go to the toilet' and as everyone burst out laughing in the dock he was then allowed to go as the judge ordered that there be no more out bursts

Then witness statements were read out about a gang of black City hooligans but not us, but it was about Daft Donald, Carl Stewart and co who had their cases dropped back at Manchester

City Magistrates months before. The jury looked over at us as I said to most of them 'what the fuck you looking at' as Maynard sat their staring right at them trying to scare them.

One of the solicitors ordered that it was to be explained to the jury that it was not about any of the defendants in the dock for the second time and from that moment on we were going to get a guilty. We did but ET, Rodney Sloan and Ian Parker got their cases kicked out but me Maynard, Brian Screeton, Stefan Nolan, Martin Townsend, Paul Morris, all got found guilty but Larry Phillips, pleaded guilty. We all got sentenced that day as me and martin got our pictures in the paper, with the headlines which read.

BOLTON CROWN COURT

MAY 31ST 1991

Two of Manchester City's most violent soccer thugs were behind bars today.

Martin Townsend and Rodney Rhoden, vicious hooligans who wouldn't learn, paid a heavy price for their part in a derby match riot which left a reds fan clinging to life.

After a month-long trial at Bolton crown court, 28 year old Townsend was jailed for four years and Rhoden, 18, was sent to a young offenders' institution for two years.

Both have a string of violence convictions and were rounded up by police in 1988 in their "Operation Omega" probe into the feared Guvnors and Young Guvnors gangs.

Rhoden and Townsend were banned from attending all football matches - Townsend for seven years and Rhoden for five. But Townsend could not keep away and travelled to Italy for the World Cup only to be booted out by the authorities.

Four other City fans were also jailed for taking part in the riot in February last year by judge John Townsend at Bolton.

An attack on Wetherby's night club by a group of up to 200 Man City football hooligans was "a serious crime against the peace of the City of Manchester," the judge said.

United supporter Gerard Conner was found in a pool of blood with a fractured skull outside the club after the attack. The judge told the six: "He will bear the consequences of that attack for the rest of his life.

"If it wasn't for the quick thinking of the police at the scene who had taken him to hospital by police van he might of died as the ambulances were on strike and you all must of known that and were therefore out to cause maximum damage to anyone who got in your way. "

Townsend and 21 year old Stefan Nolan were found guilty of causing grievous bodily harm and conspiracy to riot and were each jailed for four years.

Rhoden and 21 year old David Maynard of Moss Side, were jailed for two years each after being found guilty of conspiracy to riot.

Larry Phillips 22 from London who was in custody throughout the case as he was serving a sentence from back in January of this year after waiting a full year to be dealt with for the so - called battle on Piccadilly pleaded guilty to conspiracy to riot and was jailed for a year to run concurrent with the sentence he was serving.

Paul Morris 35 and from Glossop, was jailed for 28 days with a further 11 months suspended for conspiracy to riot. Brian Screeton 32 and 24 year old Nicky Carrington from London were cleared of conspiracy to riot.

*

The police said after the case that although there was up to 200 Man

City thugs involved they were pleased that convictions were made against six of the major players who were well known to them for some years, and that they hoped that the length of sentences handed out today would be a warning to other would be City hooligans in the near future.

He went onto say that this year had been a success as many other Manchester City Hooligans had been jailed for other serious football related offences and their operations would continue to root out all the feared Guvnors and Young Guvnors gangs at Man City.

HMP STOKE HEATH

It was back to prison again but this time it was with the big boys and for much longer as two years was a lot different from six months inside. I spent a few days in Hindley prison in Wigan before being moved to Stoke Heath prison, once in Stoke Heath to start my sentence I met up with Stefan Gaye who was the younger brother of Danny (R I P) and Paul Gaye (R I P), as he was doing bird there. I arrived on the Monday and told him that I never knew he was in jail as he had not been seen in ages.

He knew I had been locked up as he always had the Manchester Evening News posted to the prison everyday so he had read all about it. That lucky cunt in the end just laughed and said that he was out on the Friday. He knew he put me on a real downer but I wasn't really arsed as I had done bird before but this time I had to fight through the 16 months ahead of me.

I soon got settled into my sentence after two weeks and I began to enjoy the place. Most of the screws were ok in there and so were the lads, I met up again with Lee Parry from Toxteth and Terry McCann from Liverpool. They had both been in Werrington House Y.O.I with me two years earlier when we were only 16. We were now 18 and had to do our bang up. I was used to the bang up as I done it in Hindley and I think being banged up made the time go a bit faster in prison because when it was lights out at a certain time, as soon as you woke up it was like you had been asleep a few minutes.

I was padded up in a single cell and next door to me was a lad from Wigan called Gareth Meehan. He was in Wigan's Goon squad hooligan gang and he told me a few stories about their mob. I knew they had a mob (as we had a run-in with them one season when they were cutting through Manchester) we were fighting with them in Piccadilly they then chased us we soon got off and went to Brannigans to get more lads out. As we were kicking it off all the way to Victoria station they kept on turning and fighting us before the police came and chased us all away from the station.

We heard that they had a large rugby following with them but either way they were game as fuck and always have been. It's teams like Wigan that never got a mention as their mob were doing it back then and now even the teams in the north east from Middlesbrough all the way up to Darlington and Hartlepool, but it was always the cockneys who always got a mention as if they were all untouchable. Firms from down there always got a surprise when they came up north to places like Wigan, Preston or even Burnley.

A few months had passed by in there and I was taking it easy and settling in well. I had met friends from all over the country. There were lads from Stoke, one of which I knew who used to come to Manchester to the night clubs. There were also lads from Birmingham and other places – nearly all of them were in for crimes other than football violence but knew or had once in their life had seen trouble at football. I soon bumped into a United hooligan called Mossy who was from Blackburn. He was in there on remand as he had been arrested in the Operation China Dawn raid which was aimed at drug dealers on the Gooch Close estate in Moss Side. As the lads all came into the prison I knew every single one of them – there was going to be a bit of tension with another gang called the Doddington Gang from Moss Side who were in there at the time. There were a few members of the Doddington and the Cheetham Hill Hillbillies who never got on with Doddington.

Members of the Gooch and Cheetham Hill gangs would sometimes kick off with the Doddington gangs but the screws soon had enough as they knew what was going on and shipped nearly all the Doddington out of the prison and back to Hindley. The Cheetham Hill and Gooch Gangs were then split onto two different wings to ease all the tension and keep each other apart. Back at Stoke Heath there was only Paddy C from Doddington left in there and there was no more trouble after that. I soon got on the football team as we played outside teams from the local areas. Some of the Gooch lads were on the team but were not allowed to play the away games as they were a security risk. The simple fact was that the screws shit it and thought that if a load of us got passes we would all get off, the basketball team soon started and those matches were played at night time and it was a good thing as it passed the time and it made the weeks go quicker and as me and my mate from Manchester Jason Broughton were both gym orderlies it was all ok and it was also the best job in the prison and the highest paid as we were on £10 a week, so that wasn't so bad

New Year soon came and one morning as I went into the dining hall for my breakfast the senior officer pulled me to one side and said that my parole had come through – I was buzzing as I was into the start of my eighth month and I thought that I only had thirty days left until the screw told me with a smirk on his face that I would be out at the end of March.

I wasn't too bothered though as I could now put in for my home leave. I got it weeks later but it was given to me two weeks before I was due to be released so that meant that I would have a week left to do when I got back so I decided not to take it as it seemed as if they wouldn't trust me to come back even though I had been out every weekend to play football and had many chances to do one. When it came to the smack heads they got their home leave two months before their release date and they were doing a lot longer than me and they never came back, so that said it all.

My release soon came and before I knew it I was back on the streets and at home, from then on I kept away from the football and got my old job back, settled down for a bit and had a lovely son Ethan a year later that made me even more determined to stay out of trouble which I did as I now had three years left on my ban.

TOTTENHAM (H) FA CUP - 1994

The years went by and even though I still kept in touch with the City lads I never went back but still heard about the odd fight or two. It was still in the back of my mind to go back one day so one day I went to a match to have a look even though I was still on

The pitch invasion at Maine Road during the Spurs cup game.
Expecations were high so a home defeat was always likely to end in tears.

a banning order. The game was Tottenham Hotspur in the sixth round of the FA cup at Maine road. I was outside the ground as there was no point in going in from the start and getting nicked.

It never went off before the game but as I got into the ground in the last ten minutes when the gates were opened, City were losing and on the way out of the cup. The club had opened up the new all seater Platt lane end which meant the end of the big fences. As the game went on I was stood in the middle of the lads with my hood up trying to hide myself from the CCTV. Word went around that everyone was getting on the pitch as this would be the only chance to have it out with Spurs as the police would have it under control afterwards.

As word spread there was now a pitch invasion and it started from the new Platt Lane end where we had all gathered. We all got on as I still had my hood up I knew there was only one thing in mind for me and that was to stick close to the mob on the pitch. We all ran to the North Stand end of the ground where the Spurs supporters were. As we got within shouting distance of them, some of their mob got onto the pitch and started having a go at us.

The stewards couldn't control it as some of them were getting done in by some City and Spurs hooligans, the pitch was now flooded with City lads coming from all corners of the ground to get involved. I was loving it as their would now be no chance of me getting spotted on the pitch. If I did it would be 28 days back inside which was fuck all but it would have been pointless. Police horses were now making their way onto the pitch as the foot patrol officers on the pitch could no longer control it. The best thing about it was that it was live on TV. I was off there and out of the ground and away from the area like a shot, I later heard that it kicked off with Tottenham's mob near Platt Field's park as they had a few mini buses parked up. That was it for me for the rest of that season though as I had to keep out of the way so I didn't get nicked.

A WHOLE NEW ERA 1998

It was now time for me to show my face back on the football scene, the season was soon over then there would be the World Cup in France. I was on the way to France with a few City and Preston lads known as the (PPS) Preston Para Soccer, we got spotted at the ferry terminal when we reached France when a sports shop got robbed an hour later and we got rounded up and sent straight back by the English police spotters. I was now 24 and from my point of view it was a downer as I had missed all my teenage years of going to the football with people my own age but I came to terms with that a long time ago. I was the youngest at the time and people who did more than me at that time got three years minimum which was a real piss take.

Anyway the main thing was that a lot more lads were back from the wilderness, but most of the rest just called it a day as they were a lot older and most had families and a lot more than me to lose so we could understand them. As we were all out of the limelight for so many years the City mob had now re-grouped and got it together, it was no longer the Guvnors and Young Guvnors it was all one now the Guvnors. It saved all that fucking about with mobs splitting up all over the place and to save any would be undercover police getting a sniff of anything; everyone had learnt their lesson from the past.

The police now had other ideas – there were no longer any undercover operations as such but they now had the police spotters travelling everywhere with them which they used to do back in the day but not as blatant back then, their aim was now to follow you, video you and basically get to know you. Any trouble at any games they would start to do you from game to game as the sentences for fighting at one game would almost be time inside and a three and a half year ban.

As I went back to the match everything was different; new hooligans and a new turn out it was a new breed of City thugs who were not known by the police yet. On the pitch the team were having a bad time of it and they had now been in Division 1 and were on their way to relegation – what a time to start back! Most of the old heads were also back at the games but on a quiet tip and most of them could not believe what was going on with the football team; the City manager was Joe Royle. Before I got banned the manager was Mel Machin, so they had been through a total of seven managers since then while United only had two; Ron Atkinson and Alex Ferguson to date so that tells you a lot.

That season I went to a few games which followed with a few fights but nothing special, the team were playing really, really shit even though we had the likes of Kinkladze who was in a class of his own with all the skills he brought with him but the rest of the team were not up to scratch. The manager never helped the cause as he kept leaving Kinkladze out for certain games. When Birmingham City came down I wasn't around as I was now doing six months in the holiday camp they call Kirkham Open Prison for banned driving, but I heard that they were taking the piss everywhere – they were well known and were no pushovers. I heard they were walking about all over the place, as a mob walked up Claremont Road past the Claremont pub and then past the local wanna be gangsters who soon got ran off the Zulu's warriors who had pure black guys with them and yes today you could almost call it black on black crime. Not knowing that they were dealing with football hooligans as they threw bricks as they scarpered down nearby alley ways as the Birmingham mob kept coming.

I was on the phone to some City lads throughout the day and was told that Birmingham had a good mob which was no surprise to me as they had always brought one. Late in the game City got a late goal to lead 1 − 0. With a few minutes left to play it went off in the North stand with the City mob and Birmingham's. As the sides fought it out the police waded in heavy handed as usual with the City fans even though they didn't start it but were just celebrating the late goal until they were attacked by the Birmingham mob and were simply defending themselves.

The police were hitting out at anyone and everyone but and as they got in between the two sets of fans they tried lashing out at the Birmingham fans not knowing that they were not arsed about the police presence and that it was their main lads that they had hit out at. I think the officers hit out at the wrong one's which meant that it was one of their main lads and to their surprise the Zulu's attacked the police. As their mob rushed forward towards the police they all backed off as one police officer had his nose broken in the process, they must have thought that they were dealing with dickheads who would back off from them (they were wrong!).

From then on I got back into the swing of things and all the faces I knew were coming back, the likes of Maynard, Carl Stewart, Stefan and Danny Gaye, Linford Taylor, Martin Travis, Frank Crawford were all there and not forgetting the old Foot Patrol dancing crew; Samson and his brother David Samms. It was going off every week as the police watched on as they were now suspicious of everyone and had their eyes on us lot with their video cameras now running and their cameras flashing.

Then one day we were at home to QPR and had to win to be sure of staying in the First Division but we lost and the police turned the heat up with their presence as they knew we were on our way out of the top two divisions for the first time and they knew they could not let the mob we had now go into the second division as there would be no control, especially with all the teams there that had worse reputations than us. Then there was the policing side of it, as their wasn't really much police presence in the lower divisions but mainly stewards as most teams down there could not afford the cost and because there was not much point as the attendances would have dropped to under ten thousand or even lower.

That day at the QPR game I brought out my video camera on

the advice of my solicitors Burton and Copeland. They told me I was not doing anything wrong. My idea was to film them back as it was a free country and tourists can film anywhere. As it was not a crime in filming them back just as long as the video camera was alright or they were basically saying make sure I had a proof of purchase which I did and they had no excuse to take it off me or arrest me.

I took their advice and started to bring it and film them back and it soon became apparent that they did not like it as I said to the officers 'if you film me I will film you back' which made them focus the camera on other people. Then they would send the odd officer over to me to hassle me and check the camera out to see if it was not stolen which didn't make their day as the word came back that the camera was legal. As the games came thick and fast and before we knew it there was only one game left to decide if we were to stay in the first division or be relegated. That last game was away to Stoke City and a game which I could not attend as I had gone abroad on holiday a few days before hand which I was gutted about. Hmmmm.

As I was on holiday thousands of miles away I didn't get the scores until late Sunday night as the times were different and when I did eventually get the scores off Sky World news it all came to light that City had beaten Stoke but because of the results from the other games they were relegated which was a shock and an embarrassment to everyone concerned. It showed on Sky News fighting in the stands which spilled out onto the pitch at times and trouble outside the ground before during and after the game. There was even trouble with Port Vale's VLF or Vale Casuals

It was on all the news channels as there were thugs from both sides clashing with each other, all the City lot knew that stoke had a good mob as there had been fights with their mob over recent years and whenever there so called Naughty 40 had to pass through Manchester to change trains there would always be trouble. It was like every time Stoke came through Manchester and their numbers started to rise into the hundreds. The day after the two teams had been relegated to the second division the Manchester Evening News had this to report.

DESPAIR

POLICE ejected … Manchester City fans from Stoke's Britannia stadium yesterday as violence marred the saddest day in the club's history. Despite winning, the Blues were relegated to the Second Division, their lowest point in 104 years.

Although the 5-2 victory was their best away showing of the season it was not enough to save them from going down as Port vale and Portsmouth also won.

Trouble started within minutes of the kick-off at stoke when 60 City fans that were in the wrong sections of the stadium ran onto the pitch in a bid to reach the City sector. The referee stopped play while police and stewards dragged scores of struggling fans out of the ground. But the worst clashes came after the game when groups of Stoke supporters ran onto waste ground above the City coaches and began pelting them with bricks and stones.

Despite the massive security operation involving 200 police and 450 stewards it was the worst violence ever seen at the new stadium. During one flashpoint mounted police needed the protection of shields as they fought to keep rival factions apart.

Twenty fans were hurt, with six needing hospital treatment. Police said today that 28 supporters had been arrested and charged with public order offences.

Many of the 300 fans ejected claimed that Stoke City knew they were blues when they sold them the tickets. Not being able to see their team's best performance of the season was the bitterest blow of all.

IT COULD ONLY HAPPEN TO US

The new season in the second division started off well as our first game was at home to Blackpool. Their mob never showed up which wasn't a surprise they were like one of them piss take firms that only showed up at their own ground or the reason they never came was because they were shit scared to come to the hood or to Moss Side, apart from that the team just got off to a good start to the season by winning 3-0 and in front of a record breaking 32,134 crowd for a Division 2 game. That was a good sign as the fans didn't care what division we were in as they were all loyal to the team and not running off to watch United when things went wrong.

After that game in the city centre all City's mob went back to the pubs but were scattered about in different pubs as a mob of 30 walked up London Road from the Bulls Head pub towards Piccadilly they bumped into about 100 plus Huddersfield town supporters. Scuffles started then a short running battle as City's mob got ran back the way they came.

From then on the season was just a joke as we just kept taking a mob to every away game as nothing much was happening at the home games we were now travelling to places like Northampton and Macclesfield. When we did go to Macclesfield it was a piss take – the tickets were all sold out as we only had 1000 but the City fans still travelled for the short trip. As we arrived at the local train station the police were there in large numbers on horseback and on foot, backed up by their dog handlers. I don't know why because there was no one there to kick it off with or maybe the police wanted some extra training on us lot but they were so friendly, I wondered why.

As we approached the ground it was clear that there was more than a thousand City supporters there, as the police advised City fans earlier in the week not to travel without tickets as they would be turned back. The Macclesfield fans saw their opportunity to make money and sold most of their tickets for the home end, the Manchester Police spotters had now surfaced and were pointing us out to the local police as well as filming which they soon stopped as it was starting to intimidate a few of the lads. We took 200 boys with us, that was probably why the police were locked onto us. As the match began we all made our way back round the ground towards the away end. On the way round a few poor cunts had their tickets taxed as everyone now wanted to get into the ground.

Someone decided that the only way in was rushing the gate as there was only two stewards on it, so that got stormed as everyone even the normal City fans outside who travelled hoping to get a ticket got in.

The game was shit as City were looking for their first away win of the season. They missed chance after chance. The fans got behind the team as they were all over the ground. With just over a minute left as everyone was starting to leave Shaun Goater popped up to score and the City fans invaded the pitch from all corners of the ground to celebrate.

I didn't really attend any such games after that as I was working most weekends and only really took the odd Saturday off when there was a game worth going to. By now the police spotters were on my case as they were based at Greenheys Police Station. I was working at the Asda supermarket not far away and they made it their business to be seen in there while I was working. They were keeping a close eye on three others who also worked there and who were in the Guvnors. Most home games that they saw me at they would point us out to other police officers telling them where we worked. From then on I knew that a certain few didn't want to see us working there anymore and the way to do it was get someone who we didn't know to nick us on some bullshit Public Order charge, get in touch with work and get us sacked.

City we were at home to Burnley one Saturday. I did not attend the game but finished work at 4pm and made my way over to the ground to see what was happening. As I arrived with 15 minutes left to play I just waited outside the ground with a few lads who had been in the Parkside pub. They told me that Burnley had a mob so I was just waiting about to see if I saw my mate Lee Entwhistle (Twiss) who was in their Suicide Squad. The last time I saw their mob apart from when me and Anthony Wilkinson went with Twiss to their game with Bolton at Turf Moor was a few years before was when they went to Stockport County and took the piss as me, Maynard and big Steve Rhoden went to the ground.

After their game we ended up getting run off the Burnley mob as they were giving it to the Stockport County mob. We got legged everywhere and then decided to call it a day. But today wasn't about Stockport it was about Man City which is a totally different ball game. As we now made our way to the Sherwood pub on Claremont Road we were met by a large number of City lads and within minutes of their arrival 80 Burnley turned up and it went off as the City mob piled out of the pub and give it them as the police arrived to take the breakaway group back into their escort.

I could see down the road that the City lot had now charged back down the road and attacked the Burnley thugs while they were under heavy police escort. Later on in town the police blocked off York Street as City settled in two pubs next door to each other – Rosie's Bar and Athenaeum. The police were filming the two pubs as well, they were about to storm Rosie's as I walked past with Wilkinson. We were not allowed in so we stopped outside Athenaeum talking to the doorman as the police now rushed the pub some officers directed the camera on us. I thought fuck it, they film me I will film them back, so I took out my video camera from my work bag which I still had as Wilkinson had borrowed it the day before for a family party.

As I filmed the police whacking a load of City lads who they dragged out of the pub, I was pointed out and a policewoman approached and asked what was in the bag but she was really sent over to get the camera and wipe its contents off. In the end I told her it wasn't stolen and she can take my name and address even though the other officers knew who I was. I added that if there are any reports that a video camera had been stolen she has my details and that of the make of camera but she tried to grab it so I ran off down the side-streets.

She gave chase and I managed to take the tape out and hide it under a step I then decided to walk out of the alleyway as a load of officers with dogs including the officer who gave chase in the first place. I was then arrested and taken to Bootle Street police station for suspicion of theft of my own video camera. As I was taken from the custody area and taken to a cell I heard an inspector tell the police women to go back to where I was arrested and search for the tape. I thought if they find the tape that's me charged because everything on it was all true, my solicitor soon came to the station I told him I had the receipt at home.

It emerged an hour later that charges were being dropped as they were gutted and as I got my property the officer still pissed off said 'oh he pushed me' so I was re-arrested and charged with assault and released. When I got out I went straight to where I hid the tape. That was later used in court to get my charges dropped as the court advised the police that any further arrests that they might have planned for me for just being in the city centre at any time with my own property in my possession.

It was like every season from then on the police have had it in for me; pointing me out at home and away games and getting me nicked for fuck all but I always had the last laugh as I have a good solicitors firm behind me with Mr Lewis, Bryan McMahon and Co from Burton Copeland Solicitors in Manchester knew I was a target for certain officers because I have been going for so long. The days when the police knew that they could nick you anytime at a match for fuck all and get away with it are over. A hooligan conviction on your record no longer means that the courts believe everything they say.

If it was kicking off down the road with say a group of white guys the police would sometimes forget about it and decide to film all the blacks instead who were just walking towards it and doing nothing. Officers were once overheard by one of the white lads at

City say if you 'follow the blacks and you will find the trouble'. They meant that the blacks were always a target for other hooligans and just to keep an eye on them but I know what they really meant. There was a short police report after that game with Burnley which read:

MANCHESTER CITY V BURNLEY - 3/10/98
POLICE REPORT

Post-match disorder occurred when Burnley supporters were attacked by Manchester City supporters. Prompt police action prevented any serious disorder. The Burnley group were also attacked whilst under police escort back to Manchester city centre. Later that night several incidents were reported around the Chorlton Street coach station.

WIGAN (A)

As I travelled to Springfield Park it came on the local news the day before the game that there was a load of forged tickets knocking about and the police would be on the look out to confiscate them. We took a mob of about 300 and we were there by 12 o'clock at the station with a heavy police presence which was no surprise as we had a mob and no doubt that they did too.

Wigan's local pub was near the train station and it was called the Bees Knees, it was obviously shut on police advice, it was where the entire Wigan Goon Squad would hang out. It was all quiet just before kickoff we were however escorted to the ground and not by any choice of our own as we didn't need an escort because we had enough thugs to do whatever we had to do but it was a bit embarrassing being escorted through Wigan, as all the on lookers were watching the big so called Man City Guvnors getting taken to the ground by the police as if we were shit scared. It was a bit of a buzz in a way because the word did get around to their mob that we were there and in large numbers.

We were now at the ground and trying to get in I had a load of tickets which had been left at the ground for me from Richard Edghill as I gave Samson, Maynard, and Steve from Huddersfield their tickets. We made our way to the turnstiles only for the police to take everyone's tickets off them as they were now all targeting the niggers as usual, they claimed that the tickets were forged which was bullshit as I had just picked them up from the ticket office but they knew it and didn't give a shit – it was just a case of the Manchester police spotters pointing us out earlier on, so they were just using it as an excuse to get us mad so we would fall for it, kick off and then give them an excuse to nick us all.

We didn't fall for it as there was still a load of City fans outside the ground and at that point Wigan's mob came across the car park and tried to storm the City fans. We stayed where we were as the police were watching and waiting for any excuse to nick us. As everything settled down a Wigan ticket tout was selling a load of tickets for the City end, he must of had about twenty on him and wanted £15 each, (yeah right) he soon got them taxed off him, I don't know who by though but I had mine – one of the lads was cursing the Wigan fan saying did he really think that he was going to get paid off us thugs? We haven't gone that soft you know – I just laughed, it must have been his little buzz for the day.

As we were now inside the ground and still under the watchful eye of the police, the gates got stormed by about fifty City fans who either had their genuine tickets taken off them as well or just didn't have any. The game went well as Wigan put the City defence under pressure from the start only for Shaun Goater to get his 10th goal of the season and City's winner. The team needed to win as Stoke were the surprise team of the moment as they were top of the league with at least 30points and it was only the middle of October. City were contenders to go straight back up but were not doing that well as they were in mid-table.

So it was now a case of kicking it off after the match and putting City's name back on the map. If the football team were not doing anything, we had to do it as City had not been in the papers apart from when we went down to Stoke and battered them. After this game we all marched back to the town centre yet again under police escort but as we approached the centre and just yards away from the Bees Knees pub outside another pub their mob now showed up and it went off in front of the police.

They had their batons drawn as me and Chris Hayes were both hit as we tried to get out of the way of the fighting. A woman who was running across the road to get away from the trouble was also struck on the legs as the police were lashing out at anyone. They finally restored order and got us back to the train station. As we walked on the police were still filming it, this was no surprise because they had been filming from the minute we landed in Wigan until when we were about to leave. I bet they have lost the tape of the trouble in the centre as it would have shown an innocent person getting lashed with their batons, that's probably why no one from both sides got nicked. But saying that Steve from Huddersfield, Travis and a few others were pulled out during the game by the Manchester police and were told that they were seen on video fighting at Stoke which was months before, on the final day of last season when both teams when down. They were let back into the crowd soon after, the police just put the wind up them that was all.

OLDHAM (A)

It was a few weeks later when myself and all the lads met up during that time and all the talk was now about the Oldham game at Boundary Park. The City mob loved going to Oldham as it was always a good day out and we knew we could never get done and we were always guaranteed a kick-off there. Provided they showed up of course. Sometimes it was just a joke to me going there as I wouldn't kick off as I would end up talking to most of their mob, after all I did live up there for years and go fighting with their mob and just the ones that I got on with as some of them didn't like me for whatever reason. But I can guess why, there were some good lads though because you had the likes of Lee Hardman, Scott Morley, Dave Freer, Burkey, Robin Walker and Lloyd Scantlebury and co. The City lads who lived in Oldham would sometimes join forces whenever they played Leeds at the Oldham ground or we would just get our own City mob and go our own way and have some good battles up there with them Yorkshire puddings.

We had it with them at Mumps train station one night when we sneaked on and had it with them one of the Leeds boys was off his head because as it was kicking off he got hold of Cozy and kept punching him, even though everyone's fists were flying in his direction he finally left injured, but earlier on at the ground my brother nearly got stabbed during the game. As me and about ten others including Jerome Hurbert and some bitch that he was with were walking at the side of the running track when we saw about twenty odd lads heading our way, Jerome then told us to get on the other side of the gate which we did as he was a big lad then and most of us looked up to him as he was one of the main heads about the town, even though he wasn't a hooligan but he still liked to be there if it was with Oldham or City.

As the Leeds mob approached and we were on the other side of the fence and yes most of us were shitting it but I don't think Jerome was. As he stood with his hand on the gate as it was half open, the Leeds mob ran towards it saying 'come on nigger'. As we were stood behind Jerome giving him a bit of vocal support, even though we were terrified, but not letting on that we were.

As the Leeds lad got half way in front of the gate Jerome said 'come on you sheepshaggers' as they rushed it only for Jerome to slam it in their faces. It connected with at least one of them and they soon backed off as the gate flew open and we went charging out. As they stood fighting I then noticed my brother and an Oldham hooligan Eddie L, come walking towards us. My brother had his hands in his pockets trying to walk past as if he didn't know us just as a blag as always but the Leeds thugs got onto him and grabbed hold of him. My brother then head butted him as he couldn't get his hands out of his pockets. I saw the guy pull a knife out of his pocket and at that stage I ran over through the crowd of lads who were still fighting and managed to punch him at full force – he soon went flying as we all soon fled as there were no tools for us and we didn't know how many more would have been tooled up. My brother was up for it as well as Jerome but it was no point. Just then a big fat guy in his 30s shouted to us 'go go go Man City' that was the end of that – we were all on our toes. It wasn't Eddie Kelly who was if not the main man for the Service Crew but one of the older heads not forgetting we were all teenagers.

This day however was all about Oldham v City, as me, Maynard and Linford made our way to Oldham by car I got a phone call saying that everyone was at Hollinwood station. We got there in minutes only to find the train had gone. We set off to the town centre as there was a piece in the Oldham Chronicle the night before saying that the police were expecting trouble on the day of the match as there were rumours around the town that a large group of Hibernian fans from Scotland were making their way south to join up with Oldham's FYCs. As we drove through the town centre it was just full of shoppers and a heavy police presence. We left and could not find the City mob as we were starting to wonder that we were being taken for a ride at Daft Donald's expense and that a load of City lads had been arrested in the early hours of Thursday morning for all that trouble in Stoke at the last game of the season.

This new season was well under way and four months after the Stoke incident the police decided to raid the homes of 50 City fans who were later charged with various offences from public order to assault, at the same time the police in stoke were rounding up their mob too which they later called Operation Larrikin.

Police had video evidence of the troubles of that last day. You could clearly see that Stoke's Naughty Forty were well up for it. I thought that City's mob didn't want to show up today and it was looking that way and I was pissed off as I rang Daft Donald back to tell him that if no one showed up today, I wouldn't be going again. Maynard and Linford agreed as we had been charged up in the past and we still showed up for the following games. Donald just said stop panicking and get onto Rochdale road A.S.A.P – we thought that this nigger was off his head. We were not going there with less than twenty, never mind the four of us!

As we were about 300 yards away from Oldham's pub the Brook Tavern, we saw about four coaches and a load of mini buses pull away. As a mob marched down we parked up and waited until we saw who it was, as Maynard thought it was the Hibs mob. I watched to see if there were any black guys, just to narrow it down and establish who it might be, there was at least 400 plus – they walked across, most had their hoods up until I started to notice thug after thug we soon jumped out of the car as excitement took over.

The buzz soon came back as we joined up chanting 'Guvnors, Guvnors', this is what football hooliganism was all about – this was our rush, our buzz. Who needed drink or drugs to get this buzz? Most of the hooligans were labelled with it after the acid house days but it was a load of shit because the acid house and the warehouse party days had long gone. Everyone said all the thugs had gone away and were hooked on the drugs but that wasn't the case – most teams had been raided around that time and had been banned and now had re-grouped and this was City, the mob was back – good and proper! We were back in full force.

I saw a lot of City lads who lived in Oldham at the front of the mob as we all marched down Rochdale Road in the direction of the ground and now towards the Brook Tavern pub which soon had the windows put through as we passed. It wasn't until we got to the Royal Oldham hospital that the police showed up. They must have been waiting all afternoon at Oldham Mumps train station for City with all the false information they received. They were trying to keep us on our toes as their batons were drawn as there was an order from the front of the mob to walk which we did and right past Sheep foot Lane where the police were trying to push us but instead we went onto the White Hart pub.

There were about 200 now as the rest split up as a few of the lads went into the pub to find the Oldham FYC. Sheehan noticed one of their lads outside and he noticed me. It was Lee Hardman who was one of their lads, he was one of the ones you could get on with and that wasn't two faced. As soon as I said 'Lee where's your boys' as he was now with his girlfriend and obviously nothing to do with it, but he looked very nervous as anyone would have been surrounded by a mob but no one took the piss with him as he made his way through the crowd. If that had been the other way round their mob would have taken a liberty.

We finally went to the ground and in their end there were about 1000 City fans as usual. When City soon scored we were at the back and at the front jumping up and down it soon kicked off as their mob made their way over. They were slapping anyone and it was clear that all the City thugs were at the back of the stand with us and they were at the bottom giving it to the normal fans. The police soon came and put a human cordon in between them and us.

Word soon went round that they done us (not), after the match the City mob got it together outside the away end as no one moved until everyone was there as the police watched on videoing all of us as we moved off with the exact same mob as before the game. The police made sure that they were going to stay with us all the way and there were now a load of black guys marching up with us so we decided to break off out of the escort and cross over but the police were now on another mission I called 'Operation Nigger Watch'.

As the main bulk of the police crossed with us, there was Maynard, Daft Donald, Neil Crawford, Stefan and Danny Gaye, Linford, me, Dennis Edwards, Anthony Wilkinson, Paul Thomas aka Urban and about ten more from the Moss. The police didn't like it as we started calling a few white lads over to join us. In the end there was no chance of us getting near to the Oldham mob, so we decided to break off altogether and get off in the car back to Manchester. At about 8.30 that night I had a phone call off one of the lads saying that they had just done in some door men and the Oldham mob in Oldham town centre at a pub called Harry's bar. It soon hit the newspaper on the Monday, the police must have been gutted – that's what they get for following the niggers back to Manchester instead of watching the rest of the City mob.

ET – THE LUCKY ESCAPE

There was a time when City played Chelsea at Maine Road some years ago when my mate ET, who is no longer a thug as he has grown out of it, had a lucky escape. He was known to most of the Headhunters and after the game at Maine Road there was a rumour that a few Chelsea thugs were slashed up in the Moss Side area as they marched through shouting National Front.

It was no surprise, it's just like a load of black City fans from Moss Side on their patch or marching through Thamesmead estate on the way to Millwall shouting Black power, they would get popped or slashed up by the whole area. The Chelsea mob were all back on the train to London later that evening when ET appeared on the train also making his way to London that same night. He was not involved in the Moss Side incident so he was not recognised by anyone who was at the scene but because he was black he was targeted as there were 200 plus Chelsea thugs on the train and just him. Some Tottenham/ Chelsea thugs with them that day so they probably pointed ET out, as the Chelsea mob were kicking off and trying to get to him, the BTP arrived from another carriage as there were normal fans and passengers on the train.

They made their way out of the way as they obviously didn't want to be witnesses to a murder. At that point ET must have thought that he was safe as they kicked off with the police telling them that a few of their lads had been slashed by a few niggers in Moss Side. ET and the police were frightened as anyone would be stuck on a train with 200 of Chelsea's BNP head-hunters, they could do nothing to help ET as he offered one of them out for a fight. It wasn't to be as he was chased through the carriage and some of the Chelsea mob caught him further down the train – by now the police were nowhere in sight and ET was picked up off his feet as the Chelsea mob tried to throw him through the train window!

Fortunately he never went through but got a slight beating. The BTP managed to restore some order now as they got in between them and ET. He was taken to the end of the train as the police now waited for the train to pull in at a station so back up could come on. At that time it must of been the only time ET would of got goose pimples and he couldn't phone home then – there was no doubt in his mind he was shitting it as his life flashed before him thinking what was going to happen when the last stop at Euston station finally came. The BTP back up arrived in numbers to keep everyone away and from trying to attack ET again. He was told that as soon as the train pulls to a halt at Euston he would be on his own – his stomach must have been turning inside out as anybody's would in that position.

As the train pulled in slowly at Euston ET said the normal

passengers started to whisper to each other knowing what was going to happen in less than five minutes or so as the Chelsea mob shouted 'get that nigger'. The police also knew that from when that train stops with or without backup on the platform their job was done as they would be powerless to stop the Chelsea mob in the station with all the people in their way. Then there were the other football firms that would be passing through at that time

As the train slowed down to just ten mph ET was at as the door and ready for the off – he flung it open and ran alongside the train before it could stop, then up the slope and through the concourse as everyone watched. People must have thought that he had done a handbag snatch the way he was getting away or they thought it when they saw a black guy running at speed – he was off down Euston road and into the night. He soon learned that it was a lesson to him, he wouldn't ever travel to City games on the same day in future he would come up the night before and go back to London the day after the games as he didn't want to get caught again by any other firms let alone Chelsea's!

BLACKPOOL away 1999

This game was always a good fixture. Whenever we played Blackpool we could always expect a good turn out from the City thugs and there was always an expectation of a good day out. On the other hand the Manchester police would be there to make sure we didn't enjoy ourselves because from their intelligence over the years it was what they would call it a high risk fixture. I don't know why because it was the Blackpool fans who would be at risk from us!

A few lads drove down there with us as we couldn't be arsed getting on the train getting filmed and getting followed as they always do because they think by following us the ones who were known to them would lead them to something big.

As the game kicked off early it was to be one of those games where the players were still half asleep. I ended up wanting to leave but there was only a car load of us and the police would not let us out by half time so we went back to the standing terraces and sat down with our backs to the pitch and basically nodded off until we were woken by the large roar as we thought City had scored and we all wanted to get onto the pitch as planned. It wasn't to be and the game had finished. 'What a load of rubbish' the crowd chanted at the players as they walked over to applaud the crowd. And I don't know why as they were booed off at half time. Now was the time for the Manchester police to start getting busy and pushing us around. I couldn't be arsed with all that shit as I wanted to get off as we had to drop Woodie off in Rochdale and I had to go and meet some bitch in Manchester.

Me, Maynard, Woodie and Arron Davis, also from Rochdale, were in Chris's car so we tried to make our way back to the car park were Chris had parked but the G.M.P. were not letting us go back to the car and told us that we had travelled down by train so we were getting an escort back there. The amount of blacks that were getting held against the wall was disgusting and a blatant pissed take and an embarrassment in front of other supporters. There were a lot of white lads getting pulled to one side too but I counted 15 blacks in total get pulled against the wall and that was including ex-City star Steve Coward who was with at least 30 lads on the Official City supporters coach. They eventually let him go but why he didn't make a complaint after I do not know. The police saw a group of lads they seem to think were hooligans. It was a funny day with the police after all because as Woodie got back in our escort he sneaked out to the car park to find Chris and his car which had now left so we had no choice but to go on the train

As we were escorted through the streets and giving people abuse as we passed, a lot of the white lads who had sneaked out of the escort and joined with a load of Guvnors outside a pub and you can imagine how gutted me, Maynard and Woodie were as Daft Donald, Crawford, Agboola and a few blacks were stood outside a pub buzzing off us like we were a bunch of pussies being given an escort! But I give Peter Agboola his due, he got in the escort and came with us.

As we approached the bus station I saw a little disturbance up the road at a pub I later found out to be the Hop Inn. We were soon ushered on the train with a load of idiots who were singing their hearts out and giving me a headache all the way back – it wasn't until the next day when I heard on the radio news that it had gone off at that pub we passed and I phoned a few lads and heard that a few lads went in and knocked one of the so called Seaside Mafia out, then a fight broke out outside with 5 City lads and 20 odd

Blackpool then that 5 got off and came back with about 100 plus and smashed the pub to bits. I even saw a cutting what my mates from Preston showed me with a landlady on the front pointing to the windows. What a shame! The GMP was busy escorting the blacks instead of doing what they went there for in the first place.

MILLWALL home 1999

As I attended my first game back in months it was to be the MILLWALL game and needless to say it was talk of the town weeks before. This was to be the game of all games just before the Millennium. It was all over the Internet saying that they were coming to Manchester in full force and that we wouldn't know what hit us. Even the night before the TV news and the local Manchester Evening News reported that the police were taking steps to quell any trouble as soon as it starts and to target trouble spots in the city centre and around the ground.

The police also stated that they would be drafting in officers from as far a field as Preston to help patrol Maine road. The police were bigging themselves up as usual as if they had it all sorted but there was one thing they were forgetting – no matter how many officers there would be on duty they would not stop what was going to go off in the North Stand which is the area where the away fans are situated and also which was the patch for our mob.

That day everyone was to be in that stand. Early that morning I couldn't sleep dreaming about what a good day it would be. So I was up at 7.30am all washed and dressed and out. I rang Maynard and Steven Nevins, and we soon linked up after that. City's full mob were not meeting until 11am so we were driving about and ringing a few lads which we met. We ended up driving about in the city centre to keep an eye on United's mob as they were setting off to Notts Forest; we soon met up with my mates from Preston's mob; Justin Nixon and his boys who roll with Preston North Ends (PPS). There were only five of them but they were good lads. They came with us that day – we didn't need anyone else to link up with us as our mob was big enough.

At about 10.30am we drove around the city centre and saw a load of police vans heading out of the City and up the A6 towards Stockport, so I turned my hand-held scanner on to see what was going on. It came over that bronze control and silver, which is the football channel for the GMP on match days, it said all units to Stockport town centre as the United fans were being attacked by the Millwall fans who jumped off the train to give it them. The police arrived just in time to see the reds getting ran around the roundabout as the police eventually rounded up both sets of fans and sent the Millwall contingent on their way. They kindly said over the airwaves that there was an 800 plus hooligan group.

I soon rang City's mob to let them know but they were not interested in coming to town as they were busy getting pissed up in a pub near the ground and didn't seem to be in a rush to leave the place as usual but in a way there was no point in going looking for them just wait at the ground, which they did. As the Millwall lads came off the station we all got pulled by the police and checked out who told us to leave the city centre or we all would be arrested. As we were on our way we could hear the chants of 'no one likes us we don't care' as we looked over to the station their mob just kept coming out – there were fucking hundreds of them.

Justin and the other Preston lads couldn't believe what they were seeing and neither could me and Maynard. I thought straight away respect to them for bringing that many because they must

Questions asked over Maine Road violence and opposition grows to United takeover

DEMAND FOR PROBE INTO RIOTING AT CITY MATCH

BY PAUL HARTLEY

A TOP-LEVEL probe has been demanded into mob violence at Manchester City's game against Millwall.

Control leader Richard Leese said problems had been reported as the town hall wanted "a thorough investigation" into security — how the incidents happened and why adequate measures were not taken to prevent them.

Violence flared before, during and after Saturday's match as hooligans from the London club clashed with local supporters and police.

Eleven people were arrested. Five were charged with public order offences and for encroaching on the pitch. Four men were contained and two others were retained without being charged. Six police officers were also injured.

Traders whose shops were targeted in the violence after the game have criticised the police for not working that the ...

Asad Iqram ran inside his business, Ahmed, 36, who runs a jewellery business in Wilmslow Road ...

"We were busy when 40 to 50 youths suddenly came and smashed the window," he said. "They kicked the window door, charged into the shop and grabbed what they could.

"We lost a substantial amount of jewellery, although at the moment it's impossible to say how much.

"Thankfully nobody was injured, but we were all terrified."

Manchester City have defended the decision to sell tickets to Millwall fans on the day of the game. Ground safety officer Jack Richards said: "The ticket arrangements for the visitors were the same as any other game."

Fewer than 50 Millwall fans paid to see the match on the day, bringing the total number of away fans to around 1,500.

Mr Richards said: "We agreed the level of policing required. There should be no criticism of the police. They were magnificent."

Greater Manchester Police, who said the game had the highest level of police for this season, have confirmed that ...

■ Picking up the pieces: Saleem Ahmed at his jewellery shop in Rusholme

A visit from Milwall was always eagerly anticipated - here are some shots I got of their visit in 1999

have known if they bring less than they would be real trouble. After that I was on the phone to Travis, Craig and Arron to say that we better have a good mob out today or we will get done but even if we didn't I knew the lads would give them a good go even if we were outnumbered but we have always give them a good go and they knew it, which is why they brought the whole of London with them.

We managed to get a few photos of their mob before we got off to the ground to meet up with the Guvnors, Young Guvnors and the well known Beer Monsters. Everyone was out at the ground – I was proud to see faces from the past. There were at least 4 to 500 at the ground and a shit load of police with their video cameras taking pictures of us. As the Millwall escort came down Claremont Road at the side of the ground they were showered with missiles which they threw back at us as the dog handlers and the mounted section kept us apart. We soon went round to the North Stand where they were queuing up. We shouted 'we will see you in the ground'.

After all the chanting and insults with both sets of fans, City's team soon got their act together and started to score goals which triggered off what everyone longed for as the Millwall fans pelted us with seats which they had decided not to sit on. We gladly threw them right back followed by other missiles as the police intervened. Some of them were also attacked as the riot police soon stepped into the middle of us. My hood went straight up as they started to film us and gather evidence.

About 20 of us surged down to the bottom of the stand pitch side so we could take the trouble onto the pitch but the police stood in our way and stopped us going on. The players from both teams watched in amazement just before the match ended and with nearly all the police focused on the North Stand I decided to get a mob together and leave the ground early. There were at least 200 lads outside who never got into the match with Mr N Gaye, Baron Whitter and his brother Eugene Sobers from the Rusholme reds and their boys were outside waiting as they said they saw a load of police officers dragging a load of people out earlier on when it went off.

The fun was about to begin as the game was ending and everyone was firming up outside. The numbers were beginning to swell to 400 plus so we all marched round to the Millwall end which was adjacent to the Kippax. The police had the street locked off with the mounted section and the dog units, we knew then that they were keeping the Millwall fans inside for as long as possible. The Tactical Aid Unit turned up with their balaclavas on and chased us all to the next junction with their batons so we all got tooled up down an alleyway and came back at them with bricks and bottles and backed them off to the corner of Claremont Road and Yew Tree Road which was later shown the TV programme McIntyre undercover.

Our mob surprised them – they carried on pelting them with a whole range of missiles including distress flares. The police didn't know what had hit them as they thought they could still push us about and chase us off with dogs but the tables had turned as they were outnumbered and didn't realise how many boys we had until we had them on their toes. They soon responded with repeated mounted charges even though they were still being pelted. We soon re-grouped at the Sherwood pub as there were shouts of 'turn' which we did but not for long as the mob reached the Lord Nelson pub a few yards past the Sherwood pub the side street from top of Viscount Street to bottom was rammed with City's mob.

Then someone noticed a green Ford Mondeo with two plain clothes police officers in, the car was going nowhere as it was blocked in the side street right in the middle of the Guvnors. I saw the car getting smashed to fuck as the two men inside jumped out and ran for their lives. Everyone let them get away and concentrated on the car and started to move down onto Wilmslow Road as they were frustrated at not getting anywhere near the Millwall fans. That was why the police had got us as far away from the ground so they could escort them down Lloyd Street and into the City. But it wasn't that easy for the G M P as the mob now entered Wilmslow Road I saw the jewellers getting rushed and the windows went through as the shop got looted.

I was across the road stood watching as the restaurants started getting it as the police and the mounted section were a few yards away from me who were also stood watching and could not get involved as there were just too many. Shop after shop was getting looted or smashed up. I crossed back over even though the police had their eye on us as they knew who we were but we didn't do fuck all, even though they knew we were all well known thugs. I thought fuck them, I'm in the mob so I should be right with them, there is a riot going on and everyone and everything is getting it!

As we marched down onto Oxford Road a petrol station soon got hit by the young ones. The guy behind the counter and his mate tried to hold one of the City lads in the shop which turned out to be their worst mistake, as more lads piled in to do the place over. We soon moved on down Oxford Road causing havoc as an ambulance had its windows put through and other cars in the road were being damaged,

We finally made it to the city centre on the lookout for Millwall supporters who were now long gone. We re-grouped in Edwards bar in Piccadilly until about 9.30pm, when we heard on the hand-held scanner that a train containing a 100 plus group of United hooligans were approaching Piccadilly. We soon sneaked near the Station Approach right behind the police who were waiting as they knew nothing about were the City mob was. Eventually we got back to Edwards bar to get City's mob out. As we then saw the United mob singing and chanting as they marched through Piccadilly but as soon as they heard us shouting 'Guvnors, Guvnors' they soon went quiet as Tony O'Neill and his boys were attacked as we ran them through the bus station. A few of them soon turned on us but were soon attacked. The police turned up as usual as we pulled bins out and charged the police as the so called Red Army dispersed, the police reinforcements soon came and chased the City lot away as usual. This was probably because there were always blacks in the firm and none in United's not because we always kicked off with them but you never hear of the United boys kicking off with the police...

That was it that night. We got off home before we got harassed all night by the police. The next day the TV and Radio reported what had happened on Wilmslow Road with the jewellers and other shops being done over. It was all over the news that day – what a good day it had been as City was all over the news both inside and outside the ground. A programme was soon aired about that day on the McIntyre programme when he went undercover with the Chelsea mob then he came to Manchester via train to the City-Millwall match with the Bushwhackers and a few Chelsea plus Reading and nearly the whole of London as a load of teams joined up with Millwall to come and fight City.

The documentary also showed inside the ground and outside when City's mob attacked the police with missiles. There was also a programme on Channel M which shows Manchester, it showed us kicking off at the bus station after the Millwall game with United and the police in Piccadilly.

FIRST WIGAN THEN WEMBLEY

All the way through that season there was trouble along the way to the very end of the season. Some of the lads were very depressed at being in this division and they too were behind their team at every game cheering them on to do well out on the pitch and try and get us up and out of this embarrassing Division 2. The team and the club were bigger than this!

There was a good chance as Stoke, who were top of the table for months and had been 20 odd points clear at one stage, then started to slip up and lose games from February through to May. We had now won 12 games and lost 2. Our last home game was Wigan which was a night match – it was the Second Leg of the play-offs. We won by a single Shaun Goater goal that caused a massive pitch invasion which was all in good fun. As we invaded the Maine pitch I managed to get hold of the match ball which the referee was about to pick up but decided otherwise. I still have it to this day and maybe Shaun Goater should have had it as it was his goal that was to take us to Wembley for the play-off final against Gillingham.

WEMBLEY STADIUM: - GILLINGHAM PLAY OFF FINAL

This was to be our day of fate – the day which would see if we were to stay in the Second Division or to move a step forward and get back up to the First. With 40,000 fans following they couldn't disappoint. As we all met at Piccadilly on the Sunday morning we were also met by the police. It was too early for all that videoing shit and the photos being taken of us al.l I was going to get my video camera out and film them back but I couldn't be arsed.

Instead I wished I had gone to church that morning and prayed that the police would just fuck off out of our faces for once and leave us all alone to enjoy our day and stop harassing us. They were the ones who most of the time provoked the trouble because people were just going about their business trouble free. The police did not like to see that bit of joy and happiness in our faces. I thought they were also there to keep the peace and prevent any trouble from happening well they were doing a good job as usual trying their best to start it.

In 1999 I went to Wolverhampton. There were fuck all happening that night anyway, apart from people getting nicked, fucking battered and robbed in the subway near the football ground but that was basically all that happened that night.

2000 FA CUP

As January started we had Leeds United that was a fourth round in the FA cup, we need to win to get through to the next stages. It was a Sunday game again; as me and Danny Gaye were out early with Chris H in the car and went into the city centre spying on Leeds fans. We saw them come off the train at about half past eleven and they walked through Piccadilly Station, came down the approach with a load of police.

There were riot police, police on horseback, and foot patrols backed up by the dog unit trying to stop the Leeds fans from entering the city centre. As they came down the concourse onto the main road, the police put a cordon across and as soon as that happened about 400-500 Leeds United hooligans charged down at them and broke through the cordon and into the city centre without being touched by anybody.

All the City fans were at the ground because it was too early for them to go to the city centre. They all waited near the football ground. There was no trouble before hand, only a few insults as I walked passed them as they had a police escort later on. By the time City had finished the game we'd been beaten by them sheepshaggers 5-2; Bishop scored the first goal followed by another from Goater and then on form Darren Huckerby got one for Leeds.

City were out of the cup again, and that was it – the police were about to have their hands full and they knew it because straight after the match it went off everywhere. Outside the ground, from the Kippax stand we could see fighting up the road near the Sherwood pub. We just carried on walking and kept out of it – we saw a load of police charge up, they baton charged some of the City fans and after about ten minutes the road was completely blocked with hooligans and police.

The City fans then turned on the police as the Leeds fans were being escorted out of the other side of the City ground. By now the police had backed the City fans up the road away from the ground so they could escort the Leeds fans through.

I had a phone call off Neil Crawford saying that he was on

Kippax Street near Gascoyne Street, and he had just been chased by about 200 Leeds fans and there was no police around. So as we were making our way there we saw City fans outside the Sherwood still fighting with the police and then saw them tip over a van, I think it was full of Leeds. I got off to where Crawford was to see what was happening. As we got down there Maynard was with us, little Benny, Linford and a few others young lads that had nothing to do with it really, they just lived on the estate and they had nothing better to do. We were on one of the streets when we saw one of the Leeds fans come down. By this time it was pissing down with rain, all you could hear was 'Leeds! Leeds! Leeds!' This was their Service Crew.

As about four of the fans came round the corner we confronted them, next thing we knew about another fucking hundred fans came around the corner and on these streets it was fucking narrow, so you can imagine how many filled the street in one go. There were no police there or nothing and there was only about six or seven of us as we were fighting with them 'toe-to-toe'. Loads more Leeds fans came round and as they did the main hooligans that were at the back of the mob now made their way to the front. As soon as they saw a couple of black lads – they came running down to us shouting 'come on sooty', as everyone knows Leeds fans are racists it was fucking obvious they were going to say something like that.

As they chased us off we got to the end of one of the streets, we got a couple of wheelie bins and as one of them came running round I threw the bin at him, he slipped on the road, and that was a sign for us to go because there were too many of them and there was no point in us fighting them in the wet to get tripped up and get killed because there was that many of them to stand again and have it with them.

Meantime, the other City fans were on the other side of the ground fighting with the police still. After that we just said to ourselves 'fuck it' and went home. We phoned a load of boys to come down but they never came. Instead they decided to fuck off to the pub and get pissed and stay there all night.

That same day United were at Everton, I think they had a cup game as well I am not sure who they had but they got back early and we had arranged to meet them in town but nothing ever came of it. We walked across town as usual filming as we went looking for them only to be ran towards the G-MEX by the police. That was basically it for that day. It was all fucking' shit after that, I couldn't even bother going to a match after that.

We went to a Huddersfield night match and that went off before the game. It was going off from three o'clock onwards. There was a police report after that incident from NCIS saying what happened .... (Further down in the book). It was just all draws for City after that, no fucking' wins. Then the big one was Barnsley away, in the year 2000, we got there that morning and the usual shit, police waiting for us at the train station to escort us to the ground, as that happened the Barnsley fans attacked our police escorts not that we needed one. Most of us were at the back because we couldn't be arsed getting in any trouble off the police and it was the hooligans at the front that started kicking off. We stayed at the back because the police were videoing the trouble and we couldn't be arsed getting spotted so we stayed back and watched what was happening and we saw a Barnsley fan get slashed across his face, the police got involved and the person who done it never got arrested.

The Barnsley fans backed off then. As we got to the ground everyone was just stood outside chatting about what had just happened and the police soon got us in the ground. The game went on at half time in the tunnel the police had locked the bar so no-one could get a drink or hot dog or anything to eat. It kicked off in the tunnel, I saw a policeman get a door slammed in his face by one of the toilet doors when he tried to go through.

I saw a baton get stolen from one of the police officers. It was just going off in the tunnels for about 15 minutes and we were stood watching it with the Manchester police looking at us wondering why we were not getting involved so that they could get us on film and arrest us. Instead we went back down the tunnel into the main ground and told a few lads to come and get onto the pitch, this would get us on TV as the Granada Television cameras were there all the time filming the match but no one would get on it.

We were pitch side but no one wanted to know, so we stayed on the terraces while it was still going on, as we were getting beat as usual Goater popped up to get the equaliser and we ended up winning the game 2-1. After the match had finished the Barnsley boys were waiting for us, we attacked them, ran at them as the police was with us and got it all under control they took us back to the train station where we had to change at Sheffield.

When we got to Sheffield, Wigan fans were there as well, we saw a couple of lads on the other side, about ten or the Wigan fans were coming onto the platform mouthing at us, as there were about 200 of us we ran round they must have thought we were some fuckin' idiots, when we got around the corner we caught up to these lads and asked them if they knew who we were, and told them that we were Man City fans. They turned out to be Doncaster Rovers. We saw Travis talking to them like he knew them, but he didn't, he asked Travis for his phone number so that he could come to the Manchester City matches and link up with him. I intervened and told him that if he came to the 'hood, he was going to get battered and robbed, as we didn't want them down there. We didn't need those sheep shaggers, and that was that. Everyone fucked off, over the steps to the other side of the train station, the Wigan boys had just come off the train.

We were now running across to meet up with Wigan but the police had blocked it off with dogs so nothing happened in the end. But on the same day, at the same time that that was happening Sheffield Wednesday were at home to West Ham, so when we came out of the station West Ham fans were walking in and they could see how many there were of us. I don't think it was all their boys anyway. There could have been about 20 or 30 of them but the rest had no scarves on anyway.

They were letting onto us and we were giving them pure shit. Cockney bastards this and Cockney bastards that. I didn't kick off and we got the train back to Manchester. When we got there, there was a load of police waiting for us because they had heard what had happened at Barnsley and they were expecting trouble. The United fans were nowhere to be seen.

VICTIMISATION

The next game that I went was at Stockport County a couple of weeks later - we drew 2-2. It kicked at the train station, I had been arrested earlier for running across the track because we were going to miss the train, so me and Maynard and a few others fucked off across the track to catch the train. The BTP got on the train and got me and took my details and said they were going to send me a summons for running on the track. I had to give them my right details or I would have been nicked on the train. I gave them the information and got off the train at Stockport and their boys were there waiting.... Four or five of them walked passed us; a half-caste lad, and a few white lads in their late thirties thought we were all the scarf boys, all the City fans with their scarves round their neck just carried on walking. They don't have anything to do with it, they just go to the match, they sing songs and basically go in the game and enjoy it but as we walked pass the half-caste lad spotted me and I spotted him... so me, Maynard, Benny, Crawford and Chris all ended up fighting with them.

We chased them out of the station with all the scarf heads that were with us, chasing them up the ramp. As we were doing this, I phoned Travis who were were in the pub at the top of the station. I had spoken to them prior to that whilst we were on the train and they told us where they were. I told them that there were a lot of Stockport coming up and we were chasing them now so they charged out of the pub and blocked the top of the road off. It turned into a little scuffle as the police came and quickly intervened.

One of the Stockport lad's trainers came off so I threw it over the wall onto the train track. The police tried to grab all of us, but saw that there were too many of us, and turned their attention towards the Stockport lads and told the officers to nick 'em because they started it, although it was obvious to all that we were partly to blame. There was no further trouble en route to the ground so after the game we marched through the town centre with about fifty lads with the police following us everywhere, but as usual they just took the piss following the niggers so we all crossed over on one side and left the white lads on the other side.

The police crossed over with us, horses and everything as we got to the town centre and near the McDonald's it went off at some pub with the Stockport boys. Maynard got nicked but was soon released because one of the City hooligan spotters told the Stockport police he had done nothing wrong, he had been attacked, when he had been trying to go make his way to the 192 bus stop near the bus station.

We went for the bus back to Manchester, as we did that a load of police kept following in their vans, by this time there was about fifteen of us now. We all jumped on the 192 bus as I had left my car in Longsight, the police continued to follow us on the bus, so we all decided to get off the bus outside McVities in Levenshulme and walk to Burnage. The police left us alone that night and that was the end of that.

During this period, I didn't attend many matches because I was busy working at Asda as I had taken too much time off to go to the games. Most of the games now were home games and at least City were winning. We beat West Bromwich 2-1, Swindon Town 2-0, Bolton 2-0 and Crewe 4-0. Then we ended up getting beat by Grimsby away, but there were still more wins to come, all the points were vital because we were getting promoted soon and it was near the end of the season, another game was Portsmouth on the Bank Holiday Monday.

Grimsby Town away was alright, Tranmere at home we were winning all the games we needed to get promoted back to the Premiership. City fucked it up as always we were winning 2-0, and they threw away the lead at half-time old boy Lee Bradbury, got 2. After that we played the last home game which was against Birmingham.

Now we needed to win that game to get into the play offs, and also to have a chance of winning at Blackburn which was our last game away. It was a night match on a Friday when we played against Birmingham; we won 1-0 following a goal by Robert Taylor. The Birmingham lads never showed up that night either because they were hiding, or we heard a rumour that they had gone to London as one of their lads had a boxing match the night after. Whatever the reason, they never showed. Taylor had scored and we all got onto the pitch, which was shown on TV, the entire pitch was flooded with boys just before the final whistle as we all decided to pile on.

Everyone was celebrating, the commentators on TV was saying that you'd think they'd won the championship, and in truth we nearly had done, as there was only one more game to go and we were nearly up, but there was another two below us that had a chance to get up.

Now the last game was a week later, it was a Sunday game, Blackburn Rovers away at Ewood Park. We got there early. A train load of City were due in from 10am onwards and as we landed in the town an hour later we didn't see any Blackburn youth anywhere. I had loads of tickets to give away because Richard Edghill, who played for City at the time, used to sort me out.

There was a load of people outside wanting tickets up to one hundred pounds or more, but I didn't bother selling my tickets, I just sorted out my mates at a face value. As it got nearer the game we decided to make our way to the City end, as we did this there was the usual pure numbers of niggers walking with us and about fifteen or twenty of us followed up by white guys. The police decided to come up to us at the turnstiles asking us if we had tickets and we just flipped. When you see the amount of white people outside the ground, why didn't they ask them if they had any tickets? Us again! I told them that it was an all ticket game... they knew that there were some fans there without tickets that wanted to get in. They never got past the turnstiles. Crawford was there, Anthony Wilkinson, Tony Worthington, a few lads had to stay outside.

We got in, but it became obvious that a turnstile or gate was going to get rushed, because there were at least two thousand City fans outside who were locked out.

Prior to kick-off a gate to the right of where we were standing, which was a Blackburn Rover home end, got stormed by about 400 City fans who were then followed by the rest of the fans waiting outside. During the game you could see the police pulling everybody outside that were in the Blackburn end that had City tops on. City's end was full to capacity, the top and bottom tier was rammed.

Half way through the game we scored, then they equalised. In the end City won 3-1. Before the match had finished after every goal scored we invaded the pitch, it was all live on TV, and it was also a good day out as well. Peter Agboola was with us, Maynard, ET came and Larry was there, Linford, John Sheean, my Brother, we even took pictures of us all on the pitch which was later in the City magazine.

As the game neared the end it was obvious that City had been promoted again for the second season on the trot. At the start we had been relegated to Division 2, we got promoted through the play off at Wembley the season before and at the end of this season we had been promoted again back to the Premier League again.

That year had taken us into the 2000 / 2001 season, which I didn't really bother with because it was a waste time and waste of money. Travelling up and down here, there and everywhere. The only game that I went to was Liverpool in the September of that year, and as always I got nicked again. The police were always nicking me when I went to Liverpool just to find out my daughter's address, so that if ever I went on the run for anything or

*A great day to be a blue - City win at Blackburn to earn promotion,
we celebrate wildly and attract the attention of the law.*

they wanted to find me. I couldn't be arsed with it, they nicked me
and that was that.

*

Before that happened there was a game against Coventry at home
in the league, now that night after the Coventry game there was a
bit of trouble in the city centre. There were about a hundred lads
out saying that they were going to Moston for some reason, to fight
with some lads. As always, I followed up there in the car, when we
got to Moston we went up to the pub and all of a sudden a mob
came charging out. I don't really sit in pubs so I stayed outside with
my mates in the car (me, Benny and Frankie) whilst them lot ran on
to some estate chasing some lads. We didn't talk much about it, but
later on we found out that someone had been stabbed to death. We
were nowhere near the scene at the time, one of our lads rang us to
say he had got lost on the estate and we were driving around to try
and find him. We just saw a load of lads running at the car, I did not
recognise anyone as it was dark so I just reversed out of there and
fucked off home. The next day we heard on the news that someone

had been stabbed to death. It was fortunate for me I wasn't there, I didn't know until I heard on the news, and all the City fans started ringing around that one of the lads were supposed to have stabbed someone in a house.

The match at Anfield was two weeks later and the police were looking out for me, which is why they had nicked me previously to find out where I was living. There were a few lads in the ground at Liverpool at half time when we were at the bar getting something to eat saying one of the lads said that when he got nicked that the police were asking if there were any black guys there when the fighting took place in Moston. They asked them again and again if any black guys were there, are you sure there were no black guys there? I think that they were taking the piss, trying to stitch me up again anytime anything happened at a match and we never got held all the police were asking others if there were any wogs at the scene. Anyway, that night after they let me out of the police station in Liverpool they didn't do fuck all, they didn't charged me. I heard a rumour that the police were coming for me next for the Moston incident so I just decided to fuck off, I thought 'what the hell am I staying here for to get nicked for something I hadn't done?' so I just did one to Ibiza on the next flight which was on the Wednesday.

Only Gordon knew where I had gone. He got arrested for some dispute with his neighbour and they had him in the police station. Apparently Martin Townsend and Neil Holland, who was one of Stockport county's lads, was locked up at the time also in connection with the Moston murder. They told Gordon that the police were after me. As soon as Munich Gordon got released from the police station, he phoned me on my mobile to tell me that the police were going to get me. I stayed in Ibiza for two weeks then came back. I picked up my car that night and parked it outside my mum's house and stayed there that night, I hadn't even unpacked my suitcase or done fuck all.

Six o'clock the next morning the police were knocking on the door as I was in a bedroom downstairs, I looked out of the window and there were CID there and I turned round to my mum and said "Fucking hell they've come for me." I had a load of season ticket books, everything. I tried to hide them but the police found them, nicked me, took my car, took me to the police station and charged me on suspicion of murder. I was apparently the 45th person charged and they were looking for two more people – Benny and Frankie.

Now the police had said prior to my arrest that if I had not handed myself in that would put Benny's face and Frankie's face on the telly. They never did get hold of Frankie or Benny but they kept my car as a guarantee to them that if I didn't tell him where he was they were going to keep the car. I turned round and told them they could keep it! The solicitors from Burton and Copeland, Mr Lewis and Mr Harper were very helpful to me they made sure they'd made all the enquiries that were possible, made sure I came back to the police station and saw that I came back two months later. The police kept towing the car, Mr Lewis from Burton Copeland Solicitors was trying to fax Chester House for them to give me back my car because they were not charging me, they'd let me go without a charge after two months but they wanted to keep hold of the car. They tried to say that whoever had done the stabbing tried to jump into my car. Which was bullshit! It was not to be, and I was released anyway.

On the night I got released we had a cup match, it was Gillingham at home. The police were shocked to see me because it was the same police that had been at the City home game previously. There was a ginger lad and an Asian lad who were police officers stood behind us in the ground with ear pieces in. And every time I went to get something to eat or talk to one of the lads in the Main Stand where we used to sit, the police would tail me. As I walked past the police they were watching and looking for my lads to nick for the murder. I shouted to all the lads, there was like a slope that you could look down and we were at the top and shouted "everyone, the murder squad are here!" and pointed to them and they soon fucked off.

I didn't go to another game again until 2001, when I went to Liverpool away again, this time we were in the 5th round of the cup. I got nicked as usual, this time for apparently dragging a policeman off his horse or trying to throw a punch at a policeman who was on a horse. Now this was a load of shit. They got me after the match, beat me with truncheons, this was happening whilst City were being escorted. There was Maynard, Linford, Chris Hayes, David Samms, Daft Donald, Carl Stewart… a load of us were there that day. I had been taking pictures all day of the mob. ET came down from London, Larry came down from London. Everyone was there; Travis, Aaron, Craig, Cooper, were all present as I got nicked, got beaten on my legs and ankles with truncheons, because of this the City escort stopped and started fighting with the police, and the police were videoing it from the helicopters above, there was one of those video vans, videoing us. As I got nicked, I thought fuck it; this is all because of Linford, because all day before the match Linford was giving it out to the police "What you looking at? What you looking at?"

There was a load of police and Linford got on hype because every train that pulled into Lime street, about every 45minutes, would bring a mob of City fans. We were in the pub, facing the station in Wetherspoons opposite the Shopping Precinct. There were about a hundred in the pub and by 2 o'clock there were three pubs rammed with City fans. Wetherspoons, the one beside it, which I think was called the Yankee at the time near Lloyd Street. All those from the Yankee bar came over to Wetherspoons, there was about 300 in total. As we were there in the pub about 20 or so scousers across the road shouted to Chris "where's your boys?", so whilst this was going on I said to Chris, "Are these guys off their fucking head, we'll do it with fucking ten of us, we'll get ten out and give it em." But there were police outside; there were dogs, vans and horses circled around the pub. I don't know what these scousers were thinking; they must have thought that if there were that many police outside the pub, then there must be more than twenty in there. When you see that many police on horses, you must think that more than a hundred fans are in the pub.

The scousers came back about twenty minutes later with a few more boys, and we all decided to charge out and chase them up the road in front of the police. Fuck all happened before the match. The police got us in an escort and marched us to the grounds so fuck all happened. Linford would not stop giving it to the police

Action shots from our cup game at Anfield - 2001

saying "Fuck off! What you looking at you racist…" and all of that, which they were because they kept fucking pointing at the niggers. I told Linford to calm down because they're just going to nick him but in the end it was me who got licked and handcuffed.

They took me to the police station and I was pissed off because I got nicked because of Linford giving it to the police all day and they had taken it out on me. As I got into the police station to get my handcuffs off, Linford was sat there handcuffed and that made my night that, it really did, to see him in there sat on his black arse next to me. We had to go through all the rigmarole of going to court, reading all these bullshit statements what the police said. In the end when we got to court, I still have the statements to this the day where the police said I tried to either punch him on the back of the horse or drag him off, which if I did it would have been on the video, but the police apparently lost the video from the video van. They probably didn't think I would remember them filming it. We asked for the tape from the helicopter, and the prosecutor turned round and said in court that they had lost the tape. The magistrate threw it out straight out.

*

The next game that I attended was Bradford City away later that season. It was actually the year 2000; I did not go into the ground but stayed outside as there was a lot of trouble just as I got there. There was too many police there, which made it difficult to just stand around near the ground, so I decided to get off back to Manchester. I was with David Maynard, David Samms, Peter Samms and we drove back. As we got near to Manchester about half an hour later, it would have been approaching half time at the match; I received a phone call from the lads saying that it was going off. City had gone in their end and kicked it off, on hearing that we just decided to turn back round. At this point Maynard had been banned from driving and I told him to let me take over the driving, but he refused saying that he would be alright until we get there.

On the way there we got stopped at Huddersfield near the junction to the Huddersfield turnoff and Maynard got arrested.

The police searched the car and found a bag containing foil, but I never saw what was inside the bag. Straight away they phoned in for assistance. They just thought four niggers in a car, four niggers carrying drugs…they didn't tell the officers what it was all about.

Anyway, Maynard gave a blagged name and the policeman had him sat in the car and another policeman came. As the copper was approaching there was a big scuffle with Samson and myself and the police on the hard shoulder. The guy was trying to say that there was drugs in the car. Now we knew what it was, one of the guys had bought a chicken from Asda where he worked and had left the bones in the bag and did not want to throw the rubbish out of the window so he had decided would wait until we parked up. The police had seen it and just radioed through and as the other officer arrived the scuffle stopped because there would have been an accident on the motorway. We told the officer what had gone on, the other officer had stopped my mate from driving and he seen a bag in the car, and we told him it was chicken.

The officer searched it himself as we stood back on the hard shoulder and watched him. He came out and started laughing and said to the other officer "it's only a bag of chicken bones." The officer felt embarrassed but this did not stop him from nicking Maynard. We drove on to Bradford in his car and as we got there it was near the end of the match and it was going off. Apparently, the City fans were supposed to be attacking some Asian lads who lived near the ground. What I heard was that the Asian lads were throwing bricks over the wall at City fans.

It was a bit hard to believe because there were a few black guys, some Asian lads and they said that they never heard it. Apart from that incident, it was going off all over the ground. I drove down towards Manningham Lane following the police sirens it was kicking off with Bradford. There was fighting at the roundabout, toe-to-toe fighting down the road. In the end the police got in the middle of all of it and stopped it. We decided that it was time to go, because they were just nicking everyone that day, I think Craig got nicked from City and a couple of the other lads, so there was no point hanging around so we set off back to Manchester in the car.

As we drove back to Manchester, we passed through the city centre and we saw a few United boys, but they were just on their way to a pub so we didn't bother to stick around and we fucked off home. Later that night I got a phone call saying that it had gone off in town outside the blob shop pub near club Havana facing the Arndale. Some young City lads against a load of United fans, I've seen the video myself . The City lot were obviously tooled up, as well as them lot (United) but in the end they ran the City fans, but it was all captured on CCTV and it was going on for about twenty minutes, they all got nicked for that as they all got rounded up near the end of the season.

*

City played United a couple of weeks later but I did not attend because a lot of people were getting arrested a week before the game so I decided it was in my best interest to just stay away. City were going to be relegated, it was the last game of the season against Chelsea at home we got beat 2-1. In the book football hooligans volume 2 (M-Z), it shows it going off in the ground with the Chelsea fans. Now Chelsea always bring a mob every time they come to Manchester because they know that there will be a mob waiting for them because we've had a bit of a bad blood with them over the years.

We drove into the city centre that morning to be confronted by a load of police on horseback, so we knew from then that there was a big mob of Chelsea on the way and them boys ain't really fucking about either. I think the police were aware of their reputation, nothing had happened before the game because they monitored them all the way to the ground. Near the end of the game when we had gone 2-1 down, Steven Howey scored for us but it was not enough, we decided that everyone should get onto the pitch.

There were a load of lads in the North stands who had phoned us, and were waving to us to say they agreed to invade the pitch, if City were going to go down, then they could do so in style. It is well known that when City go down there is always a pitch invasion or a fight in the stands. The SKY cameras were there just filming the goals, and we all decided to get onto the pitch. I've got a few photographs of that invasion – there were five minutes to go and maybe we should have got on a bit earlier; maybe we could have held the game up a little longer, but I think we didn't have enough points to stay up. It was too late because we'd lost on points. We went over to Chelsea's end but we were still on the pitch side behind the goal post the police on horseback came on and tried to march us off, then a load of City fans came onto the pitch and started attacking the Chelsea fans with plastic chairs.

At this point we were in the corner near the Kippax stand end and there were a load of Chelsea fans shouting racist abuse at us right in front of the police on horseback. I've got no evidence of that, obviously you cannot see what they are saying, but the police were more interested in telling us to get back. By this time the whole pitch was flooded with boys, there were about three hundred of us or more, and we thought 'fuck it', we'll get on, and we've got a few pictures of it, and it just went off from there, there was fighting in the stands, a lot of the City lads got into the Chelsea end through the police cordon and started kicking off with them.

Now the Chelsea fans were giving it them back, and I think some black guys got done in but they shouldn't have been there really, they should have just backed off but obviously they did not know the script about Chelsea. It was all over the news, pictures of people's faces on the TV on the Monday, picture in the newspapers and the police wanted to question them. Apart from that it was all over, City got relegated back down to Division 1.

*

The following season I don't think that I went to any games that year because that was the year one of my son's died, in the September, around the same time that the planes flew into the building in America. When my baby died I didn't go to any games I just kept well away because my head was up my arse.

By the end of November we had Rotherham at home and we won 2-1, I was on the phone to Peter Agboola. I was on holiday, in Tenerife. I had to get away for a bit, he said it kicked off on Yew

Tree road and Rotherham got done in. I didn't go to any games that year, but by the following season I was ready to go back to the matches and I planned to return when we played Millwall on 13th January 2002. The authorities made sure me and a few thousand City fans were disappointed as there was a no go clause following the trouble during our previous meetings.

By March 2002, I had finished working at Asda in Hulme and started work for a kitchen place in Oldham. On the 8th I went to Bradford City away with Maynard and Stefan. There was a lot of police on standby that night because of what had happened the previous season when all that trouble happened and there were over 30 arrests which were mainly Manchester City fans. Stefan got arrested at the ground, I had given him a ticket which I purchased from Richard Edgehill, who was playing for City at the time. He gave me three adult tickets, but the tickets had on them juniors plus adults. The police and the stewards got hold of Stefan's tickets and said that it was a Junior and you are not getting in, so I told Stefan to wait a minute whilst I went into the ground and got him a ticket from one of the touts. I came back out and he had been arrested, we could not find him, added to the fact that he had been drinking anyway, he probably had got himself locked up on a 'drunk and disorderly' charge. He basically got arrested for nothing, we went off to watch the game and we had no idea where he was. City won, Jon Macken scoring on his debut. Lee Sharpe was playing for Bradford that night and he got a lot of abuse off the City fans who were chanting 'Munich! Munich!' then 'smack head! smack head!' because of his alleged coke habit.

After the match there was no trouble, the police ushered everyone out to where they were going. We waited around until about midnight. We still couldn't find Stefan anywhere. So we decided to drive back to Rochdale and drop some lads back home and make our way back down to Manchester.

The next game was two weeks later – Stockport County away. City got beaten, this time I was with Terry who use to work at Asda with us, he's a United fan, but he came down, we were in their end. As we got in the game we were getting phone calls saying it was going off outside, but we were in the Stockport end, so we couldn't really get out there. Mickey Francis was sitting at the City end, and a load of them got on to the pitch when City scored but it wasn't enough because they still got beat.

It was going off after the game when we were coming out. We eventually met up in the little town centre near Edgeley Park, marched through with a mob of about 200 of us, we had loads of young ones with us (who are no known as the Blazin Squad) and it kicked off with the Stockport boys, the police quickly got hold of us, and fucked us off out of there.

*

The next game was Rotherham, which was also away. This time we drove down in the car – me, Maynard, David Samms and met up with the City's mob, first at Rotherham's ground then made our way to the town centre.

The police had us all before the game in the pub car park and just blocked off the road to let us out bit by bit. The police station was nearby to where we were so there was no way that we were going to start going on with anything.

We got to the ground and there was no trouble, City's end was packed as usual, I bet it was Rotherham's record attendance in years because it was about eleven and a half thousand. After the game we were all marched back to the town centre. The City goalkeeper Nicky Weaver was with us and as a load more fans made their way out of the ground, I was talking to him on the way back. It kicked off near the train station, but we were at the top of the road near Wetherspoons walking down and the police saw three black guys and decided to round us up, got us in the van and said they were taking us to the train station. To which I said "I am not on the train I came by car" one of the policemen told him that I had come in a red car, so they took us to the car park where our car was and waited there until we drove off. When we drove off the police went another way and we spun back went back to the car park. That was the end of that.

There was not much really going on because City were winning and there was no doubt that they were going to get promoted. The next game that we went to was Wolves away. We got to the ground and there was Bernard Chaisty's brothers Mark and Simon , Aaron Davies from Rochdale, and a couple more lads. We were talking with some of the Wolves boys when the main mob come towards City's end and there was a little bit of a scuffle.

Maynard and myself did not get involved as the police were watching us, plus we had tickets for the Wolves end. We were in their end most of the game, some of their boys noticed us during the match but I don't think they were interested in starting anything so nothing happened much during that game only that City won 2-0, Shaun Wright-Phillips scored two and we were on our way.

That was the last game that I attended until the end of the season finished early that year.

It was a Sunday game, April 2002, which was against Portsmouth and we won 3-1 which meant that City were getting promoted , loads of us were celebrating . We were now back in the Premier League under Kevin Keegan, and hopefully this time we were to stay there.

From then on it was time for me to calm the fighting down at the match because I was expecting a baby, my third, so I was buzzing about it and I didn't want to mess things up. The potential for police harassment of me and the other black lads at the match was massive. They seemed to have a policy of intimidation until one of us snaps so they then have an excuse to make an arrest. But by now we were a lot smarter than that and we were not going to give them an easy ride so we all kept away.

The police had regularly come into my work to keep an eye on me or just to go into the office and tell the management stories about me so I could get sacked. To their amazement the management told them if they had evidence that a crime at a match had been committed by me then they should arrest me or stop coming into my place of work harassing him.

It was still going off and I was missing it all because it was hard to leave alone but I guess the best thing about it was that the police hadn't a fucking clue what was going on at the time and were probably gutted that they couldn't make any black arrests for a change. When I did finally attend a game at Maine road it was only a shit game which there would be no trouble so I decided to take my eldest son Ethan who was seven at the time.

I managed to get two tickets off my mate Richard Edghill. He didn't really like getting me tickets because he probably didn't want the police to know that he knew me and he always said to me with a smile on his face 'I hope your not fighting' or 'I hope you don't sell the tickets on', as it would come back on him but I told him I was bringing my son with me.

The police never liked it when he used to come out and give me the tickets or leave them at the window for me. They would always come up and look at the tickets then say 'How do you know Edghill?' I would just say 'that's my business' and walk off. They thought it was a big thing that I knew a football player, whereas I only lived five minutes up the road from him in Coldhurst in Oldham so it was nothing new to me.

Going back to the day of the game when I was with Ethan, we were going into the ground and as I guessed the police were not far behind me they were acting like a bunch of pricks following us. As we were in our seats later in the game the spotter would walk past us as we were sat in the front row in the main stand then walk round the pitch then we could clearly see them taking photos of us and videoing us. It really pissed me off. I put my hand over Ethan's face and told him to put his hood up – I don't know what harm a seven year old could do so we decided to get up and go halfway through the second half

I was really pissed off now so I phoned my solicitor to complain – it was either that or go over to the police and kick off and that is what they wanted. The solicitor just told me to calm down and he said if I'm not doing anything wrong that it is the law that I can film them and take photos back so from that day forward I started filming them and there is fuck all they could do about it

It soon started getting to the stage where they would nick me on suspicion of theft of a video camera (yeah right niggers are that broke I need to steal a £250 video camera) which was the reply I gave them on arrest. I went through the motions of being interviewed to which I made no reply as they told me it was stolen but could not tell me from where and when they charged me to which I replied 'see you in court'.

After the second court appearance I gave my solicitor the receipt which he held onto until he heard all the police evidence. He then produced our evidence which was good enough for the magistrates and enough to tell the police what they thought of them arresting the defendant for no apparent reason other than that I was filming which I am allowed to do .

He went onto tell the officer that if it was a crime to film, then they should arrest all the tourists and charge them for theft of their video cameras for no reason what so ever.

It was months before I went back to the match as I really needed to sort my head out by early 2002. I started my new job at the kitchen firm in Oldham and by April that year I found out that I was having another baby so by now Tyler was my third boy as well as Harvey, I already have a girl Leeayna. I was so proud of them including Ethan.

2006

By the time City got knocked out of the FA Cup by Oldham the year before I couldn't be arsed going as the team was getting from bad to worse by now nearly all the stars had left, there was no point me going and spending money on dead end games which the team had more or less lost before they started. Work was my main aim and interest so that's what I carried on doing as every weekend came quick it was something to look forward to as while driving up and down the country I could listen to the radio in peace away from that police presence who were always out to get us and get us banned from the games.

It must really piss them off as people can just walk in and out of any football match if and when they choose and trouble free. After the Oldham game last year a lot of lads got nicked and the ones like me who had nothing to do with it were still getting the blame. The police thought that a few of us should have got nicked even though we all arrived ten minutes after the incident. That incident at the Wagon and Horses pub in Hollinwood, Oldham, was captured on video by the police and it shows it on a DVD called British Hooligan's volume 9 – Oldham Riots. It shows most of City's mob before the game marching through Oldham town centre under a heavy police escort and there is a police officer talking as to what was happening and straight at the front is me.

IN COURT – AGAIN!

Now as time went by the police were pissed off as they couldn't stitch me up for anything as they just loved to video me and got no trouble. I loved to video them back without any trouble, but early that year City had played United at the City of Manchester stadium in January and there was a little kick off before the game with some City and United fans en route to the ground. It was nothing I was involved in, as I made my way to the ground with Carl Stewart, Paul Howarth, Peter Agboola , Arron Isreal , Arron Davies, Craig Rowland and Simon Cooper, the police were filming us all the way to the ground.

City did it again and ended up winning in style 3-1 . It was Scouser Robbie Fowler of all people who finished them off with the third goal to rub it in. The place went wild with celebrations all round the ground. I think the United team were still asleep as it we an early kick off. After the game there were about 300 plus City boys outside the ground as we all met up talking, with the police close by filming.

Guess what! My video camera popped out and their camera soon came off me! We had enough and went our own ways as we were getting off home. The rest were going on to the pubs around the ground while about twelve of us decided to go off to town to celebrate. Why would the police try and spoil our day filming us and pushing us around? Some of us were taunting the United fans and having a bit of banter with them like they would and always do to us when they beat us at their ground (that was our season over after we beat them, there was nothing more to play for even though it was January, beating them was a God send). We ended up in the city centre and I parked my works van in Chorlton on Medlock by David Samms's house and we all jumped on the bus together as David left his car as well. We eventually got to Piccadilly and went to the Millstone pub where a few City lads were.

As we arrived we saw Stefan and Solomon Gaye there, as were the police who are never far behind. I think there had been a bit of trouble inside as the police were sorting it out. It turned out to be trouble with a group of City fans amongst themselves who were by now very drunk we decided to get off now as I was going to drop a few lads off as well as Woodie (Paul Howarth) and Aaron Davis who I had to drop back to Rochdale.

There were about twelve of us now making our was down Princess Street towards the subway on the edge of town were the van was parked (outside David Samms house). As Stefan was with us (everyone knows he is a registered piss head) he wanted to stop off for a quick drink. As we approached O'Shea's bar there was about 3 police spotters outside and 2 in a space cruiser across the road which were the ones who knew us and who go to City matches. As we walked past the police on the doors they nodded to us and told us to take our hats off. We thought nothing of it as it was normal to have officers on the doors on a big match day like this as we thought there were City fans inside because as always if we went in a pub with the opposite sets of fans inside the police would have stopped us. As we walked in the pub it was rammed and the first bar we passed no one was serving, so I followed Stefan round to the other bar as I told him on the way in I was broke and it was his turn to buy a round for a change, which would of been an orange as I am a non-drinker As we approached the second bar where the bar staff were serving someone ran past me and punched Stefan in the face, then the tables went up as we backed off. I could not believe it as the police were right behind us – it suddenly clicked, United's mob were in here.

We never fought back in self defence as the police were right behind us, we just backed off as the police pushed us out. Stefan was missing and getting a kicking as was Solomon. By now we were all outside as the police grabbed us all, it was like it was a set up as the police never told us that United fans were inside so that explains why they came right in behind us but the problem was we didn't do anything and had been attacked as the police were later to find out. In the mean time we were explaining to the officers to let Woody go as he had not done a thing wrong and had walked in with us as two United fans walked outside to say he had been fighting inside which was untrue. As that was happening the T.A.G. pulled up in a van, saw a load of blacks and as the other officers were walking us across the road out of the way they saw us and drew their batons and chased us, then nicked us for violent disorder.

Arron Israel, David Samms, Linford Taylor and Solomon Gaye were taken away and later bailed to go back and as we did months later the last part of the season. Arron, David, and Linford didn't have to go back but they were soon replaced by Paul Howarth, Craig Rowland's and Stefan Gaye aka (STELLA GAYE) his nickname because of his bad drink problem – the nigga is always getting pissed and all because of the drink he loves and calls his Bitch (Girlfriend). She was not pleased!

When the video came out and it was sent to crown court it was obvious we were being charged for walking in a pub and getting attacked! Now the police want to bring up people's past. The last time I got nicked and convicted for football related violence was in 1991 when I was 18 – that was sixteen years ago. What a joke and it's all because the police want to ban us as they don't like me filming them.

In February 2007 the court case started at Manchester crown court. In the dock was myself, Stefan Gaye, Solomon Gaye, Craig Rowland and Paul Howarth (Woodie) from Rochdale. As we walked into the court room the police from the match were sat there with a little smile on their face as they had the cheek to try and say hello I blanked them because in my opinion, they are racist. Even the white lads who go to the match with us saw the same thing as they have seen it all now.

I ain't got no McCains (chip) on my shoulder and I am not one to throw the race card at anyone but how can you not see seven black guys walk right past you on the door of a pub when the police were stood on the step and give a statement that we sneaked past them! Fucking hell I know that you can't see us blacks in the dark but that takes the fucking piss. The street lighting was good and you could not miss the spring in our step not only because our trainers were a bit too tight but we had won and that was why we were out celebrating.

So we have walked in the pub as the other white lads were behind us and gone in quietly no noise or nothing when Stefan was all of a sudden punched from behind by John Catterall. We just backed off as the police were now right behind us and made our way out of the way of the trouble. As the police from the City games made it their business to help the United supporters with their attack on us by pushing us out of the pub as Solomon was being dragged about the pub. A bar stool was blasted off his head and punches and kicks were also thrown at him as the police just pushed them off him while we were outside arguing with the police about what had happened. One of the United boys was clearly seen by the police officers assaulting Solomon, who was dragged outside and sent on his way home without being nicked.

We were then chased off by the tactical aid group as Stefan was still in the pub and probably dead by now. We were soon arrested the officers who like to point us out were stood there smiling, just as they were in court. Back in the court room it wasn't going so well for the prosecution as they knew they had nothing on us or should I say we should not have been charged, let alone had the case referred to the Crown Court. The main reason why it was sent to crown because the magistrate was too scared to look at the video which was the real truth which would have cleared us all but instead racism played a part again. They decided to listen to the police and the prosecutions evidence which was about our previous offences and she had adjourned the case to read through the evidence but never bothered to watch the DVD – all she must have done was read a few witness statements which nearly all said the same thing – six black guys walked in the pub in a line and threw a punch at the United supporters.

So their statements were all aimed at us; that blacks did this and the blacks did that but in all truth of the matter it was three black guys and two white guys that walked in the pub and it was a black guy that was punched. But they could not explain themselves in the dock when it came to it as the cameras had followed us in the pub from start to finish and the DVD said it all.

My barrister ripped the police and prosecution apart when they took the stand. The judge was throwing all the police evidence out and half way through the second week of the trial the judge had heard enough as he asked an officer why they never arrested any of the United supporters, the ones who were doing all the punching and kicking apart from Catterall. He knew from the start we shouldn't have been there in the first place but had to go through the motions before he threw it out and ordered the jury back in to give us the verdicts, as directed by the judge, that there was no case to answer or not guilty. But when the judge came back after a short break and said again there was no case to answer I looked at the rest of the lads in the dock with a smile on my face like a Cheshire cat. It's like the others didn't understand what had been said until Stefan's solicitor Darren Langton gave him the thumbs up. They realised that it was getting thrown out just like I had been saying from the start.

The police were fucking gutted as they had told the prosecution to offer us a deal and drop the charge to a lesser one so they could at least get a conviction. The other lads wanted to take it just to get it over with but not me. I told Stefan, Solomon, Craig and Woodie to do what they were doing as we hadn't done anything wrong and I was running a trial and not going to give up just for the sake of the police as they wanted us banned from the start. If we had done a deal, the next time the police would see us in a pub they would just nick us for nothing and say we were fighting again and go through all this again and who would believe us?

As the case was over the solicitors and barristers were sorted out with their bottles of bubbly as a thank you from us for their hard work and understanding of the case.

Why give the police what they dearly want but they're not going to get? They should stop wasting their time targeting blacks when nothing is happening with us anymore.

I have recently started working again and have a family and kids to think about, so I have commitments to keep. I recently went to an away game this season the Manchester police were there filming us, so my video camera was whipped out of my pocket and I started to film them back. Fuck them, they film me I will film them back!

2011 - WHAT A YEAR!

I
t had been a long time since Man City had had a bit of good luck and good luck came a few years ago with the arrival of Abu Dhabi billions.

Now the tables had turned and City had all the money in the world. We can now buy who we want and score when we want! We are now regulars in Europe and, after winning the FA Cup semi final against Man United 1-0 at the new Wembley then winning the final against Stoke 1-0, a trophy – the goal scorer each time being Yaya Toure.

It kicked off at the semi's with the United lot who were doing in any City fans with a scarf, hat or any colours on. Men, women and kids were getting it – even the supporters' coaches with families on it were getting bricked off them Munich scum until our lads turned out after the game. Pictures will appear in the next book coming soon. City even made it to the Champions League for the first time in the club's history, only to go out at the same time as the reds so we have now both dropped into the Europa League – it will be interesting to see how far we get in the competition.

I went to a few Champions' League games away and as always the Manchester police travelled and pointed people out, including myself. It's like they know there is no trouble anymore or that we're not out to cause trouble unless it comes to us, so while they're busy filming me and my mates trying to stitch us all up and get us banned for just going to watch a match and not cause any trouble like the bad old days. I have employed an undercover reporter to watch every move we make and every move they make so there is no wrong doing.

A few officers who I need not mention at this stage but might do in the other book if they haven't been found out for harassing us at football matches by the reporter, I hope we win the premier league title this season

As of March 2012 we are top of the table!

EPILOGUE

I can now say I have retired from the hooligan scene. I enjoyed my time; the battles as well as all the times we got battered and ran off other football firms, over the space of 27 years. Looking back at the court cases, the stitch ups and beatings by the police in my case it wasn't a (RODNEY KING) beating it was a (RODNEY RHODEN) beating and they loved every minute of it. The police made themselves out to be heroes at all times, even when people were arrested who were thugs but not really involved in certain fights, they would always say in their statements that women and children had run for their lives to escape these brawling thugs. One example was when we had them lot in Old Trafford one Sunday in 1988 when we took a mob to Chester Road while a game between us and them was being played. We met and clashed in the middle of the road which was captured on CCTV. No one was on the road, only us and them, a bus and a few cars. A few officers wrote a statement saying there were women and kids running for their lives as an old woman was knocked to the ground as the United Hooligans were chased off. Now via CCTV the judge saw a battle of thugs against thugs. Funnily enough, when the incident came to trial the officers' statements were thrown out and not questioned as it never happened the way they said it did! That was just one example of the lies they came come out with.

That said, I've done my time. I just like going to watch the game even more now that we have come good. Everyone like me now has a family, kids, jobs and homes to take care of rather going to football to get involved in shit. Don't get me wrong – if trouble is there, I'm not getting off. All these up and coming thugs from different teams want to make a name for themselves. Some of them just came too late, like them Mugs at United. Anyone can join up with them, even the police, they just love letting anyone in. Well the police love United Hooligans because they have never kicked off with the police like we have done, never done any pitch invasions like we have, only once or twice at villa park in cup games and that's it. That's why the police hate City because we always stand and kick it with them. They hate us enjoying ourselves at matches and they forget that I got banned when I was 15 years old and got back in at 24 years old.

I love watching football and don't really regret what I was involved in. I only wish I would could have done more on camera years ago which would have justified that length of a football ban. We have a new young mob in town at Man City and they are called the Blazing Squad. I will give them a few tips even though they know how to do it.

Finally, a big mention to the lads who have passed away over the years; Mikey Williams, Steve Stanton, Ged Ganson, Paul Gaye, Danny Gaye and Larry Phillips from Edmonton North London – ex-Spurs YID and Man City

RIP lads

My engagement party at the Etihad - January 2012

POSTSCRIPT

The police spotters at City still seem to have an interest in certain fans who don't cause trouble anymore. The picture taken for the cover of this book attracted the attention of the police. Most of the people who were on it or around were arrested and questioned on bullshit charges about association with criminals. The police claimed it was a 'team photo' of hooligans, saying that certain people have been seen in my car getting a lift from the ground. The obvious conclusion to draw from this bullshit charge is that anyone seen talking to me or my mates will be arrested and banned if you plead guilty.

It's only the football spotters at the City matches who have nothing better to do than to harass, bully and stitch up people (like myself) who have served their time many years ago. We are doing nothing wrong now and just want to go enjoy themselves butbecause there is no longer any trouble they are pissed off.

The matter has now been passed to the Football Supporters Federation who are looking into a number of complaints as well as a solicitors firm who have been monitoring these events for a few years...

If people are worried and are getting this kind of unfair treatment they should start finding out exactly what information is being held on you by both the police and the club. It is possible that information will be shared between both parties.

To get the information from GMP, see here:

http://www.gmp.police.uk/mainsite/pages/subjectaccess.htm

To get it from the football club, just write a simple letter addressed to the Data Controller at MCFC and request that, under the Data Protection Act, they release any and all information held about you regardless of the format.

You should either hand deliver it and get a receipt or send it recorded delivery as if they don't reply you can complain to the Information Commissioner but they will require proof that your request has been received. They should reply within 40 days.

THE INSIDE STORY OF
MANCHESTER CITY'S
NOTORIOUS MAYNE LINE
SERVICE CREW

BY TONY SULLIVAN

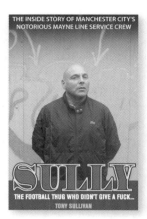

THE INSIDE STORY OF MANCHESTER CITY'S
NOTORIOUS MAYNE LINE SERVICE CREW

SULLY

THE FOOTBALL THUG WHO DIDN'T GIVE A FUCK...
TONY SULLIVAN

FOR ALMOST 25 YEARS, Tony Sullivan has been a member of some of the most violent gangs following Manchester City. He has also toured Britain and Europe as a professional 'grafter'.

Now, with his hooligan career at a close, 'Sully' looks back on this violent era and relives the good hidings handed out and the kickings received. He also details some of the stunts he and his mates pulled - using the cover of his fellow fans to 'earn' a living in an era before extensive CCTV surveillance, often with unexpected results.

Along the way he contrasts the exploits of the various supporters groups he encountered - the scouser's well known propensity for using a blade, the United supporter's unwillingness to take part in a fight unless they were certain to win it and the craziness of a typical away day in Newcastle city centre in the early eighties.

The 1990s also saw a slew of hooligan memoirs hit the nation's bookshelves, often written by people with tenuous connections to the incidents described. Others sought to celebrate hooligan culture as somekind of weekly fashion parade.

Sully has little time for either as he explains:

> *"Over the years I have been beaten, stabbed, had bottles cracked on my head and had lads threatening to come round my gaff - but you wont hear me complain. This book is a true account of those years, devoid of sensational bullshit."*

'SULLY'

Order this book for just £6 from www.empire-uk.com

GRAFTING FOR ENGLAND

THE INSIDE STORY OF ENGLAND ABROAD IN HOOLIGANISM'S GOLDEN AGE

TONY SULLIVAN

The early 1980s was a golden age for football hooliganism and shoplifting in Europe. With security forces on the continent yet to fully realise the extent of the English Disease and security relaxed in even the most expensive shops. The continent was ripe for pillage and Sully was one of many to take full advantage - funding his trips following the national team with ill-gotten gains.

As a member of Manchester City's notorious Mayne Line Service Crew he was accustomed to far stricter security in England. Using the cover of fellow England fans Tony reveals the secrets of his success in ' Grafting for England' the follow-up to 'Sully - the football thug who didn't give a fuck' published by Empire last year.

As Tony makes clear, the football wars in England didn't necessarily stop when hooligans from all over the country got together to follow the national side. Fights would regularly be sparked off between different factions supporting the Three Lions and even a trip to Wembley could catch unsuspecting patriots unawares.

Order this book for just £6 from www.empire-uk.com